CHRIS SALEWICZ has been writing about music and pop culture for over 30 years. He was at the *NME* in the late 1970s and early 1980s and has written for the *Sunday Times*, the *Independent*, the *Daily Telegraph*, the *Observer*, *Conde Nast Traveller*, *Q*, *MOJO* and *Uncut* magazines, and countless other publications worldwide. His critically acclaimed books include *Bob Marley: The Untold Story*, *Mick and Keith* and *Redemption Song: The Definitive Biography of Joe Strummer*.

CHRIS SALEWICZ

Quercus

Originally published as individual ebooks under The 27 Club series by
Quercus Publishing Ltd in 2011, 2012 and 2013

This paperback edition published in Great Britain in 2015 by

Quercus Publishing Ltd
Carmelite House
50 Victoria Embankment
London EC4Y 0DZ

An Hachette UK company

A CIP catalogue record for this book is available from the British Library

ISBN 978 1 78429 133 4
EBOOK ISBN 978 1 78429 556 1

Picture credits: Amy Winehouse *Mirrorpix/Adam Sorenson*; Kurt Cobain
Getty/Winelimage/Terry McGinnis; Brian Jones *Mirrorpix*; Jimi Hendrix
Mirrorpix/Eric Harlow; Janis Joplin *Getty/Michael Ochs Archives*; Jim Morrison
Getty/CBS Photo Archive; Robert Johnson (with Johnny Shines)
Getty/Robert Johnson Estate

10 9 8 7 6 5 4 3 2 1

Typeset by CC Book Production

Printed and bound by Clays Ltd, St Ives plc

CONTENTS

INTRODUCTION

'The 27 Club' refers to the disproportionate number of musicians who died at the age of twenty-seven, their legend as cultural deities secured forever.

As a term, The 27 Club came into common parlance in 1994, following the death of Nirvana leader Kurt Cobain. 'Now he's gone and joined that stupid club. I told him not to join that stupid club,' said Wendy O'Connor, his mother, on hearing of the demise of her son.

For the purpose of this book I have limited myself to a study of those 27-year old musical casualties who became iconic: Amy Winehouse, the most recent, passed away in 2011; Nirvana's Kurt Cobain in 1994; Jim Morrison of the Doors in 1971; Jimi Hendrix and Janis Joplin in 1970; Rolling Stones' founder Brian Jones in 1969; and the inspirational and innovative pioneering bluesman Robert Johnson in 1938.

These forever young creative geniuses are all embraced by the global imagination, giving them an apparently eternal life in the collective psyche. My aim has been to illuminate the phenomenon of these inspirational figures who seemed to unwittingly sacrifice themselves at the same age for the sake of their art.

Of these principal seven, two died from an overdose of heroin: Jim Morrison and Janis Joplin; Brian Jones drowned; Amy Winehouse seemed to literally drink herself to death; Jimi Hendrix accidentally overdosed on sleeping tablets; Kurt Cobain shot himself; and Robert Johnson was murdered, poisoned by a jealous husband.

Each of these seven musical stars had unique experiences that drove them towards their particular outlandish fame, untimely death and ensuing legend. They all had their own knowledge of celebrity, the dark romance and seedy glamour that led to membership of The 27 Club. Each tragically underwent his or her own journey of flying far too close to the sun.

There was one thing they all had in common, however: although Jimi Hendrix may have had the worst experience, each carried their own psychological issues stemming from childhood. Driven by the insecurities this gave rise to, in many ways their entire short lives can be seen as attempts to overcome and heal themselves through music. Forcing themselves ever onwards in this healing process, by the time they attained the age of twenty-seven they were all burned out, exhausted, and seeking a shift in their lives.

Although some readers will not be comfortable with this, there are esoteric explanations for the notion of The 27 Club.

INTRODUCTION

Astrologers will tell you that twenty-seven is immediately before the time in your life, at approximately the age of twenty-eight, when Saturn returns to its point in your astrological chart at birth. In terms of Saturn's return, as it is known, the age of twenty-eight is meant to mark a break with youth, and the first steps into maturity, a major transitional point in life. In other words, the members of The 27 Club seemed unable to make that evolution into adulthood, perhaps because they no longer had the mental or physical strength to do so. Could it be that their souls were rebelling? That their inner beings had really had enough?

In quasi-mystical realms the number twenty-seven contains numerologically powerful associations: when reduced to the primary number of nine, by adding two and seven together, it becomes the cube of three, itself considered a 'Magic Number'. Moreover, twenty-seven is significant for several reasons in the Bible: there are the twenty-seven books of the New Testament, for example, and the name Abraham appears in twenty-seven books, and according to the Gospel of St Matthew twenty-seven is the number of generations from David to Jesus Christ. Mary Agreda, the seventeenth-century Spanish mystical nun, reported after visions that it was at the age of twenty-seven that Jesus Christ began to preach his personal gospel.

According to researcher and author Alfred Weysen, twenty-seven is a lunar symbol which indicates the light in darkness, the symbol of divine light. And Jacob Boehme, allegedly the greatest of Christian Gnostics, born in 1575, considered the number twenty-seven as being synonymous with 'the death'.

So twenty-seven clearly appears to have numerous symbolic and mystical associations. But who were further victims of The 27 Club? Well, there was Alan 'Blind Owl' Wilson of Canned Heat, dead two weeks before Jimi Hendrix in 1970 from a barbiturates overdose – suffering from depression, he had attempted suicide some months previously. And a fellow member of the late 1960s 'underground' movement, Ron 'Pigpen' McKernan, who played keyboards, harmonica and percussion with the Grateful Dead, and who passed away in 1973, physically damaged by his addiction to alcohol. 'He was a juicer,' commented Jerry Garcia.

The previous year Les Harvey, guitarist with respected UK semi-blues group Stone the Crows, and brother of the singer Alex Harvey, had been fatally electrocuted onstage after touching an unearthed microphone. Later that decade, in April 1975, Badfinger's award-winning songwriter Pete Ham hanged himself, mired in depression. Also that year Uriah Heep's bass-player Gary Thain succumbed to a heroin overdose.

Pete de Freitas, the talented drummer with Echo and the Bunnymen, was killed at the age of twenty-seven in 1989 when his motorcycle collided with a passing vehicle. And one of rock 'n' roll's great recent mysteries received some form of closure when Richey Edwards of the Manic Street

Preachers was legally declared dead in 2008, thirteen years after he had disappeared in 1995. His car had been found close to the Severn Bridge that links England and Wales, and – although his body was never found – suspicions grew that he had jumped from the bridge into the vast river. At the time of his disappearance the allegedly 'troubled' Edwards – like all the aforementioned names – was, of course, twenty-seven.

However, none of these figures, and there are many, many more, was a household name in the manner of those – with the exception of Robert Johnson – on whom I have concentrated.

Their legend now appears to be eternal. Unsullied by age since they checked into The 27 Club, they will never check out.

AMY WINEHOUSE

'Mostly I have this dream to be very famous. To work on stage. It's a lifelong ambition'

Amy Winehouse, 1996

On Friday, 22 July 2011 at 8.30 p.m., Amy Winehouse's doctor came to her house in London's Camden for a scheduled appointment.

Permanently ensconced in her home was a minder, employed by her management company. That night he heard Amy playing drums late into the night, at one point suggesting she quieten down so as not to disturb neighbours.

At 10 a.m., the minder looked into Amy's room; she was still sleeping, he thought.

He didn't check on her again until shortly before 4 p.m., at which point he realized she was not breathing. Although a pair of ambulances arrived almost immediately, it was too late. Amy Winehouse was dead.

What was most surprising about the death of Amy Winehouse was that it hadn't happened sooner.

The actual cause – alcohol poisoning – wasn't especially

what we might have expected. A heroin overdose? A cocaine-induced heart-attack? Those were more what we were primed for . . . But didn't it feel like something we'd been waiting for? For a while, in fact?

Because the tragedy of Amy Winehouse was one of Shakespearean dimensions, of extreme arcs of crisis, despair and self-recrimination, all played out by a queen of an alternative new royalty. It was lived out in public; as her snappy, confessional songs reveal, she was not averse to self-analysis. Yet later she would be repelled by the school society, hectoring aspects of rehab.

Amy Winehouse was very much a product of her time: a pushy, north London Jewish girl, embraced by assorted family neuroses. With his perpetual hints of bad boy, her father Mitchell was her male archetype; her relationship with Blake Fielder-Civil, as specifically detailed in 'Back to Black' and 'Me & Mr Jones', is like a parody of her mother Janis's relationship with Mitch, who had an established relationship with another woman. (In fact, before she married Blake, Amy had become the Other Woman.)

She was talented to the point of genius. Amy was one of those kids who is so highly intelligent that school is habitually boring. It is significant that her favourite subject was English. She was a natural writer – you can feel it in her lines.

But she's also a symbol of her age; like everyone nowadays, she wanted to be famous. That was one of the central thrusts of her existence. But one should always bear in mind the piece of Chinese wisdom that warns you to be careful of what you wish for, because you just might get it.

For if Amy Winehouse was representative of her times, it was because of the manner in which she was also killed by celebrity culture, the Holy Grail of the twenty-first century, with the bullying paparazzi permanently on her doorstep. Amy initially seemed to welcome this, but then became devoured by it.

She also lived at a transitional period for the music business, as record companies cannibalize themselves and, suffering acute anxiety attacks, collapse into a digital world for which they are unprepared. What seemed like Amy's colossal array of influences – unimaginable for someone, say, two decades previously – was a reflection of her being a child of her age, when teenage (and even younger) music fans would swap entire laptops' worth of music, building up enormous collections. This is extremely fruitful material for study, for those who could be bothered to immerse themselves in such riches. And, of course, Amy certainly could.

With her art forced into the margins by the ceaseless psychological and cultural miasma of her life, you can almost forget the value of her music with its powerful, deep contralto vocals. But that was where her essence lay; for, although she released only two albums, Amy Winehouse, aged only twenty-seven, died a legend.

*

At first she had simply behaved as an archetypal Camden caner. 'When I first met her around Camden,' Russell Brand affectionately remembered on his *Guardian* blog, 'she was just some twit in a pink satin jacket shuffling round bars with mutual friends, most of whom were in cool indie bands or peripheral Camden figures Withnail-ing their way through life on impotent charisma.

'Carl Barât told me that Winehouse was a jazz singer, which struck me as bizarrely anomalous in that crowd. "Jazz singer? She must be some kind of eccentric," I thought. I chatted to her anyway though, she was after all, a girl, and she was sweet and peculiar but most of all vulnerable.'[1]

The facts are clear: Amy Jade Winehouse was born on 14 September 1983, to Mitchell, who was 34, and 28-year-old Janis. They were good Jewish parents and habitués of the north London Jewish neighbourhood of Southgate. Amy was the second child, born four years after her brother Alex. ('I'm Jewish, yeah?' Amy would proclaim in 2004. 'So I'm one of those people who thinks that, at the end of the day, my opinion's always right, my gut instinct is always right. I think that's a Jewish thing. Or whatever.')

Janis was American, from Brooklyn, New York. There were other relatives in Miami and Atlanta, though financial constraints meant the London Winehouses hardly ever visited them.

Amy grew up in a two-bedroom flat, followed by a 1930s semi-detached, which was in turn succeeded by a three-bedroom Victorian terrace house. When Amy was growing up with her mother and father – which lasted until the parents split up when she was nine – Mitch worked as a double-glazing salesman, rising to an elevated position within the firm.

Mitch Winehouse ended up in later life working as a black-cab driver. 'I grew up in London's East End, which is where most Jewish people come from. And we had a very, very close-knit family. My father was a barber and then he became a London taxi driver. Most Jewish guys in those years did that.'

Mitch also had been a singer, a lover of Frank Sinatra. As already noted, there is something attractively louche about Mitch Winehouse and his barrel-chested, gangster-like machismo, an echo of Jake LaMotta in *Raging Bull*. 'I was more a semi-professional singer, when I was in my twenties and thirties. I stopped when I was about thirty. I was singing in clubs, local stuff, nothing special, and I really gave it up to look after the family because I wasn't making any money at it.'

'Rehab', Amy's greatest hit, even includes a reference to her father, from the point of view of a little girl ('And my daddy says so . . .') – he is omnipresent in her life, replicated through her bad-boy lovers. (The record also contains an allusion to her manager, Raye Cosbert, another father figure.)

A man of the world, Mitch had a relatively liberal attitude to drugs. In an interview, he once stated 'my daughter isn't drug-crazed. Even when I was a young man I dabbled – what young person hasn't?'[2]

There is a sense about Amy of her always trying to make things right for Mitch – the response of many children of divorces, as they go about the task of parenting their parents, often carrying the unnecessary secret fear that somehow it was their fault that their mother and father split up. Towards the end of her life, she persuaded him to record and release an album. 'I taught Amy to sing when she was a baby,' said Mitch. 'Like all parents, you know, they sing to their children – and when her first album came out, and she was doing shows, she would get me on stage to do a couple of songs, and it's always great fun.'

Because Mitch would sing to her so much, Amy followed his example; when she first attended school, teachers would tell her to stop singing in class. At the age of four, Amy had started her formal education up on the edge of north London at the borough of Barnet's Ossidge Primary School, which had a strong tradition of musical education. Bonding with a girl called Juliette Ashby, at a very early age she formed a musical double act, with Juliette as Pepsi and Amy as Shirley, the Wham! backing singers who forged a career away from George Michael. 'I think we clicked because we were both a bit off-key,' Amy told the *Observer*. 'We had a tune called "Spinderella", which was great.'

From the off, Amy Winehouse and Juliette Ashby were troublemakers, something that Amy would recall in an interview: 'You'd get sent to the school reception if you were naughty and we were always meeting up there. We told this boy that if he didn't pull his pants down we wouldn't be his friends any more. And he did it.'

'I used to egg Amy on a bit more because she was more fearless,' said Juliette. 'One of our best routines was that one of us would run out of the classroom in tears, and the other would say that they'd have to go out and comfort her. And then we'd just sit in a room somewhere, laughing for the rest of the lesson . . . Amy was always keeping her friends on their toes. I made her a friendship brooch once and she threw it in the sandpit.'

Amy denied this: 'I never did that. She was the one with the upper hand. Juliette always had strawberry shoelaces in her bag, and you knew you were flavour of the day if she offered you one.'

After outgrowing her obsession with Michael Jackson, Amy transferred her allegiances to Madonna, listening to her *Immaculate Collection* 'every day until I was about eleven. And then I discovered Salt-N-Pepa and TLC. My first real role models were Salt-N-Pepa and Lisa "Left Eye" Lopes,' Amy said in 2007. 'Salt-N-Pepa were real women who weren't afraid to talk about men and they got what they wanted and talked about girls they didn't like. That was always really cool.'[3]

Left Eye Lopes was some role model. She was the central creative thrust of TLC, whose fabulously crafted R'n'B albums took the three-piece girl group to superstardom; 1994's *CrazySexyCool*, their second longplayer, sold 15 million copies. But the tattoo-adorned Left Eye was also feisty, and seemed like trouble, a bad girl; the same year that *CrazySexyCool* came out, she burned down the Atlanta, Georgia mansion of her boyfriend, NFL football player Andre Rison. In 2002, while working on a video in Honduras, Left Eye swerved her SUV off a road to avoid a truck; her vehicle tumbled, and she died of her injuries, at the age of thirty.

When she was thirteen, however, Amy first heard a formative influence: 'Leader of the Pack' by the Shangri-Las. The Shangri-Las' melodramatic tunes, produced by Shadow Morton, also included 'Remember (Walking in the Sand)' and 'Out in the Streets', and were masterpieces of teenage angst.

Music was in the family. Amy's father's 'beautiful' mother, Cynthia, a huge fan of Tony Bennett, had once been engaged to the saxophonist Ronnie Scott, who had founded his celebrated jazz club in London's Soho. This gave Amy something of a royal jazz lineage – her petite 'nan', something of a mystic, brought out a similar disposition in Amy, who would share her interest in the reading of tarot cards. And her Uncle Leon was a professional horn player.

Janis was a big fan of Carole King and James Taylor, and King's mellifluous *Tapestry* album was a permanent highlight of Janis's in-car entertainment, as Amy well remembered. Amy was accordingly imbued with an appreciation of two of the most skilful of the early 1970s singer-songwriters.

She would have cause to become even more familiar with the tunes. When Amy was nine, she and her brother went to live with their mother, who had split up with Mitch. They moved from Southgate to nearby East Finchley.

Janis's view of the effect on her daughter of her parents' break-up is that Amy's response can be heard in her music. 'People talk a lot about the anger in Amy's songs. I think a lot of it was that her father wasn't there. Now he's trying to make up for that and he's spending more time with her, but what he's doing now is what he should have been doing then.'

Amy was always singing around the house. Janis recalled how she would sing Gloria Gaynor's 'I Will Survive' in the bath. Otherwise, it was classic rebellion. Removed from the influence of her father from the age of nine, Amy decided to take control of her own life. Soon she was wearing short skirts and make-up. When she lost her virginity at the age of fifteen, she told her mother, whose response was to put her daughter on the contraceptive pill. But Amy's first sexual experience proved traumatic – the boy involved did not treat her well, and she continued to speak about this for the rest of her life.

When she moved on to Ashmole, her secondary school in Southgate, Amy and Juliette's mothers spoke to the teachers, and asked for them to keep the two girls apart. Such was the success of this request that the two girls hardly saw each other between the ages of thirteen and fifteen. It didn't seem to really make any difference to Amy's life. Bright and alert, she found school boring and stifling.

Accordingly, an alternative to Ashmole was sought out. The Sylvia Young Theatre School was located off London's

Edgware Road. Amy had expressed a desire to finish her education there; in an autobiographical essay she wrote as part of her application, she expressed her inner desire: '. . . mostly I have this dream to be very famous. To work on stage. It's a lifelong ambition.' At her audition she impressed Young with her delivery of the jazz standard 'On the Sunny Side of the Street'. She was given a scholarship.

Yet her personality problems assailed her. 'She wouldn't wear the school uniform correctly,' Sylvia Young told the *Daily Mail*. 'She chewed gum in lessons. She wore a silver nose-ring and, when I asked her to take it out, she apologized, removed it, and replaced it an hour later. I could not ignore it but I understood and we found a way of coexisting. She would break the rules; I would tell her off; and she would acknowledge it. She could be disruptive in class, too, but this was largely because she didn't concentrate. She was, as I have said, wonderfully clever – so much so that we decided to move her one year ahead of her age group in the hope she would feel more challenged. Despite this, she was often bored out of her mind, although not in English lessons, which she loved.'[4]

Having an older brother was useful. Amy would pick up on what he was into. As a result, she read J.D. Salinger's *Catcher in the Rye* at an early age. After she heard Alex playing Thelonious Monk's 'Round Midnight', she gave herself the task of learning about great jazz singers and musicians. 'I learnt from Ella Fitzgerald and Sarah Vaughan and Dinah Washington.

They were the most inspiring people for me when I was developing a voice. It was the first real music apart from hip-hop that ever spoke to me and made an emotional connection.'[5]

In 1997, when she was fourteen, Amy began to smoke serious amounts of weed. There were also worrying instances of self-harm – gouging cuts into her arms with a knife, for example. Later diagnosed as a manifestation of depression, the self-harming had begun at the age of nine, when her parents had split up.

In 1997 she also made her first television appearance, on *The Fast Show*; she was in a sketch titled 'Peasblossom' that went out on Channel 4 on 21 November 1997. To Amy it must have seemed mildly validating.

In the same year, Amy was very influenced by a wonderful album by a new artist – *Baduizm* by Erykah Badu, a clever, heartfelt amalgam of jazz, soul and hip-hop, which was a revelation. A very romantic, adult set of songs, it must have touched the heart of the teenage girl.

Around this time Amy's mother Janis was called in to Sylvia Young's. She told the *Daily Mail* that the principal had phoned her. He told her, '"I think you should take her away." He didn't want children who weren't going to get good grades and Amy wasn't going to. She was very bright but was always messing around.'

The same day, Janis told the *Mail*, 'I had to take the family cat Katie to the vet. I dropped off the cat, went to the school and then went back to the vet's. We had the cat put down.

My joke is, I should have had Amy put down and the cat moved on.'[6]

Despite her mother's mirth, the decision was devastating for Amy. She cried every night, burying herself in the melancholy masterpieces of Ray Charles, another recent discovery.

She was then sent to the Mount School in Mill Hill, a private school whose fees were not cheap. Although there were many musical classes, her year there was very much one of treading water; she emerged with 5 GCSEs.

After some short-term employment, Amy mustered her forces and applied to Croydon's BRIT Performing Arts and Technology School, an establishment that had the advantage of being free. She attended the BRIT School for almost a year, before finally dropping out. At this stage she was inconsistent and drifting.

However, Sylvia Young had been unhappy that Amy had been excluded from her school by the principal. Accordingly, she offered her former pupil an 'after-care' service. 'When she reached sixteen, I arranged for her to audition for the National Youth Jazz Orchestra. She was later spotted performing with the Orchestra by colleagues of pop manager Simon Fuller, the man behind the Spice Girls' success.'[7]

By now Amy was regularly smoking marijuana with her partner-in-crime Juliette Ashby. Their double-act fuelled by the weed, the pair then found employment together. Juliette's father ran WENN (World Entertainment News Network), a showbusiness news gathering service with bureaus around the world. He found positions as trainee journalists for both girls in the London office. A fellow journalist at WENN was Sean Hamilton, later to join the *Sun*.

'I remember her when she was sixteen, straight from BRIT School,' he said. 'She worked for two months as a junior showbiz reporter. She was precocious, loud, brash, rude, always swearing. She was always singing in the office.

'She was a bit of a stage-school brat. At that point her passion was jazz. She was a big smoker and liked a drink. She was hilarious and loved life.

'Her first serious boyfriend was a guy called Chris – they met at WENN. Her album *Frank* was all about him when they split.

'Around the time she was at WENN she was going out gigging with various jazz bands and learning her craft. She was on the circuit on stage almost every night.'[8]

Instead of being fascinated by the glamorous world to which she was now being given access, and perhaps swept up into it, Amy Winehouse was unimpressed, which says positive things about her character. All she wanted to do each day was get home and play her guitar, and she couldn't wait for the weekends, when there would be shows with the National Youth Orchestra.

As Sean Hamilton says, at WENN she also met Chris, her first serious relationship. The love affair only lasted for nine months; Chris was seven years older than Amy. The story of some of their relationship is elucidated on *Frank*, especially on the album opener, 'Stronger Than Me'.

Tyler James, a boyfriend from their days together at the Sylvia Young School, had been signed to a division of Simon Fuller's 19 Management. With Tyler, Amy recorded some demo tunes, before passing them on to his management company.

Nick Godwin, a manager with 19 Management, heard the demo. 'We put it on,' he said, 'and there was this amazing voice, fantastic lyrics. They were eight- or nine-minute poems. Quite awkward guitar playing, but utterly breathtaking.'

In early 2002 Godwin and Nick Shymansky, an A&R man with 19, went to see Amy perform with the National Youth Jazz Orchestra. They were stunned by her powerful act, and made her an offer of management.

Amy Winehouse and Simon Fuller always seemed an unlikely alliance. The king of moulding talent into readily marketable packages and the queen of mouldy, the girl who would be happy playing pool with the street cleaners in her local pub, and who would happily slag off Rachel Stevens, another former alumni of the Sylvia Young School, whom Fuller managed as part of S Club 7 – Amy's jibes about his artist did not please the music mogul.

In Spring 2002 her management put Amy Winehouse into Mayfair Recording Studios in London's Primrose Hill. Felix Howard was suggested to her as a writing partner. Felix had briefly enjoyed fame, even notoriety, when as an eight-year-old boy he was featured on the cover of the *Face* magazine's 'buffalo look' issue; he later danced in a Madonna video. Subsequently he had become a guitarist and songwriter/producer for EMI, his work featuring on albums by such artists as Kylie Minogue, The Sugababes and Ms Dynamite amongst others. His main task, he said, was to prevent Amy writing songs whose lyrics ran for up to ten minutes – 'folk odysseys with no chorus'.

She worked on countless tunes, although 'Amy, Amy, Amy' and 'October Song' – a tune she wrote after the death of Ava, her pet canary (who is 'reborn like Sarah Vaughan') – were the only ones that survived from those sessions long enough to be recorded on *Frank*. Altogether, three producers worked with Amy on this new material; later it was acknowledged that this may have been a case of too many cooks. So, for the recording of her first album, this was stripped down.

All the same, so strong was Amy's material that a deal with EMI Music Publishing was soon secured by Nick Godwin after he had brought her songs to the attention of Guy Mott, an executive at the company. With her advance, Amy was able to rent a flat in Camden – in a street behind Camden Road overground rail station – which she shared with her old partner-in-crime, Juliette Ashby.

Endeavouring to let Amy Winehouse develop at her own pace, 19 kept a tight lid on any news of their signing of this prodigious talent. But John Campbell, a friend of Island Records' A&R director Darcus Beese, played his pal some tunes. 'Who is she?' Darcus asked. But Campbell had been sworn to not reveal her name.

His appetite whetted, Beese – the son of Darcus Howe, one of Britain's leading black commentators and intellectuals – kept his ears open for any information about the owner of this extraordinary voice. 'I was trying to do real old-school A&R, involving a bit of detective work,' he recalled. Then, on a visit to another friend, Major, a producer who lived in Harlesden, Beese was played the same set of songs. Major, however, was under no confidentiality obligation; he told the Island Records man precisely who this singer was and who was guiding her career.

Yet on the several occasions Darcus Beese phoned 19 Management about Amy, his calls were not returned. One afternoon he decided to drive down to the company's offices, in London's Battersea, at Ransome's Dock on the Thames.

Walking into the premises, he found Amy Winehouse sitting on the floor with her friend Tyler. On a break from further Mayfair recording sessions, they were sifting through photographs of her (then) pair of tattoos, searching for a brand image that was not reliant on a picture of her face.

Darcus introduced himself. 'So what?' said the stroppy nineteen-year-old Amy. 'She already had attitude and swagger,' said Darcus. 'She was nineteen and already writing and singing songs like "You Send Me Flying" and "You're a Monkey Not a Boy". Songs that have such perception.

It wasn't pop. She waxes off the scale lyrically on the first album. She owned her material and sound. Sarah Vaughan meets Mahalia Jackson meets Courtney Love, she seemed to me. She said she was a jazz singer, but as you grow and things happen in your personal life . . . It was all her: no one came up with the sound. I told Nick Gatfield [the then head of Island Records, a former member of Dexy's Midnight Runners] that I wanted to sign her.'

At Island's headquarters on Kensington High Street, before the company bigwigs, Amy played a short set. Among the tunes she performed was '(There is) No Greater Love'.

Amy was a little mystified by all this attention. She still hadn't seriously imagined she could make a living out of music, despite it being her burning desire, as she confirmed: 'I honestly never thought I would make any money from music – I figured I'd get a job in an office or as a waitress. I never had a great plan or promoted myself, but in a way I've been working for this for years.'

Getting to know her at a respectful distance, Darcus Beese found himself even more impressed: 'When she dressed up and put on her make-up when she was going out, she'd say she was putting on her warpaint. I thought she always looked great. I think she wanted to walk down the road looking a million dollars. She'd do that if she were famous or not – she's a complete artist.'

Aware of the confusion created by the trio of producers at Mayfair, Beese had his own concept of how his new signing should progress; she needed to be guided by a single, visionary producer.

Signed to EMI Publishing was Salaam Remi. Growing up in Miami in the milieu of expatriate Jamaican musicians, Salaam Remi had produced Ini Kamoze's 1994 masterly global smash, 'Here Comes the Hotstepper'. Subsequently he had worked with Nas (by then Amy's favourite hip-hop artist), The Fugees, Toni Braxton, Ms Dynamite and Lauryn Hill. Hill's masterful solo album, *The Miseducation of Lauryn Hill,* had had a significant effect on Amy Winehouse on its release in 1998. Equally significantly, Remi produced the song 'Block Party' by TLC member Lisa 'Left Eye' Lopes, especially encouraging for devoted Left Eye fan Amy. When it was suggested she work with Salaam Remi, the choice could not have been better.

Starting on 27 May 2002, *Frank* was recorded at Salaam Remi's studio in Miami, which he had set up in his home. Salaam worked with Amy on the tunes; Amy wrote or co-wrote every song on the record. She would usually write songs while playing the guitar.

The songs she recorded for what would become the *Frank* album had the advantage of seeming like tunes you had already heard. One song for the album was written as a meditation on the break-up of her first long-term relationship, with Chris, the older guy she had met while at WENN. 'Take the Box' was literally a description of Amy's response to the split – to put all her boyfriend's 'stuff' in a box, to get rid of him. In fact, this break-up was to prove inspirational for her art; songs about the end of that love affair poured out of her, some of them coated in vitriol, like the album opener, 'Stronger Than Me', bemoaning the 'New Man' aspects of her former beau (asking him if he's a 'ladyboy'). Amy clearly liked her men strong – like her dad, Mitch.

Working on the Miami sessions with Salaam Remi was a backing singer called Jeni Fujita, who had also worked on *The Miseducation of Lauryn Hill.* Troy Genius, renamed as Troy Wilson on the sleeve notes, was a Jamaican drummer who had worked with Dennis Brown, Bounti Killa and Redman, among others. He and Remi had also worked with Alicia Keyes. For the Amy sessions, Salaam Remi brought in Earl 'Chinna' Smith, the masterly Jamaican guitarist who had worked with Bob Marley, Burning Spear, Peter Tosh, Black Uhuru and Augustus Pablo, among many others. Chinna was 'very impressed' with Amy as a person, and especially with her lyrics; his playing was all over 'Moody's Mood For Love', with its distinct reggae feel.

When Darcus Beese flew over from London to Miami to check out the sessions, he was staggered by what he heard. 'Up until then I knew she was special, but not how great. I thought new artists couldn't emulate that old stuff: people who write and bare their soul – Janis Joplin or Billie Holiday. Then Amy came along, a singer-songwriter in the true sense of the word. She was a doddle to work with: she was as musical as the musicians – she knew what was minor, or major. And I loved the detail they were putting in, like the crackle of old vinyl at the beginning of "Know You Now".'

Deviating from his original personal brief of having a single producer oversee Amy's first album, Darcus Beese made the decision to maximize the recording session's potential by also calling on the talents of Commissioner Gordon. Growing up in New York's Bronx in the early 1980s, Gordon 'Commissioner Gordon' Williams had been immersed in hip-hop culture, where he was personally acquainted with such legends as Kool Herc, and became involved with Afrika Bambaata's Zulu Nation. More recently part of KRS-One's Boogie Down Productions, he had already won three Grammy Awards for his work on *The Miseducation of Lauryn Hill* – which was beginning to feel like a key reference point for Amy Winehouse's first record.

Commissioner Gordon worked from his studio, The Headquarters, in New Jersey. He had also engineered for Carlos Santana, Whitney Houston and Will Smith. When working with Amy on *Frank*, Gordon was impressed by her knowledge of jazz and said that she knew more about it than he did. He noticed she had pictures of Dinah Washington, Ella Fitzgerald, Sarah Vaughan and Billie Holiday stuck into her lyric book.

The cover of *Frank* shows a happy, wholesome, open-faced Amy Winehouse walking a small black dog; a surprising piece of marketing – almost as though there is some uncertainty as to who will buy the record. There are hints of puppy-fat, and she's busty. Not a visible trace of a tattoo. But such an innocent image contrasts starkly with the 'adult' content of the lyrics – a 'Parental Advisory Explicit Content' decal is attached to the image.

On the record itself, Amy Winehouse declares herself to be a stroppy New Woman – as is made clear from the first lyrics on 'Stronger Than Me'. Songs like 'Fuck Me Pumps' reveal her attitude towards certain of her fellow women – she expresses her contempt for certain mutton-dressed-as-lamb, supposedly modern women, shamelessly chasing rich men as potential husbands, but ending up suffering tawdry one-night stands. And there are more songs clearly influenced by her mother and father's relationship, like 'What Is It About Men'.

To build an underground buzz, three separate nights were booked at the Cobden Club on Kensal Road in Notting Hill, beginning on 22 July 2003. On the first night Amy arrived on stage with just an acoustic guitar. When she appeared again at the Cobden, on 11 August, she had a group playing behind her.

Annie Lennox, who shared the same management, came to the last Cobden show: 'I was completely blown away. She was like a woman in her thirties, with a whole, seasoned delivery, not fazed by anything at all. I was in awe of her. I thought, wow, you have a special talent. God, you are eighteen [she was actually nineteen]: where did that come from?'[9]

'Stronger Than Me' came out as the first single on 6 October 2003, two weeks before the astonishingly self-assured debut album itself – 'at once innocent and sleazy', as the *Guardian* review of *Frank* described it. Amy was not the only contemporary artist to be ploughing the jazz furrow; new talents Jamie Cullum, Katie Melua and Norah Jones all considered themselves 'jazz' musicians. Much to her disgruntlement, Amy was lumped in with them.

A UK tour had been set up for the back-end of the year. Amy Winehouse's first major London date, at the very cute Bush Hall on Uxbridge Road in Shepherd's Bush, was on 3 December 2003. Accompanied by a drummer, two guitarists, a bass player, and a three-piece horn section, Amy also played acoustic and electric guitar. 'Long may her angst unfurl,' concluded Caroline O'Sullivan in her considered *Guardian* review.[10]

At first the album sold slowly. But on 27 May 2004, Amy won the Ivor Novello Award for Best Contemporary Song for 'Stronger Than Me'. Sales of *Frank* soared to 200,000, and the album peaked at number 13.

In March 2004, Amy appeared on Jonathan Ross's Friday night BBC1 television show. Looking glamorous in a pretty dress, her hair tumbling down to her shoulders, she described her music as 'straight jazz-hip-hop cross'. Ross questioned her about the broken romance that influenced so many of the songs on *Frank*. 'I've got about seven or eight songs about this guy . . . I was very frustrated about the way things turned out between me and him . . . I just wanted to write music that was emotional, that people would want to listen to and connect with . . . I always said I never wanted to write about love, but then I went and did that anyway,' she responded.

Later in the year, at a show in Holland, Amy returned to the same theme: 'This next song is called "You Sent Me Flying". I wrote this song about a man who I used to work for who I really liked, hmm, and he didn't like me back. So this tune is for anyone who ever liked someone who just didn't . . . care.'

'There'll be more, don't worry,' called out an audience member.

'That's cool,' retorted Amy. 'I fucked him up since then, so that's cool.'

'Where does your self-confidence come from?' Ross asked her.

Her response – all things considered – was revealing: 'My dad is very outspoken – he's a taxi driver.'

Referring to 19 Management, Ross asked if the company had tried to mould her. 'One of them tried to mould me into a big triangle shape and I said, *No-o-o-o-o*!' she laughed.

'What I like about you,' concluded Ross, 'is you sound so common.'

Amy laughed: 'They gave me elocution lessons but they didn't stick!'

Then she performed 'Love is Blind'.

Around the same time, Paul Du Noyer interviewed Amy for *The Word* magazine, meeting her early one lunchtime in a Camden tapas bar. A perceptive writer, Du Noyer immediately picked up on the 'troubled' aspect of Amy Winehouse: 'She has a striking, exotic look. Being curvy and with a pronounced bone structure Winehouse looks Amazonian in some photographs, but is actually petite in person. Yet she has a cold stare that you guess she could deploy to deadly effect. She is very bright, though not in a systematic way, as if she has learnt so much so quickly that the patterns have not yet come together in her head. She seems a forthright young woman, and her conversational manner is confrontational. By the interview's end, however, she looks preoccupied by private anxieties.'

In the interview Amy waxed ecstatic about London, which was always a subtext of *Frank*. 'Oh, I love this city! I love it. Wherever I go in the world, to land back in London is the best feeling. I get to see so many amazing places when I'm working, like Miami, and I think, I could live here. But then I go, yeah, but I wouldn't be in London.'

Frank, wrote Du Noyer, 'was her diary of a torrid adolescence – she was just nineteen when it was recorded – sung with the funky melisma of a jazz veteran and the glottal stops of a mouthy schoolgirl on the Piccadilly Line. It's a great piece of modern British R&B: for all its vintage American stylings, *Frank* could not have been made anywhere but in London, in the twenty-first century.'

When the record was thus defined to her, Amy seemed delighted by the writer's assessment: 'Thank you so much!' she beamed. 'That is the best compliment you could pay to me. The city is really important to me. I've always been a really independent girl. From the age of thirteen or so I've always found my own way in the city and there's nothing I like more than to find another part that I didn't already know. It really fascinates me. It's a really English album but I guess I'm a typically English girl.'

To the consternation of her record company and management, Amy had already questioned the worth of *Frank*; and Du Noyer followed up the theme of whether she liked her own record:

'Yes and no. If I'd been 100 per cent satisfied then I could have relaxed and gone on holiday for six months. But it's a constant thing for me to better myself. I've got a clear ambition now, to make a record of what I hear in my head. Like Stevie Wonder did. It was a learning curve. I always thought I would do music, but I certainly didn't expect to have a record deal by the time I was nineteen.'

At the end of the interview, Du Noyer mentions a poignant moment, as Amy Winehouse describes the world of promotion into which she has been pulled since *Frank* was released. 'There's nothing real in it, nothing real. Which really drains me. But you know what? It's gotta be done.'

'She suddenly seems 65 years old,' he writes.[11]

Staying in touch with her local area, Camden, Amy was interviewed at around the same time by Dan Carrier, her local paper's chief feature writer. A few days later, she dropped off a collection of vinyl presses to his home, dedicated to his young niece, a fan. 'Your uncle is cool,' an inscription read, before being signed off with kisses.

In Camden Amy Winehouse had become one of the locals. She was great company, whether you were one of the *Big Issue* vendors with whom she would regularly converse; one of the homeless, who were regular recipients of the £5 notes she would dole out; or fellow customers in the York Way fish and chip shop or the Marathon kebab shop, where she was always up for a rap or reasoning. Staggering out in her alarmingly high heels, Amy would purchase Assam or Earl Grey tea from her newsagent; tuna salad she would pick up at Cafe Villa, also in York Way, a regular haunt.

'I'd overhear her conversations with her band,' waitress Lesieli Kava told the local newspaper. 'Once, a band member was expecting his second child, and he was talking about it with everyone, and I remember she said something like, "I want that," or "I wouldn't mind that." I remember that really well because everyone started kind of teasing her about it afterwards.'

In the cocktail bar and restaurant, Made in Brasil, in Camden's Inverness Street, Amy also became a regular, even helping out with the cleaning of the place at the end of one long night. 'Amy got up and said, "I'm polishing the glasses, give me a cloth",' said the owner. 'And she stood there polishing the glasses, cleaning all the sticky liquids off the bar.'[12]

In some interviews, however, Amy Winehouse had given short shrift to her fellow artists; Dido, in particular, was singled out for contempt. Such a stance did not endear her to everybody. 'That's what my nan said to me,' she admitted later. 'See, I don't give a fuck about people who make shit music. I. Don't. Give. A. Fuck. That's it. But my nan is right when she says to me, I know you're a nice girl, Amy. I know that, your family know that, but other people don't know that. They think you're a little bitch and that's getting in the way of your music.'[13]

In the early spring of 2004, Amy had run into a man a year older than herself with whom she instantly clicked. His name was Blake Fielder-Civil, and he was a well-mannered boy. 'I used to go out clubbing with Blake. He's kind of a charming bad boy,' said a friend of his. 'He's the sort of bloke who's got all the chat – who's got a little twinkle in his eye. He'll go out and misbehave and do who knows what, but he'd never let a woman go through a door second.'[14]

A 'drop-out' from Bourne Grammar School in his native Lincolnshire, Fielder-Civil had moved to London when he was sixteen. His parents had broken up, his mother remarrying a head teacher; this meant that the family would frequently relocate to other cities, and Blake was never able to settle. In London he worked as a production assistant on music videos, and was handsome and stylish.

Amy and Blake hit it off instantly, especially sexually. It seemed as though fate had driven them together, and they felt compulsively drawn to each other. 'We loved each other intensely and probably in a really unhealthy co-dependent way,' he admitted later of what became a love story of epic proportions.[15]

But from the start, there was pain. Blake was living with another woman. He would see Amy, but then go back to his already established relationship. Amy would be left in the endless dark hurt that she would finally lay bare in the song – and album title – 'Back to Black'.

The co-dependency included physical violence towards Blake by Amy; in an interview in 2007, she confessed that, with drink taken, she had been known to physically attack him: 'If he says one thing I don't like then I'll chin him.'[16]

Amy was busy on stage during 2004. Not just in the UK, but all over Europe: in Germany, Spain, Holland, France. She performed at the Glastonbury Festival, the V Festival and the Montreal International Jazz Festival. ('It's not a quiet jazz show that needs to be in an intimate setting, not at all,' she said. 'I'm a fierce singer. I got a horn section. We got electric instruments, it's a big sound. It's not a tame thing.') She started the year with a tour of cherry-picked clubs and concluded it with a full UK tour, ending at the 5,000-capacity Brixton Academy on 19 November.

In January 2004 she was nominated as Best Female Solo Artist for the Brit Awards. 'It's a big compliment,' she told ITN following the nominations. 'It doesn't feel like me being nominated. It feels like my cousin called Amy. I never thought I'd be here performing.'[17]

She told the interviewer that, for her, the peak experience

of 2003 had been meeting the jazz and funk artist Roy Ayers. 'Getting the album finished and holding it in my hands was one of the biggest highlights.'

Passed over for awards at the Brits, on 27 May 2004 Amy Winehouse received what was for her a far more prestigious gong at the Grosvenor House hotel in London. She won the 49th annual Ivor Novello Award for Best Contemporary Song, for 'Stronger Than Me', solidifying a burgeoning reputation as one of the best songwriters of her generation.

She ended 2004 on the *Hootenanny* television show, Jools Holland's New Year's Eve special, singing Dinah Washington's 'Teach Me Tonight', her hair cascading to her shoulders, managing (despite the sexually knowing tone of the lyrics) to look almost cosmically innocent.

A year later, you would be beginning to have the impression that such a sweet façade would seem very much the mask of a wolf in sheep's clothing.

During 2005 Amy Winehouse's consumption of drink and drugs took an exponential upswing. She also experienced serious weight loss gone was the curvy figure, that collision of voluptuousness and puppy-fat. She became increasingly volatile; an anger clearly burnt within her. Unleashed by her intake of assorted substances, it would begin to assert itself in a frightening manner.

Her emotions, both positive and negative, were driven by her obsessive love for Blake Fielder-Civil. Was he a substitute for Mitch Winehouse, Amy's male archetype, to whom her charmingly spivvy new boyfriend's persona bore some resemblance? For her part, Amy would behave with Blake like a typically possessive Jewish mother, fussing over her 'baby', as she liked to call him.

During the course of 2005, Amy Winehouse was photographed with increasing regularity emerging from bars or nightclubs, looking slightly off her head. Scenting a kill, as they do, the paparazzi turned her evident vulnerability and relative innocence into a legitimate target. There was something almost frighteningly premeditated about the ongoing soap opera that Amy Winehouse became during 2005–6. Later she would confess to a television interviewer that she was 'manic depressive'.

By the beginning of the next year, Amy's lifestyle had led her to change managers. Amy and 19 parted company. Nick Shymansky, who was the same age as Amy, was one of her closest friends; but as part of her management team, he made the decision she should talk to a counsellor about her increasingly evident drinking. And in doing that, according to Darcus Beese, 'something broke'. Consequently, he was replaced by Raye Cosbert, who had promoted all her UK shows. He had first made his name putting on Public Enemy at Docklands Arena – the first hip-hop act to sell out a UK arena show – and later had promoted shows by Robbie Williams, Blur, Björk, and Massive Attack. The fact that Raye was black may have tickled Amy's ever-aware sense of street cool and been an additional selling-point; again, it set her apart – there were no other significant white UK acts with black managers.

By then, however, Amy Winehouse appeared to know no notion of restraint. In February 2006, at the annual Brit Awards, she bellowed from her table at Bono – 'Shut up! I don't give a fuck!' – as the hapless U2 frontman attempted to address the audience from the stage.[18] Here, it might be felt that Amy only personified the zeitgeist: many members of the audience no doubt identified with her sentiments. Moreover, it was becoming apparent that Amy Winehouse did not 'give a fuck' about anything. That impression was confirmed by Don Letts, the DJ and filmmaker, who found himself sharing a table with her at the Brits. 'At one point I said that I wished I had a spliff. At which she opened her bag, took out a huge stash of weed, with a grinder, and proceeded to skin up at the table. She was this Fellini-esque voluptuous girl. Feisty, determined, very to-the-point. Very confident. She was very charismatic and bubbly. And very funny.

'I knew *Frank*. When I first heard her voice, it sent shivers down my spine. It was the frightening honesty and cutting observations. I like the way the lyrical wordplay is so macho: "Fuck Me Pumps" from this little white girl.'[19]

Amy Winehouse had met Blake Fielder-Civil in her local Camden pub. She would go there to play pool and listen to the joint's excellent jukebox with its soul and Motown sounds. Their time with each other was lived out in a miasma of drugs. Most of the time they were together, they were out of it, on one substance or another. Amy of course was a serious spliff-head, but this new boyfriend didn't smoke weed, preferring harder drugs that came in powder form: coke, crack, ketamine, heroin. Smack was something that Amy had not got into. Even her dysfunctional, hyperactive mind had always processed and accepted the information that if you do heroin, it is likely to – sooner or later – kill you. Blake was also very partial to alcohol. No stranger herself to booze, Amy Winehouse now became a voracious consumer of it.

Within a month of meeting him, Winehouse had wilfully tattooed 'Blake' on her neck, something of a proprietorial statement. Above her left breast, as though on the top of a blazer pocket, she had inked the rubric, 'Blake's Pocket'. (A later, equally significant tattoo, on her upper left arm, was an image of a horseshoe, bookended with the words 'Daddy's Girl'.)

As stability was lacking in her relationship with Blake Fielder-Civil (he would go home to his girlfriend), Amy Winehouse simultaneously fell into another love affair, with a north London Jewish boy. Alex Clare (also know as Claire), a musician and chef three years younger than her, became a secondary object of Amy's affections. Then – as during 2006 Blake Fielder-Civil appeared to fall altogether off Amy's radar – Clare became her number one boyfriend. Yet he was not best pleased when, one night in the Camden music venue pub the Dublin Castle, Amy sold kisses to punters in exchange for shots of tequila. And he was even less happy when he learned that Amy and Blake had made up their differences and were back together. 'After turning up at three in the morning at The Hawley Arms,' Clare wrote on his MySpace blog in March 2007, 'I saw the ex with her ex and I saw red mist. I was shaking like a leaf and decided to get . . . leathered while she sat there inebriated and on the lap of her ex.' Clare sold his account of his adventures with Amy to the *News of the World* newspaper, who ran the story under the headline 'Bondage Crazed Amy Just Can't Beehive in Bed'.

On 23 October, Island Records released 'Rehab', the first single from her new album, *Back to Black*, itself released four days later. As a trailer for the album, and as a stand-alone self-portrait of Amy Winehouse, 'Rehab' could not be bettered. Structured like an old-fashioned R'n'B song ('Soul, doowop, girl groups,' was what Amy said she had been listening to), 'Rehab' is a formidable number, expressive of the air of colossal arrogance, complete insolence and sheer innocence effortlessly evinced by Amy. It was also utterly honest; Amy describes being sent to see a counsellor about her drinking. Her response to why she drinks? 'I'm gonna lose my baby/So I always keep a bottle near'. And then, a few lines later: 'I don't ever wanna drink again/I just, ooh, I just need a friend'. Words from the heart; a pity no one seemed to be listening.

The single reached number 7 in the UK charts; more surprisingly, it marked the American breakthrough of Amy Winehouse, hitting number 9. (As yet, *Frank* had not even been released in the United States.) It would go on to win three Grammy Awards in 2008, including Record of the Year, Song of the Year, and Best Female Pop Vocal Performance, and was nominated for two more Grammy Awards.

As with *Frank*, *Back to Black* had a pair of producers. Salaam Remi had continued his successful course with Amy. Now, providing the new album with a different feel altogether from *Frank*, were the talents of 32-year-old Mark Ronson. Born in London, but brought up in New York in a musical family (his stepfather was Mick Jones of Foreigner), Ronson, intelligent and likable, at an early age had become a high-end scene-maker, deejaying at moneyed Manhattan parties; at heart, however, Ronson, like Amy Winehouse, remained another north London Jewish kid obsessed with soul music. Signed to Elektra Records, Ronson had released one album, *Here Comes the Fuzz*, in 2003, employing a diversity of artists. Although the record was well received, it failed to sell, and Ronson was dropped by the label. Subsequently, he set up his own label, Allido Records, a subsidiary of Sony-BMG, and he became legendary for his mixing and remixing abilities.

One of Ronson's especial skills was making recorded tracks radio-friendly. As well as being an expert at drawing out the essence of a horn section – as he showed on the new song 'Tears Dry on Their Own' – his crisp drum sound, his 'beats', was perfect for pop songs. As backing group, Ronson brought in The Dap-Kings; working with Sharon Jones, the New York-based Dap-Kings had shunned digital recording, working with analogue equipment and aiming for an authentic soul-funk sound. The Dap-Kings were featured on six of the eleven songs on *Back to Black*, most notably on 'Rehab' and 'You Know I'm No Good'. Miscredited on *Back to Black*'s liner notes as Dapking Studios, several of the tunes were recorded at their Daptone Studios. (On Amy's first US dates The Dap-Kings toured with her as backing group.)

Arguably, Ronson's own career benefitted more from his involvement with Amy Winehouse than hers did – after all, hardly anyone had heard of him before *Back to Black*. And Salaam Remi had an equally significant, if not greater, role. 'Mark Ronson had access to the media with his solo material, whilst Salaam Remi is a quiet, backroom guy. But he did at least as much,' said Darcus Beese.

Whatever, the record was a masterpiece, a perfect set of songs, even down to its relatively brief running time of thirty-seven minutes. Amy again bared her soul about her relationships, specifically with Blake. 'Me & Mr Jones' had originally been titled, simply, 'Fuckery', perhaps the first mainstream UK usage of this Jamaican term. The song (its title a twist on the 1972 Billy Paul/Philadelphia International hit 'Me and Mrs Jones') detailed the unfaithful relationship that Blake had had with Amy when still with his former girlfriend, a theme examined exquisitely in the title track and on the self-explanatory 'Love is a Losing Game'. Meanwhile, there was the hilarious wit of 'Addicted', the album closer. Everything is conceptually correct in this witty tale of urban weed-smoking etiquette; at one level it is like a subplot from the sitcom *Ideal*, on the other a distinct call for . . . well, maybe just for the dealer.

Listening to the words of *Back to Black*, you felt Amy's utter vulnerability, the manner in which everyone around her was pulling her in all directions. Nevertheless – in fact perhaps because of this – the record would become the biggest selling album in the UK since the turn of the millennium; in 2007 alone, it sold 1.85 million copies. In the USA it entered the album charts at number seven.

Cynthia Winehouse, Amy Winehouse's paternal grandmother, who had once been engaged to Ronnie Scott, passed away in 2006. Later, Janis would insist that the loss of Cynthia was traumatic for her daughter, causing Amy's seeming headlong race into decline. Extremely close to Cynthia, Amy even had her name tattooed on her right arm. The two women's shared interest in tarot cards had led to Amy often having a pack in her handbag. Was this where the singer had come by the arcane information that she would not last longer than twenty-seven years of age? Her mother Janis certainly recalled her daughter mentioning this on a number of occasions. Whatever the truth, in the following months Amy frequently became a public spectacle.

In October 2006, the month that 'Rehab' and *Back to Black* were released, Amy Winehouse appeared on UK television, on *The Charlotte Church Show*. Duetting with Church, Amy closed the show with a version of Michael Jackson's 'Beat It', a tremendous, pounding performance. Although outsung by Church, in technical terms at least, Amy Winehouse's driving rendition of the song was stupendous, even though she was unable to remember all the lyrics, and was clearly bladdered. She had a new look, wearing a glossy black beehive helmet of hair, as well as numerous new tattoos; the hair made her look like one of The Ronettes, an ultimate bad girl, and Amy clearly felt that was how she should behave. On 16 November, on the BBC pop quiz show *Never Mind the Buzzcocks*, she was demonstrably off her head, at one point spitting on the floor. When Simon Amstell asked her if she was emulating Pete Doherty, Amy replied that she was meeting up with him later. As a demonstration of train-wreck television, her performance on the show set high standards.

Yet she insisted that she was cleaning up her act; having joined a gym, Amy also claimed to be running regularly. On *Hootenanny* that New Year's Eve, she looked in fine fettle, appearing with Paul Weller, duetting with him on the Marvin Gaye classic 'I Heard It Through the Grapevine', and performing solo on Toots and the Maytals' 'Monkey Man'.

But almost immediately there was further controversy. On 6 January 2007 Amy Winehouse had been booked to play at G-A-Y, at the Astoria on London's Charing Cross Road, the UK's leading gay night. Like several similarly diva-like chanteuses – Marianne Faithfull, Kylie Minogue, Judy Garland – Amy had been embraced as a gay icon. Unfortunately, as

Amy came out on stage – at around 1.30 a.m. – and began to perform 'Back to Black', she simultaneously began clutching at her stomach, rushing from the stage to throw up. She did not return to perform any more material. Afterwards, witnesses insisted that prior to her 'performance', she had smelled strongly of drink.

The next month, however, at the Brit Awards on 14 February 2007, looking extremely pretty in a yellow dress, the edge of her black bra visible in her cleavage, Amy seemed in fine form. She won the award for Best British Female Artist. Amy was also nominated in the Best British Album category, but *Back to Black* lost out to the Arctic Monkeys' debut, *Whatever People Say I Am, That's What I'm Not.* That May, 'Rehab' won the Ivor Novello Award for Best Contemporary Song.

A little later in February, the NME put on a show at the Astoria, at which Amy delivered a strong (and sober) set. As the NME night ended, a further G-A-Y night replaced it. Still in her dressing room, Amy found herself returning to the stage, redeeming herself before the G-A-Y crowd, and not for the final time that year.

On 17 March 2007, Amy made her US television debut on *The David Letterman Show*, singing 'Rehab' to close the programme. In his end-of-show rap the redoubtable Letterman compared her look to that of The Ronettes. The TV appearance was a plug for her impending three-week US tour, in April and May that year, which was largely a huge success. In an interview with *Spin* magazine, undertaken during those dates, Amy rather surprised Terry Richardson, the photographer. With a shard of broken mirror, she scratched the words 'I Love Blake' onto her bare stomach.

Because she was clearly such an easy target, the level of paparazzi attention was relentless and remorseless; visits to McDonalds, her local fish and chip shop, convenience stores – all would relentlessly be shadowed by them. Finally, under the Protection from Harassment Act, Amy Winehouse took out an injunction against a paparazzi agency; its photographers were banned from following her, or from coming within 100 yards of her home.

Yet it seemed that wherever she appeared, increasingly looking like some living piece of art, Amy was a good story. For example, when Amy went on stage (the gap of her newly missing upper right tooth evident) with The Rolling Stones at the Isle of Wight Festival on 10 June 2007, singing the Temptations' 'Ain't Too Proud To Beg' with Mick Jagger, and standing next to Keith Richards, it was as though she was confronting the mirror-image personification of her own inner demons; it was quite clear she had become the female Keith Richards. (Amy had played the festival the previous day, on 9 June.)

Meanwhile, something very significant had taken place in her personal life. Amy Winehouse and Blake Fielder-Civil got married in Miami, Florida, on 18 May 2007, a court official the only witness. Only the next year, Blake would confess to the *News of the World* that it was he who had introduced

Amy Winehouse to hard drugs. 'I made the biggest mistake of my life by taking heroin in front of her. I introduced her to heroin, crack cocaine, and self-harming. I feel more than guilty.'[20]

The notion that Blake Fielder-Civil was the dark force who drove Amy to destruction is too simplistic, however. Wilful and self-assured, Amy was by no means the innocent waiting to be corrupted that she was sometimes portrayed as. Loving the glamour of a rock 'n' roll lifestyle, she seemed to imagine that there was something 'cool' in such incessantly druggie behaviour, a seamless fusion – or confusion – of life and art; after all, she was hardly the only person in the area so indulging. Her neighbour and friend up on Primrose Hill, where he was ensconced at the home of his girlfriend Kate Moss, was Pete Doherty, seemingly never out of the media for his latest drug bust. With its legion of street dealers, Camden was notorious for its dark, sleazy side, hardly the best environment in which to clean up – even if you wanted to.

A month after his wedding, moreover, Blake Fielder-Civil was involved in an incident that would have extremely serious consequences – he and a friend, Michael Brown, assaulted a barman in the hip Hoxton pub, the Macbeth, and their victim suffered a fractured cheekbone. They were charged by the police with having committed grievous bodily harm, an imprisonable offence.

But eventually a spell in rehab for Amy Winehouse did finally come along. In early August 2007 a number of

European shows that Amy had been due to perform were cancelled; ill health and exhaustion were given as the causes. In fact, on 7 August Amy Winehouse had overdosed on heroin, ketamine, crystal meth and alcohol. Returning to London from Chicago, where she had played the Lollapalooza festival, she had gone with Blake on a pub crawl from the airport back to her home in Camden. Rushed to University College hospital by Blake after her heart appeared to stop beating, she had her stomach pumped clean. Amy later credited him with saving her life.

A week later she and Blake jointly checked into the Causeway Clinic in Essex, intending to say yes-yes-yes to rehab. After forty-eight hours, however, they were saying no-no-no. Quitting the facility, sited on an island, they flew back to Camden by helicopter. That night they went to the Old Eagle pub in Camden with Blake's parents.

On 23 August Amy and Blake checked into the chic Sanderson hotel in London's West End. In the early hours of the morning, Amy was seen running away from the hotel, bloodied and bruised, pursued by an also bleeding Blake. In the street, Amy flagged down a car filled with girls. She asked them for a ride out of there, and they dropped her off a mile or so away. Returning to the hotel a bit later, Blake and Amy clearly resolved their differences; by 4 a.m. they were strolling around Soho, arm in arm. Later, Amy claimed the injuries had taken place when she had brought a prostitute to the room, expressly for the consumption of hard drugs.

It seemed as though everything in this sordid soap opera was unravelling at breakneck speed. Amy Winehouse became a cause célèbre for well-wishers. Deciding that getting out of town was the most sensible course of action, Amy and Blake flew off to the Caribbean island of St Lucia, checking into the Jade Mountain resort for £1,000 a night.

A two-week European tour scheduled for October, honouring August's cancelled shows, went ahead as planned. In Bergen in Norway, however, the long shadow cast by their much publicized misadventures in London caught up with them – they seemed to be taking on the unsavoury mantle of Sid Vicious and Nancy Spungen. At the SAS Hotel Norge, Amy and Blake were busted for possession of marijuana, and each fined the equivalent of £350. This would have serious consequences for Amy Winehouse's career in the United States.

Yet this was only a small episode compared with what was to come. Following the assault charge made against him after injuring the Macbeth barman, Blake had sleazily endeavoured to bribe him with £200,000 – the provenance of this cash was always clear – to refuse to testify, and thereby save Blake's skin. But this pay-off had come to the attention of the police. Now, not only was Blake charged with committing a serious assault, he was also to be prosecuted for attempting to pervert the course of justice. To arrest Blake, the police used a battering-ram to break down the door of his and Amy's marital home.

A British tour was scheduled. Almost unexpectedly, all

things considered, it went ahead, kicking off in Birmingham on 14 November 2007, two days after a distressed-looking Amy had been seen outside the gates of Pentonville prison, where she had been refused access to see her husband. In Birmingham, at the 12,000-capacity National Indoor Arena, Amy came on stage an hour late, forgot the words to songs, and shouted 'monkey cunts' at members of the audience who were booing her lacklustre performance. Before the tour was even three days in, there were tabloid reports that the tour manager had quit after passively inhaling heroin on the tour bus.

It is easy to forget the extent to which the saga of Amy and Blake dominated the media in 2007. Suddenly the full degree to which the world was watching Amy's tragedy became apparent as she turned into an international incident. The head of the United Nations Office on Drugs and Crime, Antonio Maria Costa, singled out the behaviour of Amy Winehouse and her neighbour Kate Moss as reprehensible examples of glamorizers of cocaine. Costa was making a serious point – increasingly West Africa was being used as a trans-shipment point for cocaine smuggled from South America, and this was having a progressively more deleterious effect on the cultures and economies of impoverished African nations. On 21 November London's *Evening Standard* ran a front-page picture of Amy with what was clearly cocaine residue in her right nostril.

Despite ecstatic responses to her tremendous shows at

Brixton Academy on 22 and 23 November, Amy's performance the next night, at Hammersmith Apollo, found her back to her worst ways. She arrived on stage forty-five minutes late, seemed uninterested in performing, briefly walked offstage halfway through the set, and interrupted her encore of 'Valerie' by leaving the stage for good. After a date at the Brighton Centre, Amy Winehouse then cancelled the remaining eight concerts. Cancelling a tour is a hugely expensive thing to do; instead of making an expected £1,250,000 from the dates, Amy now faced costs of £500,000 in compensation. No wonder that the next year her estimated wealth of £10 million found itself halved by the *Sunday Times* Rich List. She bought a flat in Bow, and moved out of Camden.

Yet all was not a disaster. The immensely hard work she had put in writing and recording *Back to Black* was paying off globally. In December Amy Winehouse was, phenomenally, the recipient of six nominations for the annual Grammy Awards, to be held the following February in Los Angeles: Album of the Year, Record of the Year, Best Female Pop Vocal Performance, Best New Artist, Best Pop Vocal Album and Song of the Year.

In November a picture of her appeared – Amy in the street, back in Camden in the middle of the night, shoeless, wearing only a bra and a pair of jeans. On 24 January 2008, after phone camera footage had appeared in the *Sun* newspaper of her smoking crack, Amy decided to go to rehab, checking in to the Capio Nightingale hospital in Lisson Grove, close to Camden.

Was this a ruse to help her get a US work permit for the next month's Grammy Awards? The Norwegian drug bust alone would have theoretically disqualified her for such a visa. Although at first a visa was denied, this decision was rescinded on the Friday before the Sunday Grammys show. Amy, still undergoing treatment at the Capio Nightingale, decided instead to perform from London via satellite, from the Riverside Studios in west London. Performing live to Los Angeles, she sang impressive versions of 'You Know I'm No Good' and 'Rehab'. A mark of her colossal new status, Amy Winehouse won in five out of the six categories for which she had been nominated, all except Album of the Year. Then she went back to rehab.

She spent 2008 in a blur of headlines.

On 23 April she allegedly head-butted a passerby who had hailed her a taxi, and then punched a man who would not give up the pool table at Camden's Bar Tok. She was questioned by police about this, held overnight in the cells, but released without charge. Two weeks later, on 7 May, she was again questioned by police, this time over the *Sun*'s footage of her smoking crack. Again, it was announced that no charges would be brought.

Despite all this, for every down it seemed there was an up; on 22 May at the Ivor Novello Awards she won the award for 'Love Is a Losing Game' for Best Song, Musically and Lyrically. For one million pounds she performed at a private party in Moscow for the Russian oligarch Roman Abramovich and

Daria Zhukova, his girlfriend. She and Mark Ronson were reportedly collaborating on a title song for the upcoming James Bond film, *Quantum of Solace* – which was ultimately abandoned.

June 27 marked the celebration of Nelson Mandela's ninetieth birthday at a large event in Hyde Park. Amy performed 'Valerie' and 'Rehab', concluding by playing on 'Free Nelson Mandela' with that song's writer Jerry Dammers and the Soweto Gospel Choir. Archly, at one point Amy changed the line 'Free Nelson Mandela' to 'Free Blakey, my fella'.

Amy Winehouse played a respectable set on the Saturday night on the main Pyramid stage at that year's Glastonbury festival, coming on stage immediately prior to the headliner Jay-Z. As soon as she finished her performance she ran into Don Letts and his wife Grace. 'She was completely dismissive of Jay-Z, and made me miss his entrance. Then she frogmarches us onto the side of the stage, telling the security guards to fuck off, and stays there for four numbers until she got bored and wanted to do something else. She looked like she needed a good meal and maybe a good wash. She had this kind of nurse woman with her, hovering around me, vetting everyone. Then she dragged Grace off to the bathroom, and sat on the toilet, telling her a story.'

She played assorted other festival dates: T in the Park, Rock in Rio Lisboa in Portugal, Ireland's Oxegen, and both legs of the V festival.

But in July Blake, her husband, was sentenced to twenty-seven months in prison. He had already served nine months on remand.

On 28 July, Amy was taken to University College hospital by ambulance after suffering from 'a bad reaction' to prescribed medication. Later in the year it was revealed that Amy had developed emphysema from smoking crack. During late October she became an in-patient at the London Clinic for a week.

Then in the middle of December she flew to St Lucia, hooking up with a man she met on the island, 21-year-old Josh Bowman. When newspaper reports surfaced of this romance, Blake filed for divorce from prison. Even though Bowman left the island in January, Amy Winehouse stayed in the Caribbean, relatively out of harm's way – although the easy accessibility of cocaine and crack, as well as marijuana, in the region must have concerned those around her. On 13 February she was taken to hospital on the island, having collapsed while jogging. Nevertheless, while still in St Lucia, Amy launched her own label, Lioness Records; the first artist signed to it would be thirteen-year-old Dionne Bromfield, her god-daughter. Returning to the UK in March, Amy found herself in court for allegedly punching a woman attempting to photograph her the previous September. In July she would be acquitted of the charge.

Early in April, Amy returned to St Lucia and was rumoured to be recording a reggae album. She was due to return to London at the end of May, to appear on the closing night of a week of concerts at Shepherd's Bush Empire, to mark the end of celebrations for the fiftieth anniversary of Island Records, her label. On 8 May she appeared at the St Lucia Jazz Festival, but her set was farcical. Clearly drunk, she announced, 'Sorry, I'm bored,' midway through 'Some Unholy War'. Then halfway through 'Valerie', Amy walked offstage, not to return, amid booing from the crowd. Luckily, a sudden tropical downpour dampened the audience's anger. Footage of the St Lucia show appeared almost immediately on YouTube; Island Records decided that to risk her topping the bill at such a prestigious event would be ill-advised, and the Shepherd's Bush Empire appearance was cancelled. As a consequence, Amy did not come back to London until July.

Having apparently overcome an addiction to heroin while in St Lucia (she had taken a cure that Keith Richards seemed to have devised, replacing the drug with large amounts of alcohol), there were reports of her crawling around under restaurant tables, looking for more alcohol. Even while she was still on the island, her parents had appeared on ITN, worried (as ever) about their daughter, but now with fears occasioned by her alcohol consumption.

In August, she made an unscheduled appearance at the V Festival in Chelmsford, joining Pete Doherty and his group Babyshambles on stage, but not uttering a note. But then she did sing with the re-formed Specials, on 'You're Wondering Now' and 'Ghost Town'. She and Doherty had intended to record together, but when he played her a recently written song, she was dismissive: 'Is that all you've got?'

The year ended as it had begun, with Amy in more trouble. She was alleged to have attacked the manager of the Milton Keynes Theatre on 24 December during a production of the pantomime *Cinderella* – he had objected to her language at a children's event. Early in the new year, she pleaded guilty, and was given a conditional discharge.

In May she bought a mews house in Camden for £1.8 million, moving back there from Bow. Apart from an ill-advised appearance with Mark Ronson and his group The Business International at London's 100 Club in July – she forgot the words to 'Valerie', the only song she performed – Amy managed to keep a lower profile. Finally, it seemed, she was working again, writing – and perhaps recording – new songs. She promised a new album would be released in January 2011.

Perhaps she had partially calmed down because she was enjoying a new love: Reg Traviss, a 33-year-old film director, whom Amy had met in 2009. But whether she was exactly constant is another matter. One Friday afternoon in the summer of 2010, Don Letts ran into Amy, accompanied by a pair of minders and another black guy, on Portobello Road, beneath the Westway. With Don was Lucky Gordon, the Jamaican one-time lover of Christine Keeler; Lucky now had his picture taken with another English female *enfant terrible*. Almost immediately afterwards, Amy was surrounded by fans. Letts suggested they get away, and headed to his home in Queen's Park.

At his place, Don invited Amy and her crew out to his summerhouse, at the end of the garden. 'Then she disappears into the house, giggling, with this guy she was with. It was obvious what they were doing. And she comes back, half an hour later, "I'm naughty, aren't I? Really naughty." She was very vocal, as though waiting to be told off. She asked me if I had anything to drink. I had a bottle of Jack Daniels. By the time she left, at least half of it had gone.

'By now we seemed to be talking tortured souls – which she wasn't when I first met her. Back then, she seemed more like on this planet. But now even when she was straight, it was as though she was on drugs – extremely scatty. In many ways, she's miles ahead of everyone. But there's another part of her that seems almost retarded. I guess that was part of the attraction.' That October, Amy Winehouse launched a fashion range with Fred Perry, the legendary English design house beloved of Mods. To promote the line, she played a secret four-song show – including a version of Oasis's 'Don't Look Back in Anger' – in London's Spitalfields Market at the Fred Perry shop.

This low-key event seemed to have Amy up-and-running once again. A further £1 million Moscow show, described as sensational, ended the year.

In January 2011, she played five shows in Brazil, all performed at a highly professional level. However, a February concert in Dubai was controversial, blamed on malfunctioning equipment.

Having been brought up on his music, Amy Winehouse was honoured to enter London's Abbey Road Studios in March with Tony Bennett. Together they sang 'Body and Soul' for an album of duets scheduled for September 2011.

News leaked out in May that Amy had returned to rehab, at the Priory in Roehampton. The medical treatment preceded a European tour. Later there would be unsubstantiated rumours that Amy had been pressured into these dates.

Whatever the truth, the first show, in Belgrade in Serbia on 18 June, was an utter disaster, a car-crash performance. Appearing on stage drunk, clearly unable to sing, she was loudly booed. Later, a story emerged that Amy's excuse was: 'The coke was no good.' Having downed industrial amounts of Jack Daniels prior to the show, she had been relying on the fortifying effects of some cocaine she had been given to straighten her out before going on stage. The subsequent dates – two in Istanbul, one in Athens – were cancelled.

Back in London, Amy appeared unexpectedly (singing backing vocals) with Dionne Bromfield on 20 July at the Roundhouse in Chalk Farm. It would prove to be her final stage appearance.

The autopsy following her death revealed that during the evening of 22 July 2011, Amy Winehouse had literally drunk herself to death. Her body contained lethal amounts of alcohol – five times the UK drink-driving limit – and her bedroom had been littered with empty vodka bottles, the debris of her last, lonely binge. A spin was put on such an end; that Amy had given up both drugs and drink, and – returning to booze that night – had endured a fatal reaction to such a blow-out. In the light of her spectral Serbian performance, this seemed wishful thinking.

Almost inevitably, after having for a time become a national whipping-girl (someone onto whom to project every available theory about Britain's obsessively dysfunctional last-bar-open-on-the-Titanic drink-and-drugs culture), in death she was immediately celebrated as a national treasure.

Lioness, a new album, was scheduled for December 2011. It went straight to number one, but turned out to be a ragbag mix of out-takes, including several covers: a reggae version of Rosie and the Originals' 'Our Day Will Come'; The Shirelles' 'Will You Still Love Me Tomorrow', recorded with Mark Ronson; Astrud Gilberto's bossa nova classic 'The Girl From Ipanema'; her first stab at recording the Zutons' 'Valerie'; Gertrude Lawrence's 1930 standard 'Body and Soul', which Amy had recorded as a duet with Tony Bennett; and Donny Hathaway's 'A Song For You', recorded at her Camden home while working on songs for her third album.

The second tune was an original, 'Between the Cheats', a story about Blake Fielder-Civil and herself, recorded for what would have been the third complete Amy Winehouse album. In addition there was the original, ballad-style version of 'Tears Dry on Their Own', and 'Like Smoke', featuring a rap by Nas. The jazzy 'Half Time', recorded during the *Frank* sessions, featured Amy and an acoustic guitar, and 'Best Friends, Right', was laid down a few months later.

There were heartfelt messages in the liner notes from Janis and Mitch Winehouse, and thoughtful words by Mark Ronson that concluded: 'I think to myself, if I can make music and live my life with a shard of the level of honesty and integrity with which she lived hers, I will be a better man because of it.'

KURT COBAIN

'Now he's gone and joined that stupid club: I told him not to join that stupid club'

Wendy O'Connor

And so Wendy O'Connor, the mother of Kurt Cobain, reacted to the news of her son's self-inflicted death on 8 April 1994.

Kurt Cobain was not the first male member of his family to kill himself. So matter of course was suicide on both sides of his family that, as a young teenager, Kurt would joke of having 'suicide genes'.

When the future Nirvana singer was twelve years old, Burle Cobain, his great-uncle, brother to Kurt's grandfather Leland, took a pistol and shot himself, first in the stomach and then in the head, finally killing himself. A year previously, ignoring medical advice that he would face death if he did not give up alcohol, Ernest Cobain, Leland and Burle's brother, had fallen on the stairs in his house while drunk, dying from a brain aneurysm – some form of subconscious suicide, perhaps. ('Aneurysm' would become the title of a 1991 Nirvana song, the B-side of 'Smells Like Teen Spirit';

however, there seems little link to Ernest Cobain's tragic fate – Charles R. Cross, Cobain's biographer, asserts that Kurt wrote the lyrics to 'Aneurysm' about his ex-girlfriend, musician Tobi Vail.)

On his mother Wendy's side, Kurt's great-grandfather had stabbed himself in front of the entire family. Admitted to a mental hospital, he finally killed himself two months later by tearing apart his healing wounds.

It must have seemed almost an everyday occurrence, when, as an early teenager, Kurt and a pair of friends found the hanging body of a boy who had done away with himself. So, you are inclined to muse, was Kurt's end inevitable?

Surviving members of families in which suicide has occurred are frequently haunted by the fear that it runs in the family, that one day they too might take their own lives. Mental health problems run in many families, and it is worth recalling that the third single off *Nevermind* was 'Lithium', a song that took the name of the drug that allegedly 'treated' manic-depressive – bipolar, as it became termed – behaviour. This was an affliction from which Kurt certainly suffered, though it is not known whether he ever took lithium.

Yet tragedy in the family can act as a spur for other members. Was this the case with this highly sensitive and intelligent, innately artistic boy who would utterly change the course of 1990s music?

In 1991 Nirvana revealed themselves as the last Great American Rock Band, one which emerged seemingly from nowhere to sell over 30 million copies of *Nevermind*. Nirvana are as indelibly the sound of America's West Coast as the Beach Boys, but this is a different West Coast, marinaded in rain, mist and darkness. In the vanguard of what became known as the 'grunge' movement, the sludgy fusion of punk rock and heavy metal that emerged from the Pacific Northwest, Nirvana's seemingly sudden success overturned the American music business. Until then, 'alternative' music had seemed marginal at best in its sales potential, but now it was evident that there was a critical mass of fans apparently waiting for just such an act to materialize. Nirvana shook the world with their music. Their explosive arrival opened the floodgates for acts previously marginalized as part of America's resolutely independent music scene. Several such bands became part of the most exciting movement since punk fifteen years previously, of which Nirvana were direct descendants. REM – already frontrunners – Pearl Jam, Smashing Pumpkins, Dinosaur Jr., Rage Against the Machine, Screaming Trees, Jane's Addiction, and – for Kurt, the spiritual godfathers – Sonic Youth, now swept all before them.

Not only was Kurt Cobain the most successful musician of his generation, he was the rock 'n' roll god of his age: a rock star, a father, an anti-style icon, a junkie, a suicide. Yet his was also the story of what happens to a man when he gets what he wants.

Kurt took the universal pain of a child of divorce and

expressed it (the parents of Nirvana bassist Krist Novoselic and drummer Dave Grohl had also split up). His persistent feelings of utter isolation were so archetypal that he managed to truly connect with an enormous audience. Kurt seemed an almost professional loser, which was why he became such a huge star. Everyone identified with him and his struggle to be himself. Yet there was always an element of pose, and although Kurt Cobain seemed the personification of what would soon become known as Generation X 'slacker' apathy, he was also a very good actor. He was largely content to go along with anything that could boost his success, perfectly prepared to sign with a headline label, to ditch an inappropriate drummer, and to accept huge pay cheques for playing major festivals. Yet he was persistently conflicted over his role as a star, uncomfortable with the financial rewards it brought.

Nirvana were a punk act that drew on the spirit of the Sex Pistols' *Never Mind the Bollocks*, on the churning drive of Led Zeppelin and Black Sabbath, and on the melodic possibilities of the Beatles, with whose music Kurt had grown up. Many of his relatives loved the English group. 'My aunts would give me Beatles' records,' he told Jon Savage. 'For the most part it was just Beatles' records.' In fact, many of Kurt's influences were from the UK. Appropriately, at the end of 1991, when *Nevermind* was surging up the US charts, Nirvana were touring Britain and then Europe, largely unaware that their lives were about to be utterly transformed.

An anti-hero figurehead for his generation in his moth-holed thrift store woollen apparel, in January 1992 Kurt Cobain and Nirvana dislodged Michael Jackson's *Dangerous* album from its long stint at the top of the US album charts. As a cultural figure, Kurt represented a very specific moment when a unique sense of community – the global Nirvana community – emerged from popular culture. The early 1990s were a period of recession and war, both in the Gulf and the former Yugoslavia, and Kurt's hand-me-down garb was the antithesis of the designer-besotted late 1980s. His rebel music bespoke the soul of a difficult, dysfunctional individual, which was precisely the interior landscape of many of his fans.

As the Beatles had done with Liverpool, Bob Marley with Kingston, Jamaica, and Bruce Springsteen with New Jersey's Asbury Park, Nirvana put Seattle on the musical map. Seattle, which has a population of three million, has a long-standing liberal, progressive outlook, and is an affluent city. But it does not enjoy an easy climate: central to the sound of Nirvana is the mildly depressive, laconic feel of the American Pacific North-west, where rain clouds ceaselessly tumble inland from over the vast ocean and sit over the blustery city.

It was only later that it became known that Nirvana were not actually from Seattle at all. The biggest city in Washington state happened to be the one to which Kurt Cobain and bass player Krist Novoselic had eventually relocated from the logging town of Aberdeen, three hours' drive to the southwest. This is where they had grown up, a town with an 18,000 population that has an average rainfall of almost 100 inches. Grays Harbor County, in which the town is located, has one of the highest suicide rates in the United States. Later, Alice Wheeler, Kurt's photographer friend, would visit Kurt in Aberdeen. 'It would always be raining,' she said. 'You'd always witness some kind of domestic violence.'

Kurt Cobain had been born on 20 February 1967, in Aberdeen, Washington. (On that day Jimi Hendrix was in the studio in London, making one of his first recordings.) His father, Donald Cobain, was a 21-year-old car mechanic, and his mother, pretty Wendy Fradenburg, whom he had married when she became pregnant almost as soon as she graduated from high school, was only 18. Three years later, Kurt's sister Kim was born. From the age of two, Kurt showed an interest in music. This was hardly surprising, as everyone on his mother's side of the family played one musical instrument or another. Wendy's sister Mari was a guitar-playing country musician who had actually made a record. When he was five Kurt was learning to play the drums. By the time he was seven, Mari would play him Beatles and Monkees records, and was attempting to teach her nephew the guitar.

Already it was evident that the boy was a talented artist, a gift he was encouraged to explore and express. Birthday and

Christmas presents would often be gifts of new pencils or paints. For a long time he wanted to complete his education at art school. 'The plan for my life, ever since I can remember, was to be a commercial artist,' he said.[1] 'My mother gave me a lot of support in being artistic. She was really complimentary of my drawings and paintings. So I was always building up to that. By the time I was in ninth grade, I was taking three commercial art classes and I was going to art school and my art teacher would enter my paintings and stuff for contests. I wasn't interested in that at all, really. It wasn't what I wanted to do. I knew that I wasn't as good as everyone else thought I was in that town . . . I'm a better artist than probably everyone else in that school, but that doesn't say anything if you compare it to a larger city. I knew my limitations. I really enjoy art, I like to paint still. I've always felt the same about writing as well. I know I'm not educated enough to really write something that I would like to read.'

Kurt was one of those kids who finds security in burying himself in books. 'I went to the library a lot, and I skipped school a lot, especially during high school, and the only place to go during the day was the library. But I didn't know what to read, it was just whatever I found. During grade school I would read S.E. Hinton books [the most famous is *The Outsider*]. I really enjoyed those. I read a lot in class too, when I went to school. Just to stay away from people so I didn't have to talk to them. A lot of times I'd even just pretend to read, to stay away from people.'

As he grew older, Kurt had a group of very loyal, supportive friends in Aberdeen who held him in high regard, respecting the image of the consummate artist that he exuded. His semi-abstract paintings were strikingly interesting, sometimes fascinating, and he wrote witty, often extremely dark but very distinctive poetry, diligently logged away in sets of journals. (Later, seeking lyrics, he would often purloin them from his collection of poetry, noting those contrasting occasions when he wrote a set of lyrics specifically for the song in question.)

Kurt's entire life was overshadowed by the trauma of his parents' divorce, when he was eight. 'I had a really good childhood until my parents divorced,' Kurt said in 1993. 'I was ashamed of my parents. I couldn't face some of my friends at school. I desperately wanted to have a typical family. I wanted that security. All of a sudden my whole world changed and I became anti-social. I also started to understand the reality of my surroundings. Which didn't have a lot to offer.'[2]

'He changed completely,' Wendy, his mother, told Michael Azerrad, remembering the divorce. 'I think he was ashamed. And he became very inward – he just held everything. He became real shy. He became real sullen, kind of mad and always frowning and ridiculing.'

Ignoring the friends and family members who appreciated his evident talent, Kurt began to believe he was increasingly friendless, an outsider. By the time he was coming into his teens, Kurt said, 'I started to realize that I was more interested in drawing and listening to music, more so than the other kids. It just slowly grew on me and I started to realize that. So that by the time I was twelve I was fully withdrawn.'[3]

Diagnosed as hyper-active, and allegedly suffering from attention deficit disorder – which, in Kurt's case, probably only meant a restlessly inquisitive mind – he was prescribed Ritalin. This amphetamine-like drug would prevent him sleeping at night, and consequently, he was also put on downers. Eventually, sugar and red dye no. 2 were removed from his diet, and Kurt was taken off the pharmaceuticals.

When Bev Cobain, Kurt's cousin, a registered nurse with a background in mental health, was later asked if Kurt had mental health problems other than general depression, her reply was illuminating: 'Kurt was diagnosed at a young age with attention deficit disorder [ADD], then later with bipolar disorder [also known as manic depression]. Bipolar illness has the same characteristics as major clinical depression, but with mood swings, which present as rage, euphoria, high energy, irritability, distractibility, overconfidence, and other symptoms. As Kurt undoubtedly knew, bipolar illness can be very difficult to manage, and the correct diagnosis is crucial. Unfortunately for Kurt, compliance with the appropriate treatment is also a critical factor.'

'Kurt was an unstable person even before he got into the music business,' said his aunt Mary. 'There was a song he wrote when he was 17, called "Sea Suicide".'

Unable to coexist with his mother's new boyfriend, who reportedly was later diagnosed as paranoid schizophrenic, Kurt went to live with his father, Don. Don had given up his job of car mechanic and become a logger, moving into a prefabricated home in tiny Montesano, a town with a population of under 4,000, twenty miles from Aberdeen. Soon he and Kurt moved into a proper house in Montesano. Also living with them were Don's new wife and her two children, an arrangement that caused Kurt further unhappiness. Hunting in the local forests was part of everyday life in Montesano, but when his father took him on a hunting expedition, Kurt refused to climb down from the truck to take part. 'Now that I look back on it,' Kurt remembered, 'I know I had the sense that killing animals is wrong, especially for sport. I didn't understand that at the time. I just knew that I didn't want to be there.'[4]

Don Cobain did have a considerable record collection, however. Kurt began to hang out with a group of slightly older boys who were into music and smoking pot. When they came over to the Cobain home, they discovered Don's records, which included Led Zeppelin, Black Sabbath, Aerosmith and Kiss. Listening to these albums, Kurt's head was opened up to further musical possibilities, possibly assisted by the marijuana he began smoking with his new friends. 'I started turning into a little stoner kid,' he said.[5]

It hardly seems surprising that, in the manner of some lonely children, Kurt Cobain created an imaginary friend, significantly named 'Boddah', as though Kurt was searching for a guide to provide him with peace of mind.

When he was in junior high school, Kurt, encouraged by his father, reluctantly joined the wrestling team. In wrestling matches he would release some of his growing anger. 'I was a scapegoat, but not in the sense that people would pick on me all the time. People wouldn't pick on me or beat me up, because I was so withdrawn by that time, and I was so antisocial that I was almost insane. I felt so different and so crazy that people left me alone. I always felt they would vote me most likely to kill everyone at a high school dance,' Kurt said. 'I've got to that point where I've fantasized about it. But I would have opted for killing myself.'[6]

When he was turning twelve, already inspired by watching the B-52s on *Saturday Night Live*, Kurt read an article in *Creem* magazine about the Sex Pistols tour of the United States, something of an epiphany for him – it was the idea of the group that appealed to him, some time before he actually got to hear them. Searching in his local library for punk records, he discovered the Clash's *Sandinista!*, which didn't live up to what he was expecting. Although he came to like that group's *Combat Rock* album, when he finally heard *Never Mind the Bollocks*, he fell in love with it. On assorted Nirvana tunes, such as 'Territorial Pissings', you can hear that this is a vocalist who has assiduously studied the work of John 'Johnny Rotten' Lydon. The instrumental introduction to 'In Bloom' could be from a Pistols' out-take.

'The Pistols' album has the best production of any rock record I've ever heard,' was Kurt's assessment. 'It's totally in-your-face and compressed. All the hype the Sex Pistols had was totally deserved – they deserved everything they got. Johnny Rotten was the one I identified with, he was the sensitive one. The only reason I might agree with people calling our band "The Sex Pistols of the 90s" is that, for both bands, the music is a very natural thing, very sincere.'

For a fourteenth birthday gift, not long after Kurt had been diagnosed as suffering from a minor case of scoliosis (curvature of the spine), Kurt's uncle Chuck gave him the choice of a bicycle or an electric guitar. Kurt had still been playing around with a drum kit, but now he swapped instruments. He opted for the guitar, a cheap secondhand model, and was given some tuition from one of Chuck's bandmates, learning to play AC/DC's 'Back in Black'. Other songs he learned included the Cars' 'My Best Friend's Girl', Queen's 'Another One Bites the Dust', and that staple of the region, 'Louie, Louie'. From that point on, he began to write his own songs, 'really raunchy riff-rock,' as he described them. 'I would try to play as nasty as I could . . . It was definitely a good release. I thought of it as a job. It was my mission. I knew I had to practice. I had this feeling all the time – I always knew I was doing something that was special.'[7] (Unbeknownst to Kurt, the weight of playing the guitar would exacerbate the curvature of his spine. 'I had minor scoliosis in Junior High, and

I've been playing guitar ever since, and the weight of the guitar has made my back grow in this curvature. So when I stand, everything is sideways.')

At his father's insistence, Kurt had played in a local baseball league – as unwilling as he had been about wrestling. Another member of the team was a boy called Matt Lukin. It turned out that Lukin, like Kurt a student at Montesano High, was also a prospective musician, playing bass in a local group called the Melvins.

Kurt went to a Melvins rehearsal, and got drunk. But he also experienced a striking realisation: *these guys had actually managed to put a band together . . .*

Having started out as Who copyists, the Melvins by now were playing furiously paced hardcore punk, sometimes performing shows as far afield as Seattle. When other groups began to play in a similar style, the Melvins altered utterly, playing everything at an impossibly slow, doomy pace, into which – sacrilege! – they began to inject elements of heavy metal. The Melvins thereby became the forerunners of what transmogrified into grunge, exemplified on their *Gluey Porch Treatments* album, released in 1987, often cited as the first grunge record.

As fate would have it, it transpired that Buzz Osbourne, the leader of the Melvins, was in the same art class as Kurt at Montesano High School – although he was a couple of years older. Osbourne owned a book about the Sex Pistols, which Kurt avidly devoured, inking the group's distinctive logo onto desks and exercise books. Kurt Cobain had decided that somehow he would start a punk group.

Finding it difficult to get on with his father's new family, Kurt moved back to Aberdeen to live with his uncle Chuck: his mother had broken up with the boyfriend and had also lost her job, so she asked Chuck to care for her son. Kurt shuffled between relatives, including his father's parents and three different sets of aunts and uncles, moving back and forth between Aberdeen and Montesano, regularly swapping high schools. How, you cannot help wondering, could this not have exacerbated Kurt's mounting sense of insecurity and anger?

In 1983 Kurt moved back to his mother's place. Yet returning to his maternal home was not an easy experience. There were always guns around. In 1984, his mother suspected that Pat O'Connor, her new longshoreman husband, had cheated on her. Wendy came home drunk and grabbed one of Pat's several guns, intending to shoot him.[8] Fortuitously, she found herself unable to load the weapon. In the end, Wendy collected all Pat's rifles and pistols, took them down to Aberdeen's Wishkah River, and threw them in. Kurt watched as his mother did this. The next day he fished out of the water as many of the weapons as he could, and – in what could be seen as a symbolic twist – purchased his first professional amplifier with the proceeds from selling the guns.[9]

At Aberdeen High School, Kurt met a boy called Krist

Novoselic. Blessed with a satirical mind-set, Krist was extremely funny. Sometimes Kurt felt he was the only person who appreciated his uncompromising sense of humour. In Aberdeen, Krist was known as Chris, but in 1992 he legally changed it back to his Croatian name. Krist had been born to Croatian immigrant parents on 16 May 1965, in Compton, the sometimes notorious south-central district of Los Angeles, where from an early age being streetwise was a necessity for survival. In 1979, Krist's father, who had been driving a delivery truck in Southern California, learned that there was cheap property to be had in Aberdeen, Washington, where there was a significant Croatian community, as well as regular work in the local lumber mills. When they moved to Aberdeen, Krist Novoselic, by now a relatively sophisticated Los Angeleno, could not find any local kids with whom to empathize. Among other things, he was physically huge, eventually growing to 6′ 7″. The local teenagers were into Top 40 radio, while Krist dug Led Zeppelin, Black Sabbath and Devo.

By late spring 1980, his parents had made a radical decision to send their eldest son for a stay in their homeland, which was still a region of communist Yugoslavia. Becoming fluent in Croatian while there, Krist benefited from the excellent standard of education enjoyed in the communist bloc. He also discovered the Sex Pistols and the Ramones. Their music was released in Yugoslavia, which also had a strong national music scene, as Krist discovered.

But when he returned to Aberdeen, he found his parents had divorced. He also learned that the city's isolation meant he was almost alone in his understanding of punk. 'It was hard for punk to make its way to Aberdeen because of its geographic isolation,' he told Everett True. To earn money Krist took a job at Taco Bell, saving for a vehicle and musical instruments and equipment.

Kurt Cobain, who by now would always wear a grey trench coat, first became friends with Krist's younger brother Robert. The first time he visited their home, Krist was upstairs, playing punk music. Although he was a couple of years older than Kurt, the younger boy quickly registered his presence and immediately 'got' him. Krist was, Kurt said, a 'really clever, funny, loudmouth person everyone laughed at, even though he was smarter than them.'[10]

Yet they did not immediately become close friends. In fact, as always seemed to be the case, there was hardly anyone at Aberdeen High with whom Kurt felt he could empathize. Eventually, he began to hang out with the school's stoners, who were at least into rock 'n' roll. Among them was a kid called Dale Crover. Crover had just become the new drummer with the Melvins, who began to rehearse at Crover's parents' Aberdeen house. Kurt Cobain again found himself in the inner orbit of the Melvins, for whom he even auditioned at one point. 'I totally botched it. I was so nervous that I forgot all the songs. I literally couldn't play a note. I just stood there with my guitar and played feedback with a blushed face.'[11]

Yet the Melvins' discipline and belief in rigorous hard work hit a nerve in Kurt, who vowed to himself to emulate them.

Kurt and Krist Novoselic would run into each other at Melvins' rehearsals. Kurt discovered that Krist played guitar, and they would hang out and play music together.

On a punk rock compilation tape that Buzz Osbourne had put together for him, Kurt discovered Black Flag, and its iconic singer Henry Rollins. Suitably inspired, in August 1984 he sold his record collection to pay for a trip to Seattle to see Black Flag. 'Becoming a punk rocker fed into my low self-esteem because it helped me realize that I don't need to become a rock star – I don't want to become a rock star . . . I'm so glad that I got into punk rock at the time I did because it gave me these few years that I needed to grow up and put my values in perspective and realize what kind of person I am.'[12]

In 1993, Kurt Cobain expanded on this theme: '[Buzz] made me a couple of compilation tapes, Black Flag and Flipper, everything, all the most popular punk rock bands, and I was completely blown away. I finally found my calling. That very same day, I cut my hair, and I would lip-synch to those tapes. I'd play them every day. I'd already been playing guitar by then for a couple of years, and I was trying to play my own style of punk rock, what I thought it would be. I knew it was fast, and had a lot of distortion. It expressed the way I felt politically and socially. It was the anger that I felt, the alienation.'[13]

Although he had got into more conventional rock acts, like Led Zeppelin and Aerosmith, sensitive Kurt could detect that something was awry in their entire stance. 'I really did enjoy and do enjoy some of the melodies they'd written, but they were definitely lacking something, and it took me so many years to realize that a lot of it had to do with sexism, the way that they just wrote about their dicks, having sex. That stuff bored me,' he told Jon Savage.

Surprised at such a perception, Savage asked Kurt for the origins of such thinking – did it evolve from punk rock? No, he replied, his innate sense of injustice had been sparked earlier. 'It was before that. Because I couldn't ever find any good male friends, I ended up hanging out with the girls a lot, and I just felt that they weren't treated equally, weren't treated with respect, the way Aberdeen treated women in general. They were just totally oppressed, the words "bitch" and "cunt" would be totally common. But it took me many years after the fact to realize those were the things that were bothering me. I was just starting to understand what was pissing me off so much, and within that year, the last couple of years of high school, and punk rock, it all came together. I finally admitted to myself, I am not retarded.'

From around the time he turned fourteen, Kurt was smoking marijuana every day. By the time he was in his senior year, he started to ease off and ultimately quit altogether for a time, aware that the drug exacerbated the paranoia to which he was already prone. Before he quit he became a pot-smoking buddy of a kid called Myer Loftin, drawn to him because he was into similar music. What Kurt did not know at first was that Loftin was gay, which led to other students at Aberdeen High assuming that Kurt was also. Although this was not the case, he would be bullied – taking a couple of beatings – for this. 'I even thought that I was gay. I thought that might be the solution to my problem. One time during my school years, although I never experimented with it, I had a gay friend, and that was the only time that I ever experienced real confrontation from people, because for so many years . . . they were basically afraid of me, and when I started hanging out with this person who was known to be gay, I started getting a lot of shit. People trying to beat me up and stuff. Then my mother wouldn't allow me to be friends with him anymore. 'Cos she's homophobic. It was real devastating, because finally I'd found a male friend who I actually hugged and was affectionate to, and we talked about a lot of things. Around that same time, I was putting all the pieces of the puzzle together. He played a big role in that.'[14]

Ultimately, this led to Kurt having an especially sophisticated view of sexuality. In his Nirvana lyrics, Kurt would often say the unsayable: 'Everyone is gay!' he declared, on 'All Apologies' – a song that also contains the lines, 'Everything is my fault / I'll take all the blame.'

Once again, Don Cobain decided to intervene in his son's life, and try to put it back on course. Kurt was persuaded to move back to Montesano, where his father cajoled him into sitting an entrance exam to serve in the US navy. Kurt passed the test with flying colours, but refused to sign up to be a sailor.

Returning to Aberdeen, Kurt moved in with Jesse Reed and his family. Jesse was a friend whose born-again Christian parents endeavoured to set him on what they considered to be the correct path in life. Jesse's father, Dave, had an unconventional past as sax player in the Beachcombers, a 1960s garage group. Although he would be obliged to attend church with Jesse's parents, they provided a stable home life for Kurt. At the age of seventeen, under the Reeds' influence, Kurt was baptized. For a few weeks he declared he was a Christian. Kurt was looking for something. Something he never really found. But at least he felt a little more self-confident. In August 1984, Kurt had sex for the first time.[15]

On his eighteenth birthday, on 20 February 1985, the Reeds threw a party for him at their house. As a present, his aunt Mari gave him Stephen Davis's *Hammer of the Gods*, a revelatory, warts-and-all Led Zeppelin biography. Kurt was touched. '. . . it was nice to know people care about ya,' he wrote to her in his thank you letter.

By now Kurt's life mainly consisted of smoking large amounts of marijuana. Three months later, realizing that he was way behind on graduation credits, Kurt dropped out of high school, only weeks before he was due to have graduated. Somehow, he had decided, he would make his future in music. A high school dropout? You can't get lower than that in America. Considering his low self-esteem, such loser status may well have appealed to Kurt.

Despite the Reeds' generosity towards him, something of the feral seemed to have developed in Kurt. On one occasion when he forgot his key, he smashed a window to get back into their house. And was summarily told to leave.

Kurt briefly moved back to his mother's. After Wendy had told him that if he didn't get a job, he would have to move out, Kurt moved into an apartment with Jesse Reed. Ironically, in order to pay for this, he did get a job, working at a restaurant on the coast, then returning to Aberdeen High – as a janitor. Going back to his high school in such a lowly role sapped him psychologically, and after two months he quit.

He then turned on Jesse. After defacing Jesse's high school yearbook – a rebuke to Jesse for having graduated? – Kurt kicked him out of the apartment, which they had shared for three months. Kurt hung on to the place. Eventually, he ran out of money and, in autumn 1985, was obliged to up sticks. Broke and homeless, Kurt slept wherever he could: in the local library; on his mother's porch. Although there is an element of self-mythologizing here, it's true that he very occasionally slept under the North Aberdeen Bridge, near his mother's place. The bridge crossed the Wishkah river, and Kurt prided himself on his ability to catch fish from its waters, which he would then eat. (Later he was told that the Wishkah was so polluted that any fish caught in it were certainly poisonous.)

That winter of 1985, Kurt put together his first group, to which he gave the cartoon-like hardcore name of Fecal Matter. Playing his own material, Fecal Matter also consisted of his friend Dale Crover on bass and another boy, Greg Hokanson, on drums. On one occasion they managed to secure a support slot with the Melvins, playing a Washington state coastal town. But Kurt and Dale Crover could not get on with the drummer, and decided to concentrate on recording together. Driving up to Seattle, they paid a visit to Kurt's aunt Mari, who owned a four-track TEAC tape recorder. Mari was amazed at how angry Kurt's vocals were, on tunes with such titles as 'Bambi Slaughter', 'Laminated Effect', 'Sound of Dentage' and 'Downer', a different version of which would appear on *Bleach*, the first Nirvana album. The sound of these tunes was like a cross between the Melvins and Metallica, reliant on heavy riffing and largely devoid of melody.

Later, with Buzz Osbourne on bass and Mike Dillard, once of the Melvins, on drums, Kurt practised the Fecal Matter material, but eventually this project evaporated.

For around eight months, Kurt moved into the home of his friend Steve Shillinger. Shillinger's father taught English at Aberdeen High, and taking in waifs and strays was commonplace for the family. However none had ever stayed as long as Kurt did, who kept his sleeping bag behind the couch on which he slept. During this time, Kurt Cobain embarked on a side career as a graffiti artist. Largely this consisted of absurdist gestures, such as spray-painting 'QUEER' on trucks bristling with rifle-racks. Once he was picked up by the police and fined for such behaviour. (In his pocket when he was busted was a copy of a cassette by hardcore outfit Millions of Dead Cops.)

In 1986 Kurt managed to play his first live show, in a performance space in the state capital Olympia, fifty miles east of Aberdeen. Buzz Osbourne was on bass, and Dale Crover played parts of a drum kit, as Kurt recited some of his poetry over their instrumental backing – he had had to get drunk to do so. But local groovers Dylan Carlson and Slim Moon were impressed, telling Kurt afterwards how great the show had been. Kurt also started to hang out with a local drug dealer, and in the middle of the summer, this character shot Kurt up with heroin. This was the first time he had ever experienced the drug. 'It was such a scarce thing to find heroin in Aberdeen that I just thought I would try it,' he said.[16]

As her son was still essentially homeless, his mother put down the initial $200 deposit on a rundown wooden house at 1000 East Second Street in Aberdeen, near to where she lived. Melvins' bassist Matt Lukin moved in with him – useful, as Lukin was a carpenter, and plenty of work needed to be done on the two-bedroom property. Not that Lukin's efforts were always noticed. By the time that Kurt had been living there for only the briefest time, the place looked like a parody of a teenage apartment – the floor was littered with empty beer cans and it stank. In the bath Kurt installed a family of turtles, raising the question as to where he actually washed.

Despite having taken a job as a janitor at a resort hotel – he spent most of his time sleeping in the rooms – Kurt was still always broke. By now a seasoned drug user, he needed to find a cheap high, and soon discovered the opiate properties of assorted cough syrups.

That winter, however, Kurt badly burned his left hand. He had been cooking French fries and managed to cover his hand in boiling fat. At first he was told he would never be able to play the guitar again. While he recuperated he was unable to work, which meant he had even less money than previously. Rice was almost all he could afford to eat. Yet he was able to play guitar, and spent most of the several months of his recovery improving his skills on the instrument.

During this time, for about a month, Kurt also began to rehearse with Krist Novoselic, playing with a local drummer called Bob McFadden. Together they would travel to Olympia, which lay on the Puget Sound waterfront and was respected as a regional centre for the arts. There, Kurt had discovered another musical scene altogether, one of a relative sophistication that was largely drug-free. Its focus was K Records, an indie label. K was also a local distribution network for British indie acts such as the Vaselines, Young Marble Giants and Kleenex. K was run by Candace Peterson and Calvin Johnson. Johnson's band Beat Happening were the kings of this self-consciously naïf scene, which prided itself on its geeky, nerdy nature, in which everyone – unlike Kurt with his long blond tresses – had short hair. Free-thinking and bohemian, everyone around this scene played in each other's groups. Kurt was very taken with the notion of K Records, and had its logo tattooed on his left arm. 'K Records and that whole scene in Olympia turned me on to so much amazing music. The Pastels and the Vaselines and all that stuff. Every couple of years I feel that I've gone as far as I can with being introduced to something new, and then something like that hits me and it gives me life for a few years . . . I was turned on to the whole 4AD thing, the Raincoats and the Young Marble Giants. It was like the first time that I heard punk rock, 'cos there were all these bands from the last fifteen years, and I'd try to find all these records, and it was a whole scene, these bands that had been going on for like ten years, and it had the same impact on me. It was a completely different world.'[17]

The K scene was extremely purist, and Calvin Johnson's first name led to Kurt dubbing its devotees as 'Calvinists'. The overriding attitude was not dissimilar to that at, say, the UK's *Sniffin' Glue* fanzine which, in 1977, had railed against the Clash for signing to a major label. While on one hand Kurt was extremely taken with such a stance, it was also incompatible with his secret ambitions, a source of extreme inner conflict in the coming years.

Meanwhile Krist Novoselic had bought a VW van with his Taco Bell earnings and become the driver for the Melvins. He also became involved with a Melvins side project, the

Meltors, who would play Melvins covers. Krist became the Meltors' bass player. Some outsiders, like Slim Moon, the founder of the Kill Rock Stars label, thought him to be the coolest member of the Melvins scene. But others noted how much he drank, and his confrontational tendencies. Unlike most of his young male contemporaries in Aberdeen, however, Krist had a girlfriend, Shelli.

In his autobiography, Krist Novoselic wrote about his initial impressions of Kurt: 'Kurt was a completely creative persona – a true artist. When I first met him, he had just got a job and found his own place. What a den of art/insanity that was. He tried to make his own lava lamp out of wax and vegetable oil (it didn't work). He sketched very obscene Scooby Doo cartoons all over his apartment building hallways. He made wild sound montages from obscure records. He sculpted clay into scary spirit people writhing in agony. He played guitar, and wrote great tunes that were kind of off-kilter. Kurt held a sceptical perspective towards the world. He'd create video montages that were scathing testimonies about popular culture, compiled from hours and hours of watching TV.'[18] A longstanding problem for Kurt, however, was the fact that Krist's mother never cared for him.

For his part, meeting Krist made a considerable difference to Kurt's life: 'I hated everybody. I always managed to have at least one close friend at a time, through most of my life. There have been years where I would just put up with my best friend, and not really like the person. But since I've been in the band and since I've known Krist . . . I have a handful of friends that are great . . .'[19]

In 1987, a year after Kurt had given Krist the Fecal Matter cassette, they formed a group, with Krist on bass and Dale Crover on drums, which they called Skid Row. 'Their songs were basically riffs,' Slim Moon said. 'They'd play a riff for a long time and Kurt would scream into the microphone, then he'd drop the guitar and play with the digital delay and make crazy noises instead of a guitar solo, and then he'd pick the guitar back up and play the riff some more. Right away, he was a showman.'[20]

Soon, after Kurt had watched a television show about Buddhism, Skid Row's name was changed to Nirvana. 'It means attainment of perfection,' explained Kurt.[21]

Part of the Olympia K Records scene was a girl called Tracy Marander, arty-looking and unusual with her vivid red hair. When she and Kurt first met, she was living in Tacoma, outside Seattle. Even though she was slightly larger than him, Kurt went for this stylish, exotic girl, and she became his first girlfriend. In the autumn of 1987, Tracy relocated from Tacoma to Olympia, renting an apartment at 114 ½ North Pear Street. Kurt, now in his twentieth year, moved up to live with her, along with a rabbit he kept in a cage on top of the fridge. After he had painted the bathroom bright red, Kurt spray-painted the words 'RED RUM' – an allusion to the horror film *The Shining* – on a wall. Living-room walls were covered with pictures and articles taken from the pages of *Melody Maker* and *NME*, which he would buy on import. Despite his evident eccentricities, people in Olympia's first impressions of Kurt were that he was a sweet guy.

Historically, the Pacific Northwest has leant towards the political left. As state capital, stylish Olympia was endowed with myriad cultural facilities for its citizens. This included KAOS radio, which was reputed to have the most comprehensive library of independent music of any station in the USA. Any record on an independent label was guaranteed to be played on KAOS, part of some unwritten charter of the station. (Even in the very early days of Nirvana, the group were regularly playing or being interviewed on KAOS: April 1987 was the month of their first broadcast, when they played eleven songs during an early-hours show.) Unusually, there was also an ethos in the city of paying serious respect to women musicians, a stance echoed by K Records. Amongst those so honoured were such British female acts as the Slits, the Raincoats and the Marine Girls. After having hung out with Myer Loftin and gained an understanding of a gay frame of mind, Kurt Cobain's sensibility was again widened, as he came to appreciate not only a feminine but also a feminist point of view. The extent to which Olympia was both hardcore and 'Calvinist', simultaneously liberating and trammelling, and how precisely this came to define a part of Kurt Cobain, should not be underestimated.

Krist Novoselic and his girlfriend Shelli also moved up to Olympia, Krist taking a job as an industrial painter at the

Boeing aircraft factory. Later they would shift residences to Tacoma. Briefly Kurt and Krist formed a group covering Creedence Clearwater Revival tunes called the Sellouts, but after a few attempts to play taverns, they abandoned the project. Later, there were those who were reminded of Creedence's John Fogerty when they heard or saw Kurt sing.[22]

In the winter of 1987, the pair started playing with another drummer, Aaron Burckhard, an Aberdeen local who worked at Burger King and hung around with the Melvins. Aaron was more into conventional heavy metal, and he had a moustache, an aesthetic issue for Kurt and Krist (and, indeed, for the owners of the record label to which they would soon sign). Rehearsing at his house, Kurt applied himself with assiduous effort. 'We would play the set and then I would just start playing those songs again right away,' he said.[23] He had made a decision to get a record out as soon as possible.

Kurt was very influenced by Big Black, Killdozer, Scratch Acid and Sonic Youth – groups that he was really into and had read about in the Massachusetts-based *Forced Exposure* fanzine. He was also getting into the Sonics, the original early 1960s garage band from Tacoma: 'The Sonics recorded very, very cheaply on a two track you know, and they just used one microphone over the drums, and they got the most amazing drum sound I've ever heard,' Kurt told an interviewer on CITR-FM. 'It's still my favourite drum sound. It sounds like he's hitting harder than anyone I've ever known.'

In the Tacoma of 1987, the atmospheric Community

World Theater, a former porn cinema, became an important venue, where most acts played for nothing. The early Nirvana frequently appeared there. When the Sub Pop scene hit, as it did imminently, Tacoma was a big part of that phenomenon, largely because of the venue.

In an unfashionable part of Seattle was located Reciprocal Studios, the base of a producer called Jack Endino. His ramshackle premises were hardly state of the art. But it was there that Endino had produced a number of revered local acts: Mother Love Bone, Mudhoney, Soundgarden. Jack Endino was the producer Nirvana wanted to work with.

On 23 January 1988 Nirvana drove down to the Seattle studio. In six hours, for $152.44, they put down and mixed ten complete songs: 'If You Must', 'Downer', 'Floyd the Barber', 'Paper Cuts', 'Spank Thru', 'Hairspray Queen', 'Aero Zeppelin', 'Beeswax', 'Mexican Seafood' and 'Pen Cap Chew'. For the session they had reverted to using Dale Crover on drums. That night Nirvana had a show at the Community World Theater, where they played the songs in the order they had been recorded. As soon as the concert ended, Dale Crover hit the road to San Francisco for dates playing with Buzz Osbourne in a re-formed Melvins. Before he left, he recommended an Aberdeen drummer, Dave Foster. But after Foster was arrested for beating up someone who had been hitting on his girlfriend, his driving licence was revoked.[24] As he could no longer drive to rehearsals, Kurt and Krist worked briefly again with Aaron Burckhard. But he was held overnight for drunk-driving and for abusing the arresting officer, who happened to be black.[25] When let out of jail the next day, he said he was too hungover to come to rehearsals. Accordingly he was also out of the group.

The band found yet another drummer, Chad Channing, born on 31 January 1967. While Kurt and Krist were spending a brief spell under the name of Bliss, they played with Chad's group, Tick-Dolly-Row. The two Aberdeen boys were impressed by Chad's fibreglass drum kit, but they didn't really communicate. Eventually they were introduced at the farewell show of a group called Malfunkshun at the Community World Theater. Unenthusiastic at first, Chad soon succumbed, going over and jamming with the pair at Krist's home, where he and Kurt had constructed a rehearsal studio. Chad and Kurt were not dissimilar: softly spoken, creative, very sensitive. Like the other two members of Nirvana, Chad was the product of a divorce.

On 24 April 1988, they played their first concert together, at Seattle's Vogue. A review of the group, the first ever published, in *Backlash*, a Seattle music free-sheet, concluded with a radical prediction: 'with enough practice, Nirvana could become . . . better than the Melvins!'

Seattle was beginning to reveal that it had a very specific scene of its own. As Olympia had hinged around K Records, so Seattle's burgeoning musical movement was largely underpinned by the Sub Pop label. Sub Pop sprang out of a fanzine,

Subterranean Pop, which Bruce Pavitt, then living in Olympia, had started in the early 1980s in order to pick up additional graduation credits. Moving to Seattle, he would put out cassettes with the magazine, working with Jonathan Poneman, who became his business partner. In 1986, Sub Pop put out its first album, a compilation that included Sonic Youth, Scratch Acid, Wipers and Naked Raygun. 'Sub Pop was cultivating a certain vibe, à la Blue Note or Factory,' Bruce Pavitt said.[26]

Part of that 'vibe' was the release of original-sounding singles, for which the Sub Pop pair had spotted the worth of Nirvana. So it was that on 11 June 1988, Nirvana recorded 'Love Buzz', their first single, a cover, written and originally recorded by the Dutch group Shocking Blue in 1969. Sub Pop had suggested they record this song, their favourite from the live set. Produced by Jack Endino, the B-side was entitled 'Big Cheese', an original credited to Kurt and Krist that would also appear on their first album.

In November 1988 Sub Pop released 'Love Buzz' as the first single in the Sub Pop Singles Club, a subscription service by which subscribers received new releases by mail every month. Realizing that exposure through the American media was almost impossible, its owners took the same route as another son of Seattle, Jimi Hendrix. Hendrix had moved to Britain to break the charts, then emulated this success in the USA. As the UK music press was available widely in America on import, Bruce Pavitt and Jonathan Poneman concentrated on promoting Sub Pop through the British papers. In February

1989 they paid for *Melody Maker* journalist Everett True to fly out to Seattle and document the scene in a series of articles. When True arrived, Kurt Cobain defined the sound of the city to him: 'Hard music played to a slow tempo.' Yet Nirvana were by no means at the forefront of this new Seattle scene. It was significant that their 'Love Buzz' single was restricted to the Sub Pop Singles Club, meaning the record never had a true release of its own. This distressed Kurt, and also reflected the fact that most locals were underwhelmed by Nirvana.

Prior to the show at the Vogue that secured them their deal, Kurt Cobain had suffered from stomach ache and vomited. Simple nerves, perhaps, as suffered by many performers and sportsmen. Except that from then on the stomach pains never really went away, and Kurt was obliged to adapt his life to cope with this constant torment.

But the source of his stomach ache was more than nervousness, and it intersected with the very source of his art. Because Kurt was so sensitive and so intelligent, and could feel and perceive so much, he was extremely hurt and frustrated that everyone else didn't see and sense what he glimpsed. Stomach pain also ran in the family. 'It's a psychosomatic thing. My mom had it for a few years in her early twenties, and eventually it went away. She was in a hospital all the time because of it.'[27]

He would spend the next years of his life in thrall to this debilitating illness, enduring numerous hospital visits and doctors' examinations, all to no avail. Later, in 1993, he would explain: 'Most of the time I sing right from my stomach. Right from where my stomach pain is. That's where the pain and anger comes from. It's definitely there: every time I've had an endoscope, they find a red irritation in my stomach. But it's psychosomatic, it's all from anger. And screaming.' The pain in Kurt's belly was now added to another constant hurt: the backache he suffered from his scoliosis, exacerbated by his guitar playing. 'That really adds to the pain in our music. It really does. I'm kind of grateful for it.'[28]

In September 1988 Krist temporarily broke up with Shelli. Krist no longer had regular work, while Shelli had a night-time job. Although Krist was obliged to move back to Aberdeen, to stay with his mother for a time, he was now able to play music full time, and Nirvana could practise above his mother Maria's hairdressing shop. Yet the split put pressures on Kurt and Tracy, especially from Tracy's end, as she certainly did not want to split up with Kurt. As a salve to his girl, and after listening to the Beatles' *Meet the Beatles* album for hours, Kurt wrote her a song, 'About a Girl'.

Now there were more live performances, all over Washington State. Kurt became legendary for his readiness to smash up his equipment at the end of shows. On 30 October 1988, at a show at a dorm in Evergreen State College, Kurt smashed up a guitar for the first time. And on this first significant tour, they would pick up cheap guitars from pawnshops to be destroyed onstage that night. Similarly, Kurt would seek out effects pedals wherever they travelled. But onstage it was often Krist Novoselic who stood out more than the guitarist. 'Kurt is a really good songwriter, but to the extent that those songs became full and alive, that was Krist,' said Jonathan Poneman.[29] Others also noted that Krist was far more confident and at ease with himself than Kurt, rather more in charge. Yet Kurt had an intensity that you could feel, and you knew he was the creative force in the band.

Sub Pop recognized this. They had decided they wanted Nirvana to record an album, with Jack Endino once again producing. On Christmas Eve, 1988, Nirvana were back at Reciprocal Studios for the first recording session for what would become known as *Bleach*. There would be five more sessions, each of around five hours, until the record was completed on 24 January. Total recording costs came to just over $600 for a record that ultimately would sell one and a half million copies.

Now Kurt revealed a side that others might not expect, visiting the local library and reading books about music business deals. Aware that Sub Pop made it a statement of their company's 'cool' that the label would not issue contracts – secretly because these leftie bohemian 'businessmen' didn't know what a record company contract looked like or might contain – Kurt brought this to the attention of Krist. One night a drunken Krist turned up at Bruce Pavitt's home. He demanded a three-album, three-year deal with Sub Pop, and that they would receive $6,000 in year one, $12,000 in year two, and $18,000 in year three. Sub Pop agreed.

In December 1988, another Nirvana tune appeared, on the *Sub Pop 200* box set. 'Spank Thru' (written by Kurt, with masturbation as its subject) was a really great song, with a burning drive. The song had been recorded on 6 November 1988, but was one of the earliest of Kurt's tunes, first heard on the Fecal Matter tape. It also set the template for the dynamics in almost all Nirvana songs: slow and quiet, followed by loud, fast and forceful.

The recording of *Bleach* was followed by a two-week West Coast tour, bottom of the bill to Mudhoney and the Melvins. There were worries over Kurt's abilities to sing and play guitar simultaneously, so a second guitarist was added. Jason Everman – who had given Nirvana the money to record *Bleach* – got the gig. On 11 February 1989, famously, as though in an effort to upstage his legendary Seattle forebear Jimi Hendrix, Kurt played guitar standing on his head, in San Jose, California.

In 1989 Nirvana would play over a hundred shows, five times what they had managed the previous year. When not on the road, Kurt would stay at home at the Olympia apartment he shared with Tracy. There he would paint all day. 'He'd paint with whatever medium came to hand,' she said. 'Acrylic paints, magic marker, spray cans, blood, pen, pencil – and on whatever improvised canvas he could scarf up at local thrift stores: often the back of board games. On rare occasions, he'd even paint using his own semen. He'd paint aliens, diseased children, grossly distorted childhood images utilizing pop iconographic figures such as Batman and Barbie.'[30]

On 9 June, with Mudhoney and Tad, Nirvana played bottom of the bill at Sub Pop's Lamefest '89 at Seattle's Moore Theater. It was a big event – a year previously these acts couldn't have played such a venue to a packed-out audience. *Bleach* was released days later. Sub Pop were amazed that the record immediately started to sell, as essentially, Nirvana were an almost unknown band. As soon as the record was out, Nirvana set off on their first US tour. They played twenty-six dates, mainly in bars, never earning more than a hundred dollars a night. They often slept in their van, but were tremendously excited that they were now living the full rock 'n' roll travelling band life. Although at first there was rarely a large audience, soon attendances picked up, after college radio began to play tunes from *Bleach* such as 'School' and 'About a Girl'.

Jason Everman, prone to metal rock-star-like movements onstage that jarred with Kurt's 'purist' posture, did not seem to fit in. On 18 July he played his last show with Nirvana, at the Pyramid Club in New York City, part of the New Music Seminar. His fate was sealed after Kurt and Krist got drunk one night – as they seemed to most nights – and then scored some cocaine. While high on the drug, the pair decided that Jason had to go. Jason later joined Soundgarden as bassist.

It was a three-piece Nirvana that undertook a fourteen-day Midwest tour that started at the end of September. The tour began in Minneapolis. That day Kurt suffered so much from stomach ache that he collapsed, violently vomiting, even when there was nothing left in his stomach. He was taken to a hospital but no specific condition was discovered.

Back in the studio, Nirvana recorded an EP, *Blew*, named after its title track. Other songs were the previously released 'Love Buzz', 'Stain' and 'Been a Son'. Three thousand copies were pressed, but it was only released in the UK. There was a specific reason for this. On 20 October 1989, Nirvana and Tad, who would be topping the bill, boarded a plane in Seattle for the ten-hour flight to London, before driving three hundred miles to Newcastle in the northeast of England. This was the first of thirty-six shows in forty-two days. With eleven people jammed into a Fiat van it was almost impossibly claustrophobic, especially for someone claiming to suffer from a fear of confined spaces, as Kurt now was.

The upside was that almost all of the dates were sold out – *Bleach* was in the Top 10 of the UK indie album chart – including the show in Berlin the day after the Berlin wall had come down. Six songs into that show, Kurt destroyed his instrument and stormed off. Exhaustion seemed to have led to feelings of melancholy followed by downright depression. In Rome Kurt clambered up the speakers, then onto the balcony, still strumming his guitar, hollering at the audience that he was going to jump and kill himself. ('Jump!' called the audience.) Backstage he smashed microphones and burst into tears. Jonathan Poneman from Sub Pop was there. According to Kurt, as soon as he claimed to be leaving Nirvana, Poneman offered to sign him as a solo artist. But Bruce Pavitt and Poneman had made a major strategic error. They had arrived backstage at the Rome gig as a measure of support, flying in from Seattle. By thus indulging in long-distance air-travel, staying in hotels more luxurious than anything the band members had ever seen, they earned Kurt's abiding enmity. 'Though Nirvana would stay on Sub Pop for another year, in a progressively worsening marriage, Kurt had already emotionally jettisoned his label,' said his biographer Charles R. Cross.[31]

Kurt pulled himself together and the tour moved back to London for its final show, on 3 December, at London's Astoria. Although *Melody Maker*, which had championed Nirvana, turned against them, Keith Cameron of *Sounds* proclaimed them 'the most amazing band I'd ever seen.'

The next day Nirvana recorded a session for John Peel, the revered BBC disc jockey and relentless champion of the underground.

Back in the USA, Nirvana played some Californian dates, before another national tour. Now they were pulling in audiences of a few hundred. Despite the buzz of being championed by Sonic Youth, who had come to see them on the previous tour, the band played badly at their New York Pyramid Club show. Sonic Youth's Kim Gordon and Thurston Moore were in the audience, along with Iggy Pop; and, significantly, Gary Gersh, an A&R man for the Geffen label.

Despite their growing buzz, when Nirvana played a Seattle New Year's Eve show at the end of 1989, only fifty people turned up. In the venue's dressing room, Kurt wrote on a wall: 'Do it again for another!' – an expression of his altruism towards his fellow man. 'He was so personable and so fucking cool,' said his friend Amy Moon, who was there that night. 'Kurt was totally a listener . . . One of the few people I've met who listened to what you said.'

Back in Olympia, in March 1990 Kurt and his friend Damon Romero decided one night to rent a video, choosing Alex Cox's *Straight to Hell*, a spaghetti thriller starring former Clash singer Joe Strummer. Although the film had been critically trounced, Kurt – unsurprisingly – liked it. He and Romero also noted the presence in the film of a girl they had noticed in a club in Portland, Oregon: Courtney Love.

On 3 April 1990 Nirvana arrived at Smart Studios in Madison, Wisconsin, the premises of Butch Vig, not only a record producer but also a drummer. Kurt believed – correctly – that Vig could achieve the drum sound he felt was so absent from their recordings, and which increasingly he believed Chad was unable to deliver. In a week they recorded eight songs, including 'In Bloom', 'Breed' and 'Pay to Play'. They were intended for the next Nirvana album, which Kurt had decided should be titled 'Sheep'.

As doors were opening professionally for Nirvana, others were closing emotionally for Kurt Cobain, now once again drinking heavily. On Tracy's birthday in late April, she received a phone call from Kurt, on tour. He told her that he still wanted to be her boyfriend, but no longer wanted to live with her. Unusually, Kurt then had sex with a girl while on the road in Texas, the one time his bandmates recalled him behaving in such a manner. He cursed himself afterwards for his weakness. It was an unsatisfactory, depressing experience, and he later told Tracy about it.

Nirvana were also aware that their relationship with Sub Pop was becoming problematic. Like many independent labels, Sub Pop was forever stymied by its distribution network. Nirvana would arrive on tour in a town and find no copies of *Bleach* in the local stores. By the summer of 1990, Sub Pop were aware that Nirvana had decided to leave the label.

Moreover, the group leaving Sub Pop would be without a drummer. In mid-June Kurt and Krist took the ferry over to Bainbridge Island to let Chad know that he was out of the group. The same week Tracy moved out of the apartment, which Kurt took over.

The truth was that Kurt had fallen for another girl, Tobi Vail, an Olympia musician a year younger than him with an enormous knowledge of punk music. She had also had a better education than Kurt. A feminist, who had coined the phrase 'riot grrrl' and was forming a band called Bikini Kill, Tobi's rants about sexual politics fascinated Kurt – who was obliged to put to the back of his mind the porn magazines he had leered at in the van in Europe. However, as

Charles R. Cross recalled, a person with such views was not precisely who Kurt was looking for: 'What Kurt was searching for in a relationship was the kind of family intimacy he had lacked since early childhood; but Tobi rejected the traditional relationship he sought as sexist.' Yet his endless late-night discussions – and less frequent late-night sex – with Tobi had been inspiring. 'Punk rock is freedom' was a rubric he coined while hanging with Tobi, and he would quote it at every opportunity.

Kurt and Krist were now sending cassettes of their Butch Vig sessions to major labels. Punk purist Tobi declared that she would never sign with a major. Did this manifest some inner conflict for Kurt Cobain? On a radio interview in April, he had declared: 'We don't have any interest in a major label. It would be nice to have better distribution, but anything else that goes on major labels is just a bunch of shit.'

Then Kurt did the precise opposite, enlisting the assistance of Susan Silver, Soundgarden's manager. Kurt and Krist met Alan Mintz, a top-end Los Angeles-based music business lawyer who understood the Butch Vig tape, and vowed to sign them to a major. After the relative success of *Bleach*, and many positive reviews, there was already a considerable buzz over Nirvana.

Nirvana were scheduled to record another single for Sub Pop. They brought in Dan Peters from Mudhoney on drums and recorded the tune 'Sliver', while Tad, busy recording an album, took time off for a meal. As far as Kurt's writing went,

'Sliver' was a serious development. It told the autobiographical story of a boy who is left by his mother and father to be baby-sat by his grandparents. 'It was also,' according to Charles R. Cross, 'one of the first Nirvana songs to use contrasting dynamics, which would become a signature for the band: the verses were quiet and slow, but the chorus came in as a thunderous wall of sound.'[32] The song ends with Greta Garbo's moody (and misquoted) imprecation, 'I want to be alone.'

For an August tour of the West Coast with Sonic Youth, Dale Crover was brought back in as drummer. When he had to return to the Melvins, in came Dan Peters, for a show on 22 September, at the Motor Sports International Garage in Seattle. Although Dale was told Nirvana were getting ready for a UK tour, he would not play with them ever again. In the audience was someone Buzz Osbourne had brought along – Dave Grohl. Grohl was legendary for the power with which he hit drums and for his across-the-kit attack in the group Scream, a Virginia hardcore outfit.

Dave Grohl had been born in Warren, Ohio, on 14 January 1969. At the age of twelve he had begun to play guitar. When he formed a punk band, Freak Baby, Dave became so dispirited by the ineffectual drummer he decided he could do better on the kit himself. At sixteen, Dave discovered Led Zeppelin and – specifically – the drumming of John Bonham.

Kurt and Krist had been in San Francisco and, hearing Scream had a great drummer, had gone to see them play there. Twenty days after the Motor Sports International Garage concert, Dave drummed for the first time with Nirvana at the North Shore Surf Club in Olympia. 'We knew in two minutes that he was the right drummer,' said Krist.

Almost immediately afterwards they were off to the UK for a five-date sell-out tour. 'It looks like it's gonna be pretty easy to find a big deal, we've just got to try to keep from being fucked,' Kurt told Liz Evans for *Raw* magazine in England. Clearly he was utterly aware of Nirvana's position and his group's emerging potential. 'It's a hard problem,' he agreed. 'Because we feel that we're diverse and accessible enough to try to infiltrate into more than just one market. We feel we can appeal to more than just the Metal or the Alternative Rock market. We want to try to be mainstream too. We want to reach the Top 40. Even if the whole of the next album can't get across to that type of audience there's at least a hit single or two in there.

'Our next album is going to be so diverse that we really have no choice but to cross over. We can't be classified into this simple heavy Grunge Rock category anymore. We've moved a long way on from there.'

Back in Seattle, Kurt and Krist were flown down to LA by MCA Records for an unfruitful meeting with label executives. Meeting up with Sonic Youth, who happened to be in the city, Nirvana were urged by these alternative standard-bearers to check out their own management, Gold Mountain, and to sign with Geffen Records – Sonic Youth were on the label's DGC imprint.

In Olympia Dave Grohl moved in with Kurt, who had been living on his own and seemed in an increasing state of isolation, especially as he and Tobi were hardly seeing each other. Now, however, Dave started going out with Bikini Kill's Kathleen Hannah, and Kurt and Tobi would often be with them. At Kurt's house one night, Kathleen Hannah added a piece of graffiti to a wall in the apartment shared by the two Nirvana musicians: 'Kurt smells like teen spirit,' a reference to the Teen Spirit deodorant that Tobi used. By November, however, Tobi had dumped Kurt, which he did not take well. He retreated into himself again, often seeming to seethe with rage, his mental state exacerbating his permanent stomach pains.

But the breakup was positive for his art. In subsequent months he wrote a string of his best songs, all of them about Tobi, including 'Aneurysm', 'Drain You', 'Lounge Act' and – most significantly, of course – 'Smells Like Teen Spirit'. He also introduced a new personality into the writings in his journal: her name was spelt 'heroine'. This wilfully coy use of the word heroin – as though by so archly misspelling it, he removed the danger – perhaps concealed his true feelings about, or fear of, females. He promised Tracy, with whom he had had something of a reconciliation, that he only would do the drug occasionally.

When Kurt signed a publishing deal with Virgin, his first payment came as a $3,000 cheque. He spent $1,000 at Toys R Us, his purchases including a couple of air rifles, with which he shot out the windows at a nearby building housing the Washington State Lottery.

Days later, Nirvana were visited by John Silva, the partner of former Led Zeppelin publicist Danny Goldberg at Gold Mountain Management, who oversaw the career of Sonic Youth. Gold Mountain secured Nirvana a deal with DGC, the same Geffen imprint to which Sonic Youth were signed, for $287,000, a very substantial advance. (It was not until 30 April 1991 that the contract was finally completed.) From the advance Kurt received wages of $1,000 a month. Although for years he had been living on far less, the $250 a week was somehow never enough. After falling behind on his rent, Kurt for a time was reduced to living in his car. For much of the time he ate only corn dogs – hardly the best diet for a man incessantly plagued by violent stomach pains.

To record their first album – what would become *Nevermind* – Kurt and Krist wanted to continue working with Butch Vig. While they were in Los Angeles recording, Courtney Love began to call by to see Kurt. Since they had first met at a show in Portland in 1989, she had been very taken with him. 'I just thought he was really beautiful. He was really cool and he had really beautiful hands,' she said.[33] With worrying prescience, Kurt's first impression of Courtney Love was that she looked like Nancy Spungen – 'Nancy' as in 'Sid'n'Nancy'. Running into each other at a Butthole Surfers show at the Los Angeles Palladium, Courtney showed her affection for Kurt by hitting him in the belly, before – as though in some primitive mating ritual – they began wrestling with each other.

A highly intelligent woman, Courtney Love was clearly driven towards stardom. In March 1990, she had started the group Hole. A former stripper and Oregon reform school alumnus, she had lived in Liverpool in the UK, on the scene with the Teardrop Explodes and Echo and the Bunnymen. She had also had a film part – the one Kurt had seen – in Alex Cox's *Straight to Hell*. And she could talk until hell froze over. According to her former longstanding boyfriend from Portland, Courtney's ambition was tempered by conventional belief: 'She thought it was a male-dominated world. She thought the only way she could achieve stardom was through a man.'

At first Kurt was intent on not getting into another relationship. His purpose in Los Angeles was to make a successful album; he was inspired by the city's spirit-lifting ceaseless sunshine, a considerable contrast to that of Seattle. Sound City Studios in Van Nuys in the San Fernando Valley was the reasonably priced recording complex recommended to Nirvana by DGC. The first record made there had been Neil Young's masterly *After the Goldrush*. Later in the 1970s Fleetwood Mac had recorded their enormously successful *Rumours* album at Sound City. As Kurt was not acquainted with any local heroin dealers, he resorted to drinking codeine-based cough syrup throughout the sessions. Purist Kurt would often refuse to record a second take.

The record was finally mixed by Andy Wallace, who had worked magic on Slayer's *Seasons in the Abyss*. 'Wallace sweetened the sound, filtering the raw tracks through various special effects boxes, cranking out about one mix a day,' said Azerrad.[34] The record was completed, at a cost of $65,000, by mid-June 1991. Almost immediately Kurt found himself suffering from that sense of being utterly underwhelmed and empty – on top of the overriding depression to which he was always prone – that often follows the successful completion of creative work.

But for now it was on with the show. Nirvana undertook a week-long West Coast tour, supporting Dinosaur Jr. The shows, which included dates in Denver, Los Angeles and Santa Cruz, were notable for revealing the audience's air of expectation about Nirvana.

Then, in August, it was back to Europe. Once again, Nirvana were the opening act for Sonic Youth, on a tour with plenty of festival dates. On 23 August, they played Reading Festival, on the main stage at 2 p.m, before a 50,000-strong audience. Flinging himself into the drum kit, Kurt suffered a minor shoulder dislocation. Backstage was Courtney Love, with her then boyfriend Billy Corgan of Smashing Pumpkins.

Back on the West Coast, at a sound stage in Culver City in Los Angeles, Nirvana filmed a video for 'Smells Like Teen Spirit'. It was a parody of a high school gym performance, with an elderly janitor mopping the floor – as Kurt had done at his former high school.

The cover image for *Nevermind* was established. It featured a picture of five-month-old Spencer Elden, a naked baby swimming. At least subconsciously, this was an expression of the excess of water signs in Kurt's astrological chart. This was something he was acutely aware of, and a clue to his almost overwhelming sensitivity – he would even refer to his astrological sign in his eventual suicide note. An addition to the image was a dollar bill suspended in the water to which the baby appeared to be heading – a twist that was Kurt's idea. The baby's penis was clearly visible, surviving suggestions from censorship-wary DGC employees that it might require airbrushing out.

As though facing down fate, *Nevermind* was released on Friday, 13 September 1991, with an album launch party in Seattle. Kurt found himself embarrassed at how the local scene would respond to his record company's inevitable over-zealous dressing of the hip Re-bar with a myriad Nirvana posters. Neatly pressed company employees had flown up en masse from LA. After *Nevermind* had been played twice, a cringing Kurt had the DJ replace the Nirvana music with cheesy disco and New Wave. Then the event erupted into a food fight, at which point Nirvana were asked to leave.

On 16 September, three days later, the trio played an instore show at the city's Beehive Records. Fans appeared from as far away as Montesano. 'I realized that if people you went to high school with – especially in Montesano – were aware that I was a rock star in Seattle, then it was getting kind of big,' Kurt said.[35] In response, all three Nirvana men went out and got drunk.

Was there another dimension to Kurt's cynicism? For an ultimately fatal subplot developed almost simultaneously with the release of *Nevermind*. The same month that this ostensibly mainstream album came out, Kurt had consciously decided to become a 'heroine' addict.[36] He later wrote down his experiences of the drug for a treatment programme. He said he had first tried heroin in Aberdeen in 1987, and until 1990 had done it around ten more times:

'When I got back from our second European tour with Sonic Youth, I decided to use heroine on a daily basis because of an ongoing stomach ailment that I had been suffering from for the past five years, [and that] had literally taken me to the point of wanting to kill myself . . . the only thing I found that worked were heavy opiates . . . So I decided, if I feel like a junkie as it is, I may as well be one.'[37]

He also wrote that after he and Courtney Love, a different 'heroine' who would bear his daughter, would later spend a fortnight coming off the drug, 'I instantly regained that familiar burning nausea and decided to either kill myself or stop the pain. I bought a gun but chose drugs instead. I stayed on heroine until one month before Frances' due date.' Later it would sometimes be asserted that it was Courtney who had got Kurt into heroin. But the opposite is true. She had developed a heroin habit in Los Angeles in 1989, but had successfully undergone treatment and come off the drug. When she and Kurt first fully got together, Courtney was so smitten that the relationship continued despite his ongoing use.

For some time, Kurt had wanted to become part of a sort of Sex Pistols-like punk act, exploding quickly and suddenly. When they had been about to sign their deal, he had joked of getting the DGC advance and immediately splitting up. An emulation of the Pistols seems to have been an aspect of Kurt's thinking, certainly if we recall how Courtney reminded him of Nancy Spungen. But did some part of Kurt also want to be the tragic Sid Vicious? As things would turn out, such a conceit would not prove to be too far-fetched.

Although they would become increasingly dominant in subsequent months, such extra-curricular interests needed to be put to one side. On 20 September 1991, Nirvana embarked on a headlining North American tour, on which they were at first supported by the Melvins.

A month into the shows, they started moving up the West Coast from San Diego. If they were lucky, Geffen Records had expected *Nevermind* to sell 50,000 copies. So when the album began to sell in unanticipated amounts they quickly had to order further pressings. 'The album had sold 100,000 copies by San Diego, 200,000 by LA, and by the morning they hit Seattle, for a Halloween show, it had gone gold, selling half a million,' wrote Charles R. Cross. In Seattle Nirvana played the Paramount Theater. Kurt's guitar had a message stuck on it: VANDALISM: BEAUTIFUL AS A ROCK IN A COP'S FACE.

This was a gesture which might be felt to be playing to punk's lowest common denominator.

The night of the Seattle show, at which Kurt had insisted they be supported by Tobi's Bikini Kill, his former girlfriend ended up as one of the clump of friends sleeping on the floor of Kurt's hotel room. 'It was a small irony,' said Cross, 'that Tobi was sleeping on his floor the day he'd sold half a million copies of an album that was ostensibly about how she didn't love him.'

In November, Nirvana were off to Europe again. Courtney's group Hole were booked onto the same circuit, their schedule commencing a fortnight later. At first their blossoming love affair was complicated by the presence of another American woman, Mary Lou Lord, with whom Kurt had had an affair earlier in the year, and who surprised him by turning up at Nirvana's Bristol show on 4 November. Kurt told her of the growing severity of his stomach pains.

He was aware, however, of the imminent arrival of Courtney, and in a very public way, Mary Lou learned that her relationship with Kurt was doomed. Appearing on *The Word*, a Friday night 'youth' television show, Kurt announced to the British nation, 'I just want everyone in this room to know that Courtney Love, of the pop group Hole, is the best fuck in the world!' Suddenly, as a result of this declaration, Kurt Cobain was fodder for the front pages of the mass-market media.

And Kurt was adept at giving the media what they desired.

On 27 November, Nirvana recorded a slot for BBC television's long-running chart show, *Top of the Pops*. 'Smells Like Teen Spirit' was charging up the UK singles chart – reaching number 9 that week – but in his performance Kurt sent up such glory by dropping his voice an octave and changing the opening line to 'Load up on drugs, kill your friends'. Meanwhile, Krist and Dave made it obvious that they were miming playing their instruments.

The European tour ended with a date in France on 7 December, then Nirvana flew back to Seattle; there Kurt was astonished how successful they had become in their homeland during their overseas absence. 'We'd finished the ['Teen Spirit'] video and they started to play it while we were on tour,' Kurt said, 'and I would get reports every once in a while from friends of mine, telling me that I was famous. So it didn't affect me until probably three months after we'd been famous in America . . . a friend of mine made a compilation about all the news stories about our band that was played on MTV and the local news programmes and stuff. It was frightening: it just scared me.'[38]

After a brief end-of-year West Coast tour, concluding at San Francisco's Cow Palace on New Year's Eve, the band flew to New York. Nirvana were scheduled to perform on *Saturday Night Live* on 11 January 1992. The previous day the band did a photo session with Michael Lavine at his Bleecker Street loft. Kurt, his hair dyed bright red, nodded out several times, the effects of heroin now evident to those around him. 'I remember people having to go out and score dope. I remember Kurt telling me that the reason that he loved Courtney so much was that she was the only girl he knew that would stand up at a party and smash a glass table to bits just for the hell of it. I remember thinking that was a pretty odd reason to love someone,' said the photographer.[39]

By the end of 1991, sales of *Nevermind* in the United States were growing exponentially. But the album seemed unable to climb higher than the number 6 slot. The week after Christmas, however, its sales catapulted when kids went out and spent their present money – or returned unwanted album gifts. In those seven days 400,000 copies of *Nevermind* were sold, and the album knocked Michael Jackson's *Dangerous* off the top slot in the *Billboard* charts, where it seemed to have taken up permanent residency. Suddenly they were the biggest group in the world. 'Nirvana is that rare band that has everything: critical acclaim, industry respect, pop radio appeal, and a rock-solid college/alternative base,' trumpeted *Billboard*, the American music business trade paper.

Now, with their album at number 1, Nirvana would appear on *Saturday Night Live*, a show that commanded huge viewing figures and was also extremely credible. Yet for this performance on American network television, Kurt was smacked out. He had to force himself not to throw up, and his eyes looked sunken into his head – a sign he had shot up earlier in the evening. But he rose to the moment with blistering performances of 'Smells Like Teen Spirit' and 'Territorial

Pissings', before stabbing his guitar neck through several speakers while Dave Grohl tossed his entire drum kit about the stage.

As the show's end credits rolled over the conclusion of their performance, Nirvana decided to do their utmost to 'piss off the rednecks and homophobes', in Kurt's words, as he later claimed credit for something Krist Novoselic had instigated. On camera the bass player came over to Kurt and French-kissed him, a gesture both loving and supportive.

During an interview following the performance, Kurt 'borrowed' $40 from the journalist, enough to buy a handy amount of smack. Kurt got off on the seedy social underbelly that is a feature of the ritual, lonely world of heroin, especially in New York City, where he would line up with other addicts to score smack in Alphabet City on the Lower East Side. What was on sale on the East Coast was China white – stronger than the Mexican black tar heroin available on the West Coast.

And it was in Manhattan that the full extent of Kurt's heroin problem became apparent to those around him. Returning to his hotel, he climbed into bed next to Courtney. When Courtney Love woke the next morning, she found Kurt had overdosed on heroin. She managed to revive him. As a counterpoint to such darkness, it was around now that Courtney found out she was pregnant. She claimed she stopped using drugs as soon as she learned this.

With his girlfriend pregnant, Kurt temporarily rose to the

responsibilities of impending fatherhood. After flying to Los Angeles, both he and Courtney checked into a motel. This was on the advice of a doctor whose chosen field of expertise was rapid detox. He felt they needed to be somewhere quiet and discreet. Under the influence of sleeping tablets and methadone, they both endured this shock treatment – feverish, puking, and devastated from diarrhoea. Halfway through this process, Kurt was obliged to be in a video being made in LA for 'Come as You Are', the next single off *Nevermind*, but he only did so on the understanding that the film would not feature a single clear image of his gaunt, blotchy face.

As so often with Kurt he had more than one reason for trying to get clean. Yes, he was allegedly readying himself for the birth of his child. But at the end of January Kurt was due to fly to Australia, followed by New Zealand, Hawaii and Japan, for a tour, and he was worried that in these unknown territories he wouldn't be able to score.

The tour proved as deleterious as Kurt had feared. Hardly speaking to his bandmates, and doubled up from stomach pain, he ended up being prescribed Physeptone, a synthetic heroin substitute – or methadone, as it is better known.

In Japan the record company was at a loss as to how to behave after Kurt's controversial declaration on arriving in the country, announcing he was there to 'repay the cunts for Pearl Harbor'.

Then he was off to the land of Pearl Harbor itself, Honolulu. Courtney had joined Kurt in Japan. During the plane flight the pair agreed to marry in Hawaii. A prenuptial agreement was signed by both parties. (Although Kurt had yet to receive the colossal amounts of money that would shortly flow his way from the success of *Nevermind* and lucrative live shows, he knew full well he could build significant wealth. But their relationship would not be financially one-sided: Hole were about to sign a deal with DGC for a million dollars and a higher royalty rate than Nirvana, which was important for Courtney's self-esteem.)

On 24 February 1992, Kurt and Courtney married on Waikiki Beach. Kurt wore blue-check pyjamas – habitual garb for him by now. Courtney wore an antique silk dress that had once belonged to Frances Farmer, the actor, also from Seattle, who at the peak of her career had suffered egregious mistreatment of her mental health problems.

For the wedding Kurt arranged for Dylan Carlson to be flown over from Seattle to act as his best man. A subtext to this role was Kurt's inability to find quality 'heroine' on the island but by the time of the ceremony he was slightly out of it on smack.[40] The sentiment of the occasion could still reach him, though, and at times he burst into sobs. 'She's my one and only chance,' was how he defined Courtney Love to Dave Grohl.

None of Kurt's family had been invited, and Kurt had banned Krist's wife Shelli from the event because he believed she had been talking behind Courtney's back. The next day, when Krist and Shelli flew out of Hawaii, they believed that

Nirvana had broken up. 'Kurt's a fucking junkie asshole and I hate him!' Krist cried to Shelli. After the wedding, he and Krist could never be the same. Although he and Dave had also been like brothers, Kurt was now talking about firing the drummer. Kurt really had formed Nirvana to have a group to play his songs. So for the sake of personal expediency he had no problems with the idea of dumping Krist and Dave. He made them sign a retroactive deal over songwriting credits, giving himself the lion's share of songwriting royalties – perhaps not unreasonably, as essentially the songs were all his.

Nirvana did not in fact perform for another four months. This was unsurprising, really, as over the ensuing spring Kurt did little except take drugs after he and Courtney had flown back to Los Angeles. Dave Grohl was furious: there had been plans for a lengthy arena tour that spring, which had been aborted.

There were occasional efforts at self-control. In March Kurt entered an inpatient dependency unit at Cedars-Sinai hospital in Beverly Hills, where his heroin intake was swapped for methadone. In an interview that appeared in *Rolling Stone* the next month, Kurt expounded his personal worldview as he imagined it the instant of the interview: 'I don't even drink anymore because it destroys my stomach. My body wouldn't allow me to take drugs if I wanted to, because I'm so weak. All drugs [do is] destroy your memory and your self-respect and everything that goes along with your self-esteem. They're no good at all.'

In April Kurt and his new bride flew up to Seattle to look for a house to buy. On a visit to his sister Kim in Aberdeen, he threatened her that if she ever used heroin, he would get a gun and kill her. Kim was aware that Kurt was projecting his own inner hell onto her.[41] In January Kurt had been spending $100 a day on heroin. Six months later it was up to four times that, a staggering amount.

At the beginning of the summer, Nirvana were thrown back together, honouring a booked European tour which kicked off with a Dublin date on Sunday, 21 June. Five days later they played the massive annual Roskilde festival in Denmark, outside Copenhagen. There were further festival dates, in Norway, Finland, France and Spain. And in late August, Nirvana returned to the UK, to again play Reading festival, this time headlining. The show began with Kurt singing a couple of lines of Bette Midler's 'The Rose' after being wheeled onstage in a wheelchair by *Melody Maker* journalist Everett True.

While onstage at Reading, Kurt may have had something on his mind. In an article published in the September edition of *Vanity Fair*, which appeared in early August, Courtney Love confirmed to writer Lynn Hirschberg that she and Cobain had been using heroin early in her pregnancy. The article, still on the newsstands on 18 August 1992, the date of birth of Frances Bean Cobain, would have devastating implications. Although both Courtney and Kurt claimed that Hirschberg took her words out of context, child welfare services launched an investigation questioning their parenting abilities. Although the investigation was eventually called off, it was not before Frances had been removed from her parents' custody for a short time, beginning when she was two weeks old.

Returning to Los Angeles from a triumphant visit to England at the beginning of September, Kurt decided once again to enter a treatment programme, this time at Exodus in Marina del Rey. Was the new responsibility of fatherhood weighing on his conscience? Or was it fear of the consequences of the *Vanity Fair* article? At Exodus he was prescribed buprenorphine, an anti-addiction drug which also had the effect of immediately relieving his stomach pains.

Kurt took a brief leave of absence from Exodus to appear on the MTV Awards show. When Kurt announced he wanted to play 'Rape Me', a new song, the MTV bigwigs were apoplectic. On learning that the MTV employee assigned to deal directly with them would be fired if they played the song, the band agreed to stick to the agreed number, 'Lithium'. Live, to the MTV executives' horror, Kurt played the opening chords of 'Rape Me' . . . before strutting into 'Lithium', as promised. Backstage Kurt and Courtney, with Frances on her lap, found themselves face to face with Axl Rose, an especial bête noire of Kurt's on account of his absurd rock star posturing, and his model girlfriend – rock star model girlfriends were sneered at by Courtney as an ultimate cliché. When Courtney asked Rose if he would be Frances's godfather, the Guns N' Roses man was not oblivious to her intended sarcasm. 'You shut your bitch up, or I'm taking you down to the pavement,' he threatened Kurt. Kurt responded with a smile: 'Okay, bitch. Shut up.'[42] Rose and his girlfriend departed, tails between their legs.

The next day there was a Nirvana show in Portland, followed by a benefit against music censorship in Seattle. At the 16,000-seater sold-out Seattle date, Kurt's father Don showed up backstage, the first time Kurt had seen him for eight years. Also present was his mother Wendy and his sister Kim. When Kurt began to raise his voice towards his father, Wendy led the others out of the dressing room. Later – unusually – Kurt walked to the stage in utter silence to perform the finest show Seattle had ever had from Nirvana. Don's reappearance would grant Kurt songwriting material, specifically for the autobiographical 'Serve the Servants'.

For some weeks Kurt and Courtney stayed in assorted expensive Seattle hotels, Kurt worryingly registering as Simon Ritchie, the real name of Sid Vicious. They had bought a house overlooking Lake Washington, some thirty miles away, and it was being substantially rebuilt and renovated. As cigarette burns and drug detritus built up in hotel rooms which they would request were never cleaned, invariably they would finally be kicked out of these assorted lodgings. During this time in Seattle, in October 1992, Nirvana recorded several songs, mainly as instrumentals. The demo session was with Jack Endino, the *Bleach* producer, and many of these songs would later be re-recorded for *In Utero*.

That autumn of 1992, with Frances still kept from them, Kurt and Courtney seemed on the edge of madness. Cracks were very visible. When Victoria Clarke, an Irish journalist, announced she was proposing to write an unauthorized biography of Nirvana, Courtney was enraged. She called up Clarke and – accompanied by Kurt – left a 31-minute harangue on her answering machine. Some of Kurt's threats went as follows: 'At this point I don't give a flying fuck if I have this recorded that I'm threatening you. I suppose I could throw out a few thousand dollars to have you snuffed out, but maybe I'll try the legal way. First.' Surprisingly vicious words from a man who, in 1992, was the world's leading stoner anti-hero.

Two weeks before Christmas 1992, a 'new' Nirvana album was in the stores. *Incesticide* was a collection of fifteen tunes, some previously released. Tracks included 'Dive' and 'Sliver' from the 'Sliver' single; cover tunes like the Vaselines' 'Son of a Gun' and Devo's 'Turnaround' from *Hormoaning*, a Nirvana EP released only in Australia and Japan in 1992; 'Downer' from *Bleach*; and 'Mexican Seafood' from a 1989 Sub Pop compilation. The cover art was a painting by Kurt. Hardly promoted by DGC, whose desire to have more Nirvana 'product' on sale was presumably balanced against the intended release the next year of a brand new album by the band, the record almost immediately sold half a million copies in the US, where it made the Top 40.

In January 1993, Nirvana played a pair of enormous festival

dates in Brazil. The first show, in Sao Paulo, had an audience of 110,000. Kurt was drinking and taking pills and could hardly play. Much of the set consisted of cover versions: when playing Queen's 'We Will Rock You', Kurt changed the lyrics to 'We will fuck you'.

After performing 'Territorial Pissings', Kurt dived into the audience, smashed his guitar, and lobbed pieces of it to the crowd. Some forty minutes into the set, a frustrated Krist hurled his bass at Kurt and walked off stage. Contracted to play for ninety minutes to secure their mammoth fee, the crew were obliged to fetch Krist to finish the set. When Krist returned, he picked up his bass from the stage, not bothering to retune it. At which point a guitar tech rolled a cantaloupe melon onstage. Kurt started smashing the fruit on his guitar strings, playing his guitar with it. Then the band switched instruments, with Kurt on drums, Krist on guitar, and Dave on bass. A portion of the audience walked out in disgust.

'The band started to really fail me emotionally,' Kurt said, in a partial explanation to Jon Savage, 'because a lot of it had to do with the fact that we were playing a lot of these festivals in the daytime. There's nothing more boring than doing that. The audiences are massive and none of them care what band is up on stage. I was just getting over my drug addiction, or trying to battle that, and it was just too much. For the rest of the year I kept going back and forth between wanting to quit and wanting to change our name, cos I still really enjoy playing with Chris and Dave and I couldn't see us splitting up because of the pressures of success. It's just pathetic, you know: to have to do something like that. I don't know if there is much of a conscious connection between Chris and Dave and I, when we play live. I don't usually even notice Chris and Dave: I'm in my own world. I'm not saying it doesn't matter whether they're there or not, that I could hire studio musicians or something. I know it wouldn't be the same.'

The next Brazil show was in Rio de Janeiro a week later: Kurt opened the performance with a few lines from Electric Light Orchestra's 'Telephone Line'. Kurt, who had had a row with Courtney, had been threatening to jump out of a high window of his hotel. Eventually the tour manager found Kurt a hotel with a room on the ground floor, which was a doss-house compared to the palatial five-star hotel into which he had been booked.

In their time off between the two Brazilian shows, the three group members were supposed to be working on new songs, sessions already having been booked for recording a new album. After his first night in his down-at-heel hotel, Kurt showed up the next day at the demo studio in Rio, ready to work. He had with him the first version of a new song, 'Heart-Shaped Box', which they played at the Rio show on 23 January, along with another newie, 'Scentless Apprentice'.

Kurt was insisting that the new album would be entitled *I Hate Myself and I Want to Die*. Several times in his journals he had written this phrase. 'When Kurt used to come out with that I Hate Myself and I Want to Die stuff,' said Jon Savage, 'people would completely miss his sense of humour. He was being very ironic: I asked him about this when I interviewed him.'

On Valentine's Day, 1993, Nirvana journeyed to Pachyderm Studios, in woodland near tiny Cannon Falls in Minnesota, to begin recording their new album. The facility had been selected by Nirvana's record company for its pastoral isolation – one that would hopefully ensure the absence of negative characters. Steve Albini, former member of Big Black, a major influence on Kurt, was producing: Kurt loved some of his other productions, notably the Pixies' *Surfer Rosa* and the Breeders' *Pod.*

After six days, the group had down the basic tracks. The entire album took half as long as *Nevermind* to make. Among the songs were 'Heart-Shaped Box' and 'Pennyroyal Tea', 'two of Nirvana's most accomplished works,' according to Charles R. Cross.[43] Yet Courtney Love's own, tighter lyrical writing had clearly influenced her husband. Over subsequent weeks, the *I Hate Myself and I Want to Die* title was changed, first to *Verse, Chorus, Verse*, and then to *In Utero*, a line from a poem by Courtney.

In March 1993 Kurt and Courtney moved into a relatively modest rented house at 11301 Lakeside Avenue NE in Seattle, as the house they had bought was several months from being ready to live in. To get around the city, Kurt bought a grey 1986 Volvo 240DL, stylish and safe.

A social worker from Los Angeles flew up to Seattle and

declared herself satisfied that Frances was being cared for correctly. But the controversy over Kurt and Courtney's child's custody had cost almost a quarter of a million dollars in legal fees. Inevitably, there was a problem with nannies. Unable to cope with the 'bohemian' lifestyle of the parents, they seemed to arrive and leave the house as though through a revolving door.

Kurt's relationship with Don, his own father, remained largely unresolved. That spring of 1993, Kurt wrote a letter to Don which he never sent. It concluded: 'I've never taken sides with you or my mother because while I was growing up, I had equal contempt for you both.'

The huge success of Nirvana was played out against the background of assorted vicious territorial wars in what was now former Yugoslavia. For Krist Novoselic, with his Croatian blood, this must have been deeply troubling. On 9 April 1993, Nirvana played at a benefit for Bosnian rape victims at the Cow Palace in San Francisco. They showcased eight new songs, all of which would be on *In Utero*. Also on the bill were L7, the Disposable Heroes of Hiphoprisy and the Breeders.

Meanwhile, waiting in the wings was the release of *In Utero*. Despite having wanted Steve Albini to produce the record, Kurt now thought the sound was a little too raw. Scott Litt, who had produced four REM albums, including 1992's massive breakthrough *Automatic for the People*, was brought in to make 'Heart-Shaped Box' and 'All Apologies', both obvious singles, more radio-friendly. Acting in archetypal punk situationist manner, Kurt threatened to release the original Albini mix album as *I Hate Myself and I Want to Die*. A month after this, he said he would release the remixed record, with the title *Verse, Chorus, Verse*.

On a more domestic level, on Sunday, 2 May 1993, police and an ambulance were called to Kurt and Courtney's rented Seattle house, following reports of a drug overdose on the premises. Kurt had come home smacked up, and when challenged by Courtney, he had retreated to a locked bedroom.

Kurt had taken to disappearing off into Seattle's druggy hinterlands, specifically Aurora Avenue, with its drug connections, hookers and seedy motels: Kurt loved to check into the Marco Polo Inn, where he would hole up doing heroin. 'There were many overdoses and near-death situations, as many as a dozen during 1993 alone,' wrote Charles R. Cross.[44]

Yet on the part of Courtney, there were serious and strenuous efforts being made in the spring and summer of 1993 to get clean. She was attending Narcotics Anonymous, drinking only fruit juice, and taking advice from a psychic. Later, however, there would be relapses. Yet her husband was increasingly withdrawn, in a state of acute depression. The junkie's world is one of secrecy and sneakiness, not exactly conducive to positive character development, and one in which addicts are prone to fits of status anxiety and one-upmanship. It was during those months that Kurt declared he was going to get into crack, a drug neither he nor Courtney had previously abused.

On 1 June 1993, Courtney staged – in the jargon of dependency therapy – an 'intervention' at the house, in which friends would express their concern, urge Kurt to sort himself out, and offer assistance to do this. His friend Nils Bernstein was there, as well as his mother Wendy and Krist. 'You could see in Kurt's face that he was thinking, "Nothing in your life relates to anything in my life,"' remembered Nils. In front of them, on the wall with a red marker, Kurt scrawled, 'None of you will ever know my true intent'.[45]

A month later, on 1 July, Hole played one of their first shows in months, at the Off Ramp in Seattle. Kurt was there, very evidently off his head on something – he had to be helped to walk. Brian Willis of the *NME* went back to the house with Courtney. Kurt – who by now seemed to have come down from his drug intake – was at home. However he kept out of the way as Courtney played Willis *In Utero* – the first time a member of the press had heard the record.

As dawn broke Kurt brought them hot chocolate and muffins.

This is what Brian Willis wrote: 'For someone who's been through so much shit in the past two years, whose name's being dragged through acrimony once again, who's about to release a record the whole rock world's desperate to hear and be faced with astonishing attention and pressure, Kurt Cobain's a remarkably contented man.'

In Utero was released on 14 September 1993. If anything, it was an even greater record than *Nevermind*. The album entered the US album charts at number 1, selling 180,000 copies in the first week – even though the US super chains Wal-Mart and Kmart refused to stock it. This was in response to the song 'Rape Me', which was actually an anti-rape, life-affirming song, as much about Kurt's imagined treatment by the media as sexual brutality. 'One of the reasons I signed to a major label,' said Kurt, 'was so people would be able to buy our records at Kmart. In some towns, that's the only place kids can buy records.'

Although Kurt had declared at the beginning of 1993 that he wouldn't tour to support his new album, his arm appeared to have been twisted. Could the lure of money have played a part in this? Kurt's income for 1993 was already estimated to be over $2 million, but with touring he could come close to making double that figure.

On 18 October 1993 a 41-date tour of US arena-size venues – the longest ever Nirvana tour – kicked off at the Arizona State Fair in Phoenix. It was the first time Nirvana had played an arena tour, and they had augmented their sound accordingly. Brought in on guitar was Pat Smear, who in 1976 had started the Germs, releasing 'Forming/Sexboy' in 1977, considered the first LA punk record. Mixed race, Pat had great positive energy, and was very funny. Also onstage with the band was cellist Lori Goldston, a classically trained musician from Seattle.

During the tour there was increasing distance not only between Kurt and the rest of the band, but evidently also between Kurt and the accompanying Courtney. Kurt hated the celebrity world of which she seemed increasingly enamoured. There was also a rift with his management, especially with John Silva, who now referred to Kurt as 'the junkie'. Two tour buses were used – one for Kurt and Pat Smear – which also meant Courtney, and one for the rest of the group. Kurt was drinking little on this tour. But others noted how isolated he seemed.

On 21 October, the *In Utero* tour reached Kansas City. Kurt was driven over to meet his hero and fellow junkie William S. Burroughs, who lived in nearby Lawrence. Afterwards, Burroughs said the subject of drugs never came up once. He spent much of their time together extolling to Kurt the virtues of Leadbelly, the blues legend.

At Inglewood Forum on 30 December 1993, as Krist started singing the Kinks' 'You Really Got Me', Kurt left the stage and returned with a drill, which he drove into his guitar before picking it up and spinning it over his head with the drill still attached. Meanwhile, 'big hair' rocker Eddie van Halen turned up drunk backstage, wanting to join them in their set on guitar. 'No, you can't,' said Kurt.

The next day, New Year's Eve, Nirvana were shown on an MTV special, *Live and Loud*. Also on the bill were Pearl Jam, the Breeders and Cypress Hill. The show had been prerecorded on 13 December at Pier 48 in Seattle, a ferry terminal. It was an event riven by tensions, with Kurt seeming out of it – as did many people in the audience and backstage.

Meanwhile, in real time on New Year's Eve, Nirvana were playing the Oakland Coliseum Arena.

After dates in Vancouver, the *In Utero* tour wound up on 7 and 8 January at Seattle's Center Arena. This would be the last time Nirvana played in the United States.

They would soon be on the road again. The *In Utero* tour was heading for Europe, with thirty-eight shows in sixteen countries. The Lollapalooza travelling US festival had made an offer to Nirvana of $7 million to headline that summer's shows. Everyone involved felt they couldn't refuse, except for Kurt. Despite his objections, Lollapalooza was placed on Nirvana's schedule for that summer.

By now work had been completed on the house he and Courtney had bought at 171 Lake Washington Boulevard in the Denny-Blaine district of Seattle (a neighbour was REM's Peter Buck); although the house was scarcely furnished, they moved in; bewildered by the size of his new five-bedroom home, Kurt created a space for himself in the walk-in wardrobe room off the main bedroom; he also became fond of hanging out in a conservatory over the garage at the rear of the property.

During January Courtney was touring overseas with Hole: just as well, as Kurt's drug use – heroin and cocaine now – had created a distance between him and his wife. Ostensibly living on his own at the house, during the month off before the European tour started, Kurt spent much of the time on Aurora Avenue, doing heroin.[46]

But from 28 to 30 January Nirvana returned to the recording studio, for what would be their final time recording together. Kurt did not bother to show up on the first two days, arriving late on the third day. The only completed tune that emerged from the sessions was 'You Know You're Right', with lyrics that were a pointed attack on what he considered to be the misery of his life with Courtney. 'I have never failed to fail', the final line, were words that seemed like an acute summation of Kurt Cobain's low self-esteem. That this was the last line Kurt Cobain would ever put down on tape imbues them with an extraordinary resonance.

Nirvana flew to Paris on 2 February 1994 for an appearance on a French television show. The tour proper opened in Cascais in the Portuguese Algarve on 6 February. The opening act for the first shows were the re-formed Buzzcocks, stalwarts of 1976 Manchester punk rock, a personal choice of Kurt.

Following a date in Madrid, the tour's second night, Kurt called Courtney, in tears. She was in Los Angeles, staying at the Chateau Marmont, the epitome of LA decadence. Although friends would assure him that it was not the case, there were rumours that Courtney had resumed her fling with Billy Corgan, and also that she had been seeing Evan Dando of the Lemonheads. An intended stay of two days at the Chateau turned into weeks, and Courtney was three weeks late when she arrived in London, supposedly to join the *In Utero* tour. On arriving, she was meant to immediately board a flight to Rome, but Courtney decided instead to spend time in the English capital.

In mid-February, the tour was in Paris. Kurt did a photo session for a French magazine: one of the shots was of Kurt with the barrel of a rifle in his mouth.

Seven days later, Kurt Cobain turned twenty-seven. He spent the day depressed, as he had been throughout the tour.

After the second of two nights in Milan, he told Krist that he wanted to cancel the rest of the dates. As the next show was in Ljubljana in Slovenia, and relatives would be travelling there from neighbouring Croatia, Krist demurred. Kurt agreed to carry on.

On 1 March in Munich before the final show of that leg of the tour – a further pair of German dates would be cancelled – Kurt spoke on the phone to Courtney. The ensuing row drove him to phone his lawyer to say he wanted to initiate divorce proceedings. Deeply pained, Kurt was aware that this would set in motion for Frances precisely the trauma he had undergone as a child and from which he had never recovered.

Kurt was also ill, suffering from bronchitis and severe laryngitis. After the Munich gig, he and Pat Smear flew to Rome, Kurt checking in to room 541 at the swish Excelsior Hotel. Courtney, due to arrive with Frances, was late.

When she finally made it to Rome, Courtney discovered that Kurt had filled their room with red roses. He was making a big effort. Immediately he ordered champagne from room service, telling his wife how much he had missed her.

Courtney's response was to take sleeping tablets and go to bed. Kurt was distressed.

That night Kurt took an overdose of sixty Rohypnol tablets. When Courtney woke at around 6 a.m. she found her husband lying on the floor, blood seeping from his nose. In his hand, on hotel stationery, was a three-page note to Courtney. He had written that she no longer loved him, and was unable to cope with the pain of 'another' divorce. Courtney later burned the note.

Taken by ambulance to the Umberto 1 Polyclinic Hospital, Kurt had his stomach pumped out, and was put on a life-support machine. But he only fell deeper into unconsciousness.

CNN mistakenly announced his death. His management company released a statement saying that Kurt had 'inadvertently overdosed on a mixture of prescription medicine and alcohol, while suffering from severe influenza and fatigue.' Few were fooled.

The next day, 5 March, twenty hours after he had fallen unconscious, Kurt awoke, and wrote a note: 'Get this fucking catheter out.'

On the flight back to Seattle on 12 March, a day after the second leg of the *In Utero* European tour should have commenced, Kurt could be overheard by fellow passengers loudly demanding a Rohypnol from Courtney. She said she no longer had them.

Back at home in Seattle, there was palpable hostility

between Kurt and Courtney. Kurt locked himself away in his bedroom, surrounded by guns. On 18 March, Courtney called the police, telling them Kurt's behaviour was suicidal. Kurt responded by saying he had locked himself in his room to keep Courtney away. The police took away Kurt's weapons: a Colt AR-15 semi-automatic rifle, a Beretta .380 and a pair of Taurus handguns, along with twenty-five boxes of ammunition and a bottle of unidentified pills.

On 18 March, furious at Courtney for her ceaseless haranguing of him over his drug usage, Kurt walked out of the house. There was evidence of serious hypocrisy on Courtney's part: 'On one line Kurt rang me to get some speed,' recalled Dylan Carlson of this period, 'and the other line goes and it's Courtney wanting me to get her some dope. And neither wants the other to know.'[47]

Kurt and Dylan Carlson now disappeared for several days, heading for Aurora Avenue, and the Marco Polo motel. There, Kurt OD'd on heroin, another friend saving his life by walking him round the room. They also spent nights at the nearby Crest and the Seattle Inn. Kurt hung out in such Seattle bars as the new and hip Linda's Tavern on East Pine Street in Capitol Hill, and at friends' apartments.

After what had happened in Rome, Kurt seemed a changed man. Dylan, and also Krist, worried that his brain might have been affected. Dylan told Charles Cross that 'after Rome, he seemed monochromatic.'[48]

Behaving like a teenage runaway, his time away from

home that March allowed Kurt a measure of relatively anonymous freedom, a chance to become who he used to be. But there was a financial problem. On the second day, according to Charles Cross, Courtney managed to persuade his bank to cancel her husband's credit cards.

Kurt called Krist Novoselic, and his old friend came over to see him. Krist wanted to take Kurt up to a cabin in the country, where he could withdraw from drugs. But first they needed something to eat. Although Krist suggested an upscale eaterie, Kurt insisted on going to a specific Jack in the Box. When Krist realized that the fast-food restaurant was located next to the apartment of Kurt's dealer, he was furious. They had a stand-up row, and Kurt disappeared and went home.

But there was a plot afoot. An intervention had been planned for 21 March, which Kurt learned of after Krist spilt the beans. Instead, it was moved to 25 March. When it took place, Kurt was smacked up. It doesn't appear to have been a very rational encounter, with Courtney threatening Kurt that if he didn't stop doing drugs, she would divorce him, and his access to Frances would be limited.[49] Eventually, Courtney left the house for a flight to LA, where she herself was to undergo drug therapy, as she had promised during the intervention. She never saw Kurt again.

The next day Kurt overdosed once more while sitting in his parked car, after visiting junkie friends. On realizing the state he was in, they had made him leave, terrified he would die there. He eventually came to, in even greater emotional pain than ever.

Kurt agreed to treatment. On 29 March Krist, trying to help his old buddy, came to take Kurt to Sea-Tac airport for a flight to Los Angeles, where he was scheduled to enter the Exodus Recovery Centre. But Kurt had had second thoughts. After trying to get out of Krist's car on the I-5, he then hit his bass player in the face. The last a sobbing Krist, Kurt Cobain's closest friend, saw of him was as he ran manically away through the airport.

The next day Kurt decided to submit to the programme. Before going, according to Charles R. Cross in his biography, Kurt persuaded Dylan Carlson to use his name to purchase a gun – in case of prowlers, he said. Together they bought a Remington M-11 twenty-gauge shotgun and shells. Kurt also did as much heroin as he could manage during the day. That night he flew to Los Angeles.

At Exodus he was not placed in the locked-down psychiatric unit. Had the facility known of the truth about the Rome overdose, he would have been.

Another patient at Exodus, one from Kurt's world, was Gibby Haynes of the Butthole Surfers. He and Kurt would spend time together, smoking cigarettes in the garden, joking about the guy who broke out by climbing over the rear wall – even though the front gates were never locked. On Friday 1 April, Kurt seemed truly happy, almost ecstatic. When Frances briefly visited him, brought by a friend, he was all over her, tossing her up in the air and making her laugh, holding her closely and tenderly whispering in her ear. His thinking was clear, and there was almost a glow about him.[50]

Late that afternoon he spoke to Courtney. 'Just remember, no matter what, I love you,' he told her, and put down the phone.

At 7.25 that evening, Kurt Cobain climbed over the rear wall, the same act of stupidity he and Gibby had joked about. Three hours later, he was taking off from LAX to Seattle. His credit cards reinstated, he had been able to buy a first-class ticket. Sitting next to him on the plane was Duff McKagan, the bassist with Guns N' Roses. The two musicians had a secret link: Duff McKagan was also an addict, though he was making active efforts to come off drugs. For most of the two-and-a-quarter-hour flight, they talked and drank. 'And he was pretty down,' the bass-player thought. But there was not one mention made of 'heroine'.

At Sea-Tac, Duff met his driver and thought they should give Kurt a lift, maybe take him back to Duff's place and try and cheer him up. When he turned round to suggest this, Kurt had vanished.

At 1.45 a.m. Kurt reached home. The oil-fired central heating in the house had run out of fuel.

At around 7.30 in the morning, Kurt called a cab. He told the driver he needed to buy bullets. Nowhere was yet open downtown. Kurt got the driver to drop him off on seedy

Aurora Avenue, where it is thought he checked into either the Crest or Quest Motel. Nearby was a drug connection, and at one point Kurt was seen at a Jack in the Box restaurant.

On Sunday, 3 April, Kurt went for supper at the Cactus restaurant in Seattle. He was with a woman, who may have been his heroin dealer, and a man. Kurt began his meal with banana pudding sautéed in brown sugar and rum, junkie food. His credit card was declined. Again, Courtney had stopped his flow of his own money. Writing out a cheque clearly caused him some difficulty: he wrote the amount where the name of the payee should be. Again he was seen at Linda's Tavern, an etiolated, spectral figure drifting through.

Kurt Cobain was not seen alive again.

BRIAN JONES

'Peace, peace! He is not dead, he doth not sleep –
He hath awakened from the dream of life'

From stanza 39 of Shelley's *Adonais*,
read by Mick Jagger at the Rolling Stones'
July 5 1969 Hyde Park concert,
two days after the death of Brian Jones

At the time Brian Jones died there was no widespread public awareness that his position in the Stones had become contentious, or of exactly why he had left the group a month previously. Information about the split is largely based on the unfavourable testimony offered up by celebrity witnesses, most notably other members of the Rolling Stones. Keith Richards, for example, has never pulled any punches in his assessments of Brian. 'I never saw a guy so affected by fame,' said Richards in *Life*, his autobiography, 'the minute we'd had a couple of successful records, zoom, he was Venus and Jupiter rolled into one. Huge inferiority complex that you hadn't noticed . . . he became a pain in the neck, a kind of rotting attachment.'

'Brian, in many ways, was a right cunt,' is another of Keith's assessments of his former friend. 'He was a bastard. Mean, generous, anything. You want to say one thing, give it the opposite too. But more so than most people, you know.

Up to a point, you could put up with it. When you were put under the pressures of the road, either you took it seriously or you took it as a joke. Which meant that eventually – it was a very slow process, and it shifted and changed, and it is so impossible to describe – but in the last year or so, when Brian was almost totally incapacitated all of the time, he became a joke to the band. It was the only way we could deal with it without getting mad at him. So then it became that very cruel, piss-taking thing behind his back all the time . . .'

What is strange about Keith's ceaseless dismissals of Brian is that they were once close. Such egregious assessments, moreover, were amplified by contemporary *éminences grises* like John Lennon. The former Beatle famously said of Brian to Jan Wenner that, 'He ended up the kind of guy that you dread he'd come on the phone, because you knew it was trouble.' Those much-quoted words, however, only set the tone for a more measured appraisal which Lennon finally gave to Wenner: 'He was really in a lot of pain. But in the early days he was alright, because he was young and good-looking. But he's one of them guys that disintegrated in front of you.'

It's possible that the remorseless teasing he received from the other Stones played a part in Brian's 'disintegration'. Pretty Things' singer Phil May recalled[1] that once, when the Rolling Stones had a gig in Portsmouth, Brian was driven down to the south coast port in his old Rover, the fastidiously punctual musician wanting to be at the venue early. When his car broke down, Brian waited for the rest of the group's limousine to drive past, and attempted to flag it down. But the other Stones drove past him laughing, and played the gig without him. On another occasion while on tour, Brian was suffering from a sore throat. They stopped at a chemist's for Brian to purchase an antidote, but then, at Keith's urging, drove off and left him, surrounded by screaming girls.[2]

Such anecdotes contribute to the myth of Brian Jones as a kind of pathetic loser with perpetually bruised feelings. Yet in actual fact, Brian Jones was a consummate artist ceaselessly channelling his abundant creativity into driving the engine of what became the Rolling Stones.

When the first music, images and performances of the Rolling Stones emerged, it was Brian Jones who incontestably and effortlessly captured the attention of female and male admirers alike. With his glimmering, thick golden hair, girlishly handsome face with its knowing, hard but seductive eyes (it seems almost unsurprising that he was a father at the age of sixteen, and would have four more children), and his consummate and dramatically different sense of style, he appeared like a Greek god. For almost all of his time with the group, when you thought of the Rolling Stones, you first considered Brian Jones – not really Mick Jagger, and certainly not pimply Keith Richards. Much more than by Mick Jagger, the initial visual identity of the Rolling Stones was personified by Brian Jones, its prime exponent of foppish narcissism. 'Brian Jones was the most stylised, and stylish, British rock star there has ever been,' said Paul Gorman, author of *The Look*.[3]

Ray Davies, not yet leader of the Kinks when he first encountered Brian, recalled him as being 'probably the most conceited-looking person I have ever met. But he was also one of the most compelling musicians ever on stage.'[4] 'He was the nasty one . . . the whole nasty image of the Stones really started with Brian, not Mick. Because Brian was a bitch!' said Alexis Korner, an important mentor of the Cheltenham boy.[5]

By 1965, the Stones were working with a young photographer, eighteen-year-old Gered Mankowitz, shortly to take the cover picture for their *Out of Our Heads* album. Mankowitz was fully aware of who was the star of the group: 'In those days Brian had the most formed image, the most evolved image, the most groomed image. He was the one who physically was the most confident.

'Mick and Keith were still kids in a way. They were still finding a space, a place. And that's why Brian appears in the front of the grouping in the *Out of Our Heads* cover. There's no doubt about it: even from Brian's haircut you can see he really was the most evolved and the most charismatic.' So much so, in fact, that in a poll in *Record Mirror* in September 1965, the same month that *Out of Our Heads* was released, Brian Jones was voted 'The Most Handsome Man in Pop'.

Brian Jones's smirking, studied air of dissolute elegance impressed Gered, who clearly saw the group's founder as the architect of its image; Mick Jagger and Keith Richards were far less sophisticated. 'There was a studenty thing about them, an art school thing. Brian had an element of showbusiness about him. He was more advanced in that way. That's what I mean by charisma; he had a presence to him; he'd got an image together; he'd made a conscious effort to look the way he did, whereas everybody else was just evolving, Mick and Keith particularly, and shaking off the ordinariness of early '60s British teenagerhood.'

Not only was Brian Jones by far the most charismatic performer in the early days of the Rolling Stones, he was also the most musically talented. As Clash guitarist Mick Jones commented, 'Brian Jones would just need to look at a newly discovered instrument to know how to play it.' It was Brian who introduced the sitar into the pop charts, on the masterly 'Paint it Black'. He was forever pushing further texture and daring inventiveness into the Stones' sound: the dulcimer on 'Lady Jane', the flute on 'Ruby Tuesday', the marimba on 'Under My Thumb'. Into Eastern music even before George Harrison, Brian Jones was one of British pop music's great innovators; through his recording in Morocco of *The Pipes of Pan at Jajouka*, he was the first significant British musician to discover what became known as world music.

Convinced of his status as founder of the Rolling Stones, however, Brian early on made what can be seen as a huge tactical blunder: it emerged during the group's 1963 tour with the Everly Brothers that he had negotiated himself wages of five pounds a week more than the rest of the group when signing a management contract. This was a key moment. 'That was the beginning of the end for Brian,' said Keith.

Yet the most legendary functioning rock 'n' roll outfit today would not have existed without his having started them.

On the evening of 7 April 1962, Mick Jagger had borrowed his father's car for the ninety-minute drive from Dartford in south-east London to Ealing on the fringes of the capital's western suburbia. With him was Keith Richards and their mutual friend Dick Taylor. All were members of the Blue Boys, a group that had played no further afield than their respective living rooms.

They were heading for the G Club, which had been started in a basement by Alexis Korner, doyen of British blues. The billed headliners at Ealing on that Saturday night were Alexis Korner's Blues Incorporated.

But when Mick, Keith and Dick arrived at the venue, the music that sailed up to them as they stepped down into the tiny, smoky club was a tenor sax solo by Dick Heckstall-Smith. The gang from Dartford were unimpressed, feeling this to be more in the vein of trad jazz than blues. Until Alexis Korner stepped forward and announced, 'This is Elmo Lewis. He's come from Cheltenham to play for you.' And then the group kicked into 'Dust My Broom', the Elmore James classic, on which a flaxen-haired, handsome young man took up his Hofner Committee electric guitar to devastating effect. 'They were stunned,' Dick Taylor recalled the response of Mick Jagger and Keith Richards. 'Just when it seemed there was no one else who understood, here was a kid our own age, playing bar slide blues. Mick was knocked out.'

Keith also was awestruck by what greeted them onstage. 'It's fuckin' Elmore James,' he gasped. 'I said, what? What the fuck? Playing bar slide guitar.'

'At the beginning,' Alexis Korner noted later, 'Mick and Keith hero-worshipped Brian. He seemed about twenty years older than them.' On vocals on that performance of 'Dust My Broom' was another prospective blues singer called P.P. Pond. P.P. Pond was actually Paul Jones, the singer with a blues group called Thunder Odin's Big Secret. Brian Jones had sat in with them on a few occasions, and that Saturday at the G Club Alexis Korner had given them the break of playing as interval group. Although the voice of P.P. Pond and the exciting slide guitar of Elmo Lewis gelled so well, this was the last time they would play together. Paul Jones would become the singer with Manfred Mann, another blues-based London group who would have considerable success. That evening, however, it was the guitarist with whom the Dartford boys were absolutely taken, an individual who managed simultaneously to appear slight and stocky. After Brian had come off stage, Mick, Keith and Dick spent some time talking to him. They were enormously impressed by Brian, who already had two children of his own, while they were still living at home with their parents.

Lewis Brian Hopkin-Jones had been born on 28 February 1942 in Cheltenham, Gloucestershire. Both his parents were university-educated; his mother Louise was a piano teacher, while his father Lewis was an aeronautical engineer.

Brian was the eldest of their children. Barbara was four years younger than him, but another sister, Pamela, who was two years younger than Brian, had died when she was two. Around this time Brian developed asthma, which would return afterwards during taxing situations. Later, his parents would shelter Barbara from her reprobate brother. There were suggestions that Pamela's death had caused Louise Hopkin-Jones to project all her love onto her new daughter, withholding affection from her son. Perpetually shocked by his teenage behaviour, Brian's parents put up an emotional brick wall against him, which only seemed to harden the resolve of their sensitive but tough son.

Brian easily passed the eleven-plus – he had an IQ of 135 – and won a place at the local Pate's Grammar School, which had a dress code of straw boaters in the summer and mortar-boards in winter. But this former church choirboy rebelled against the establishment's atmosphere of stifling convention. For organizing a revolt against prefects, Brian was suspended for a week from Pate's.[6] He spent his days away from school swimming at Cheltenham Lido. Brian was a very strong swimmer, and when he returned to school he had attained high status amongst his peers. Despite his behaviour, his headmaster, Dr Arthur Bell, retained fond memories of the boy.[7] 'Brian was a very clever boy, but introverted, with-drawn, with a pasty face and with his father on his back all the time. He wasn't a bad lad.' Dr Bell noted that his father would frequently arrive unannounced at the school, complaining about the behaviour of his son. 'Once he demanded that I get his boy to get his hair cut, which of course had nothing to do with me.'

Brian's parents were ambitious for their boy, wanting him to become a classical musician. By the age of twelve, he was an exceptional guitarist, as well as being adept on the piano and clarinet. After fourteen-year-old Brian sold his clarinet and took up the saxophone, however, he revealed his interest in jazz, especially the work of innovative sax player Charlie 'Bird' Parker, with whose music his parents had no truck whatsoever.[8] He also took up playing the washboard in a local skiffle group.

In 1971 his father Lewis was interviewed for *A Story of Our Time*, a programme on BBC Radio 4. 'There came this peculiar change in his early teens,' he said. 'At the time, I suppose he began to become a man, where he began to get some resentment of authority. It's something we hear an awful lot about now less about then. But it was becoming apparent in him

'He seemed to have firstly a mild rebellion against authority, which unfortunately became stronger as he grew older. It was a rebellion against parental authority and it was certainly a rebellion against school authority. He often used to ask, why should he do something he was told, just because the person who was telling him was older?'

There was a further problem thrown up by these shifts in

Brian's behaviour. Near his school was Cheltenham Girls' Grammar School, a repository of fine young ladies. Brian, aware of his extreme good looks, would boast to his classmates that he had 'gone all the way' with at least one of them. Disbelievers were soon disabused when a scandal hit prim Cheltenham: a fourteen-year-old girl had become pregnant – and the father was 16-year-old Brian Jones. Contrary to Brian's entreaties, the girl refused to have an abortion, giving birth to a son, Simon (originally Barry David), who was adopted.[9]

The year was 1959. To the good burghers of the respectable, uptight spa town of Cheltenham, Brian was considered the lowest of the low. This was despite his educational achievements: he had nine O-levels, and distinguished A-level passes in chemistry and physics. A figure of shame to the area's nattering nabobs of negativism, he was given no emotional support whatsoever by his family. And there came a further shock: Brian had also impregnated a local married woman, who bore him a daughter the following year.

Virtually run out of town, a shamefaced Brian left Cheltenham. Armed with a guitar and a little money, he hitchhiked through Germany and Scandinavia in the new style of the beatnik. He suffered many difficult experiences, partly because he spoke none of the appropriate languages. Attempting to earn a crust, he would play music in bars and cafes.

When he returned to Cheltenham in 1960, the spa town had undergone a cultural shift. Coffee bars, with their gurgling

Gaggia froth-making machines, were suddenly commonplace, a suggestion of the beginnings of a new youth culture. Around Christmas that year Brian met a pretty 16-year-old girl called Pat Andrews. She was working class, and therefore not good enough for his parents. Pat was attracted to Brian because of his bad reputation. On getting to know him, however, she was amazed by his knowledge of music. 'He was so up and down,' she later recalled. 'Seventy-five per cent of the time Brian was miserable because he was so thwarted musically at home. He felt deeply that he got no encouragement.'[10]

Brian took a job as a coalman. But then he landed on a post more appropriate for someone of his educational qualifications – as a junior assistant in the architects' department of Gloucestershire County Council.[11] Although he was hardly regular in his attendance at this job, he still applied to enter Cheltenham School of Architecture. He was refused.

Yet Brian's musical interests predominated, and he found himself involved with local groups: he played with the Cheltone Six and had begun playing alto sax with the Ramrods, who – in the manner of the times – played instrumental rock 'n' roll.

Finally finding a cheap flat to rent, and therefore time to himself, Brian at last discovered American rhythm and blues, adoring the music of such artists as Muddy Waters, Howlin' Wolf and Elmore James. He would hunker down in his small flat, assiduously trying to figure out how, say, Elmore James played slide guitar – eventually he found a piece of piping in a plumber's yard that fitted his finger. Speaking to BBC Radio One, years later, Bill Wyman eulogized about Brian's slide playing: 'He was a brilliant slide guitar player and the first slide guitar player in England that ever was.'

In 1961 the white British blues musician Alexis Korner came to play at Cheltenham Town Hall. When Brian managed to meet him, the blues maestro was impressed with Brian's knowledge of the genre. He urged him to move to London, offering to let him sleep on his floor. For a time Brian hitchhiked to London every weekend, staying at Korner's Bayswater home. Korner had distinct memories of their first meeting:[12] 'This pent-up ball of obsessive energy, talking away nineteen to the dozen in an incredibly intense manner . . . I vividly recall the first time I met Brian, but I can't for the life of me remember where I first met Mick.'

Brian's weekend trips to London, inevitably involving staying up late jamming with Alexis, frequently left him exhausted. After missing Monday work one too many times, he was fired. Instead, he took a job as a bus conductor. Inevitably sacked from that employment, he took a more appropriate position, working behind the record counter at Cheltenham's branch of the Curry's electrical chain store.

But life was about to spring a surprise: Pat Andrews, aged sixteen, became pregnant, giving birth to a baby boy on 23 October 1961. To purchase a substantial flower arrangement for his girlfriend, Brian, penniless as ever, sold four of his precious record albums. The boy was named Julian Mark, in tribute to Julian 'Cannonball' Adderley, the bop saxophonist, but was more commonly known simply as Mark.

At a new flat he had taken, Brian began to entertain visiting jazz and blues musicians: Sonny Boy Williamson, Muddy Waters and Howlin' Wolf were among those whose noisy visits, sometimes attracting attention from the local police, scandalized the neighbours in this quintessentially Conservative town.

Brian made a decision: he had to move to London. Yet the controlling hand of his father was hard to avoid: clearly still misreading his son, Lewis Jones arranged for him to study at the London College of Applied Optics.[13] While briefly there, miserably whiling away his days, Brian set about exploring London by night.

At that first meeting at the G Club, Keith Richards especially was extremely impressed by Brian Jones. 'Brian was really fantastic, the first person I ever heard playing slide electric guitar,' said Keith. 'Mick and I thought he was incredible. He mentioned he was forming a band. He could easily have joined another group but he wanted to form his own. The Rolling Stones was Brian's baby.' Quickly they discovered a deep empathy between the three of them; like Keith and Mick, Brian thought he was the only white musician in the world who was into that music.

A Blues Incorporated splinter group emerged, which

included Korner, but mainly featured members of the Blue Boys – Jagger, Richards, and Dick Taylor. Brian Jones would sometimes sit in, and occasionally another vocalist was employed, a callow youth nicknamed Plimsolls because of his footwear. Although Plimsolls could hardly play at all, he was known to have a reasonably moneyed background that allowed him to be the possessor of a new Kay guitar. He had another sobriquet, Eric the Mod, and would soon enjoy greater success when he transferred all his attentions to the guitar and reverted to his full name of Eric Clapton. For now, however, whenever Keith's or Brian's guitar went on the blink, they would talk to Plimsolls and borrow his nice new instrument.

In May 1962 Brian Jones placed an advertisement in *Jazz News*, asking for musicians interested in forming a group with him. Ian 'Stu' Stewart, who had an administrative job at Imperial Chemicals Industries, was the first person to respond to the audition that Brian held on the second floor of the Bricklayer's Arms in Soho's Berwick Street. When Mick Jagger, Keith Richards and Dick Taylor turned up at the Bricklayer's, Stu was there, playing piano in leather shorts.

That was the first rehearsal by the core of the group that became the Rolling Stones. Ian Stewart noted the immediate empathy between Brian and Mick, and that this seemed to intimidate Keith. But Stu also could see that despite the relationship springing up between Mick and Brian, Mick and Keith were set in stone as a double act. For example, whenever there were opportunities for a 'blow' with other musicians, including Brian, at a couple of Soho locations – a pub in Lyle Street, a joint in a Wardour Street alley – Mick always announced, 'I'm not doin' it unless Keith's doin' it.'

But things were moving on for all concerned. Tucked away in the news pages of the 19 May 1962 edition of *Disc*, a tabloid music paper, was a small headline, 'Singer joins Korner's Blues Inc.' This was the first mention in the British music press of the name Mick Jagger, and inevitably it was accompanied by that of Keith Richards, sharing the guitarist billing with Brian 'Elmo Lewis' Jones.

> A nineteen-year-old Dartford rhythm and blues singer, Mick Jagger, has joined the Alexis Korner group, Blues Incorporated, and will sing with them regularly on their Saturday dates at Ealing and their Thursday sessions at the Marquee Jazz Club, London.
>
> Called 'The Rollin' Stones' ('I hope they don't think we're a rock and roll outfit,' says Mick), the line-up is: Jagger (vocals), Keith Richards, Elmo Lewis (guitars), Dick Taylor (bass), 'Stew' (piano) and Mick Avory (drums).

At this stage 'the Rollin' Stones' – to all intents and purposes a splinter group from Blues Incorporated – were very definitely Brian Jones's group, and he was not at all happy about such a prominent billing for Mick Jagger. 'Brian came up with the name,' said Keith Richards. 'It was a phone call – which cost money – and we were down to pennies. We'd got no gas and we were freezing our balls off, no water, everything was cut off. We got a gig at last, so we said "Call up *Jazz News*. Put in an advert." So Brian gaily dials away – and they say "Who?" We hadn't got a name and every second was costing a precious farthing. There's a Muddy Waters record face down – *The Best of Muddy Waters* – and the first song was "Rollin' Stone Blues". Brian had a panicked look on his face – he said "I don't know . . . the Rollin' Stones." That's the reason we're called the Rollin' Stones, because if he didn't open his mouth immediately we were going to strangle him and cut him off. Not a lot of thought went into it, in other words.'

In June 1962 Mick made a final break with Korner to join up with Brian Jones, Ian Stewart and guitarist Geoff Bradford, who was into ethnic blues of the ilk of Muddy Waters, John Lee Hooker and Elmore James. ('The idealism of Geoff Bradford was to be a key part in Brian's musical education,' said Bill Wyman later, 'and in the policy of the Stones.' A blues purist, Geoff Bradford considered Chuck Berry, Bo Diddley and Jimmy Reed to be commercial exploiters of the form.) With him Mick brought Keith Richards and Dick Taylor.

In July 1962 Blues Incorporated were booked to appear on *Jazz Club*, on the BBC's Light Programme. The booking was for the same day as the group's regular night at the Marquee club on Oxford Street. To fill in for Korner's group, Mick Jagger agreed to play with Brian, Keith, Stu, Dick Taylor and a drummer called Mick Avory, later of the Kinks. Harold

Pendleton, who ran the Marquee, said he would acquiesce only if John Baldry's group could top the bill, with the Stones playing support, for which they would be paid a fee of £20. Jagger immediately agreed, and a small story appeared in the next issue of *Jazz News*: 'Mick Jagger, R & B vocalist, is taking a rhythm and blues group into the Marquee tomorrow night while Blues Incorporated does its Jazz Club radio broadcast gig.'

The Marquee gig was set for Thursday 12 July 1962, a night steamy with summer heat. The very first set played by the group under the name of the Rollin' Stones at the Marquee ran as follows: 'Kansas City', 'Honey What's Wrong', 'Confessin' the Blues', 'Bright Lights, Big City', 'Dust My Broom', 'Down the Road Apiece', 'I Want to Love You', 'Bad Boy', 'I Ain't Got You', 'Hush Hush', 'Ride 'Em on Down', 'Back in the USA', 'Up All Night', 'Tell Me That You Love Me' and 'Happy Home' – all within the space of fifty minutes.

All that summer the Rollin' Stones assiduously rehearsed. 'Brian really got into Jimmy Reed,' remembered Keith. 'He would sit around for hours and hours, working out how Reed's sound was put together. He'd work at it and work at it. He'd really get it down. Brian didn't consider [Chuck] Berry to be in the same class, but when we proved to him that he was, he really started to dig him. He'd work with me on Berry things. We really got into that. We were working out the guitar parts and the rhythm, which was 4/4 swing beat, not a rock beat at all. It was jazz swing beat, except there would be another guitar playing. He was a good guitar player then. He had the touch and was just peaking. He was really working at it. He said that we were just amateurs, but we dug to play.'

Brian Jones had a job as a sales assistant at the Civil Service store in Victoria, eagerly filching cash from the till. He found a place to stay in Powis Square in London's Notting Hill – precisely where Mick Jagger's character lived in the film *Performance*. According to Keith, it was at this time that Mick once went round to Brian's flat when Brian wasn't there, and 'screwed Brian's old lady'. Pat Andrews, the 'old lady' in question, adamantly denied this.[14] Mick had turned up there, drunk, in the middle of the night, having been to a party and unable to return to Dartford. The next morning, when Brian went off to work at the Civil Service store, Mick was still asleep. 'I made him coffee and sat on the edge of the settee to give him the mug,' recalled Pat Andrews. 'Mick swung up grinning. He put his arm around me and made a pass. I wasn't interested. Brian was a very jealous man, but I had never been unfaithful to him and I wasn't about to start with Mick. I loved Brian.'[15] Mick Jagger stuck around until Brian returned at the end of the day. Needing a 'babysitter' for the evening so they could all go out, Mick had an idea who to ask. 'That was the night I first met Keith,' Pat Andrews remembered. 'I never liked Keith. He was lazy, slovenly . . . compared to Brian, Keith had no class.'[16]

Soon, however, Pat Andrews made a decision. She realized

that Brian was not prepared to give up the Rollin' Stones and become a good family man. Leaving only a note, one day in September 1962, she took Brian's son Mark and departed their Powis Square home.

At this point Brian Jones moved into a new flat that Mick Jagger and Keith Richards had found, at 102 Edith Grove, on the border between Chelsea and Fulham. Brian also left the Civil Service store to work in a similar capacity in the electrical department at Whiteley's department store in Bayswater, which sold records. Soon, however, he was sacked for stealing money. He only avoided a criminal prosecution by claiming he had become mentally unhinged due to the break-up of his relationship.

Having lost his job, Brian was at 102 Edith Grove most of the time. Unemployed and presumably unemployable, Keith also had nowhere else to spend his days. The pair would pass each day playing together, 'figuring out Jimmy Reed and stuff,' according to Keith. 'This was an intense learning period. We would love to make records, but we're not in that league. We wanted to sell records for Jimmy Reed and Muddy Waters and John Lee Hooker and Howlin' Wolf. We were missionaries, disciples, Jesuits. We thought, "If we can turn people on to that, then that's enough." That was the whole total aim . . . the original aim. There was no thought of attaining rock 'n' roll stardom.'[17]

Soon it was the turn of Keith Richards to move into 102 Edith Grove full-time: 'I started to crash there sometimes, so as not to have to go home . . . Mick went through his first camp period, and started wandering around in a blue linen housecoat. He was into that kick for about six months. Brian and I used to take the piss out of him. I never consciously thought about leaving Dartford, but the minute I got out I had pretty strong instincts that I'd never go back. There was no way I was gonna stay there.'[18]

Edith Grove was archetypal rented accommodation of the era: a gloomy brown-painted hallway, with linoleum-covered stairs and a communal toilet on the first-floor landing. Brian had taken over the double bed in the front room, which he shared with a mahogany radiogram (in time this would turn out to be a tactical error). In the rear bedroom of the flat were three single beds, one Mick's, one Keith's, and one for a young printer and music fan who was brought in to share the rent as fourth lodger in the eccentric household of 102 Edith Grove. His name was James Phelge, an apprentice lithograph printer who worked near Fulham Broadway.

'I think Brian's much-talked-about isolation from the band started back in the Edith Grove days,' Phelge said later. 'His choice to use the lounge as his own bedroom and not share with the others perhaps became the starting point for his estrangement. Nobody thought much of it at the time, but by not sharing the bedroom Brian was missing out on the closest parts of the friendships that developed. When you shared one room you talked to each other at all hours. You could lay awake for a couple of hours talking and joking as Keith, Mick and I would, and that seemed to make you closer. In missing this, Brian created a gap between himself and the others. It was as if somehow a small piece of his relationship with Mick and Keith always remained missing. Despite all that has been said and written about Brian no one would have wished him harm. When you are with someone sharing your last food and money to survive it makes a bond you never forget.'

Edith Grove stank of grime and the raging hormones of only just post-adolescent boys. A couple lived on the next floor who seemed to vaguely disapprove of the Stones. Keith, Brian and Phelge found out where they left their key while out at work, and would raid their flat for milk, bread and coffee.

Then Brian and Keith rigged up their microphone to the electric light flex in the centre of the living room, so that it hung down level with everyone's faces. Keith and Brian tried out Everly Brothers-type harmonies together. 'There was a time when Brian and I had decided that this R & B thing was an absolute flop,' said Keith. 'We weren't getting away with it. Brian and I were gonna do an Everly Brothers thing, so we spent three or four days in the kitchen, rehearsing these terrible songs.'

While they were working together like this, Phelge noted that Mick seemed somewhat moody when he arrived home at the end of the day. 'It's because he's feeling left out,' Brian explained. 'He doesn't like it because I'm doing something with Keith. I knew it would upset him. Don't take any notice.'

Phelge was a jazz fan. One day he and the Stones' prospective new drummer, Charlie Watts, came back from an outing to Whiteley's in Bayswater where Phelge had picked up a copy of Miles Davis's *Walkin'*, which was reduced because it had lost its original sleeve. The card sleeve in which it came had had its details handwritten by none other than Brian.

Stuck at Edith Grove with Brian on their own most days, Keith soon experienced a revelation: 'I went out one morning and came back in the evening and Brian was blowing harp [harmonica], man. He's got it together. He's standing at the top of the stairs sayin', "Listen to this." Whooooow. Whooow. All these blues notes comin' out. "I've learned how to do it. I've figured it out." In one day.[19]

'He dropped the guitar. He still dug to play it and was still into it and played very well but the harp became his thing. He'd walk around all the time playing his harp.'

Yet there was a permanent kind of quiet desperation about both Brian and Keith. Still a student at the London School of Economics, Mick was far less insecure and more relaxed about the future than Brian and Keith – the Rollin' Stones was all they had, which wasn't the case for the singer.

Accordingly, Keith and Brian would play music every day. From the start, however, Keith claimed that Brian would try to play Mick and Keith off against each other. 'Like when I was zonked out, taking the only pound I had in me pocket . . . Or he'd be completely in with me trying to work something against Mick.'

A friend of Brian's from Cheltenham was in the Territorial Army. With the eighty pounds he earned from his annual two-week military stint, he would come up to London to hang out with Brian. Brian proceeded to extract almost every penny of his pay from him, including the entire purchase price of a new guitar and a set of harmonicas. Out walking in the bitterly cold winter weather, Brian demanded the 'friend' give Keith his sweater, at the same time as making him walk twenty paces behind them. (So how did Brian treat his enemies? wondered Keith.)

Bill Perks – who soon renamed himself Bill Wyman – had now joined the Rollin' Stones as bass player, following an audition on Friday 7 December 1962. When Dick Taylor announced he was giving up the group to study at the Royal College of Art, Bill had been recommended.

At the beginning of January Charlie Watts finally gave in and joined the group on drums. 'Brian saw in Charlie . . . what he had in abundance and demanded from any musician: commitment and idealism,' said Bill. At this stage Mick Jagger was only the singer. It was still clearly Brian Jones's group, and he and Keith Richards worked out on guitar whichever songs the Stones would play.[20] 'The Stones took its musical stance entirely from Brian's passion for American rural blues music,' remembered Bill of that time. Brian's role as group leader even ran to being in charge of the finances, a situation that shortly would create considerable controversy.[21]

'Brian had a presence that was definitely electric,' said Bill

Wyman, who became a close ally of the blond Stone. 'Mick did too, in a strange way, but I always felt Mick's personality was more self-consciously constructed: I don't remember him having the same sort of magical aura in those early days. When we were playing blues, I don't think anybody took much notice of Mick. Much more important was what sound Brian was playing on the slide guitar and harmonica. Mick played harmonica too, but Brian was better, more imaginative.'

There was some sign of movement. Taken under the wing of Giorgio Gomelsky, who ran assorted venues, they had been offered a regular slot, a Sunday night residency, at the Station Hotel in Richmond in west London, a font of hipness. On the posters that Giorgio quickly had printed up, the group's name was misspelt 'Rolling Stones'.

Errant consonants notwithstanding, the group decided to play their final show at the G Club in Ealing; they could afford to drop it, as the Station Hotel in Richmond paid just as much. At that final G Club date, Brian was confronted by the sight of a new girlfriend, Linda Lawrence, moving to dance in front of the stage, at the very moment that Pat Andrews walked in with Mark. From the stage Mick saw what was happening, and started chuckling while still singing. Keith caught the mood, and also began to laugh. Brian's eyes were downcast, however. But in fact neither of the girls knew who the other was, thereby saving Brian's bacon.

If any further proof was required of the mushrooming chic status of the Rolling Stones, it came on 21 April. A frisson ran through the audience at the Richmond Station Hotel as the crowd parted for first John Lennon, then the rest of the Beatles, who had been appearing on the *Thank Your Lucky Stars* television programme, filmed in neighbouring Twickenham. They stood and watched the set, which the Stones concluded with a lengthy version of 'I'm Moving On'. The personable Liverpudlians were not at all standoffish and congratulated the Stones on their music. Afterwards, the Beatles went back to 102 Edith Grove with the Stones.

Astutely identifying who really motored the Beatles, Brian talked at length with Paul until 4 a.m., perhaps recognizing a like mind and drive. Seizing the moment, Brian and Keith were out of bed bright and early the next morning, heading off to meet the group at their hotel. The Beatles invited them to come and see their show at the Royal Albert Hall the following Thursday.

That day, 25 April, Mick, Keith and Brian caught the 31 bus up to the junction of Kensington Church Street and Kensington High Street and walked along to the Albert Hall on Kensington Gore. To get them into the building, the Beatles' road crew handed the three Stones guitars belonging to John, Paul and George, which they carried in through the back door of the hall. There they were mobbed by girls who thought they were the Beatles. Brian loved this – now he wanted to be a star.

Meeting the Beatles was psychologically important for the Stones. It also greatly impressed Andrew Loog Oldham, a 19-year-old slick and stylish hustler who had worked on publicity for 'Love Me Do', the Beatles' first single. In partnership with Eric Easton, an old-school manager of such music acts as guitar maestro Bert Weedon, he offered to manage the Rolling Stones.

At Easton's offices off Baker Street on 6 May 1963, the Rolling Stones management contract with Oldham and Easton was signed by Brian Jones on behalf of the group for a term of three years. Mick and Keith waited nearby in one of London's ubiquitous Lyons corner houses. Before Brian signed, he nipped across the road to confer with his compadres. Back with Andrew Loog Oldham and Eric Easton, he made a deal on the side that he would be paid £5 a week more than the other members.

Radical changes were mooted by the group's new management team. Eric Easton had only become involved in the project because he wanted to drop Mick Jagger as vocalist, and get in a 'proper' singer. At first Brian seemed perfectly amenable to this. According to Bill, there was dark plotting by Brian Jones about this potential change: Stu had overheard Brian telling Easton that Mick's voice was not strong and they should be careful if they needed him singing every night, and that, if necessary, they should get another singer. 'As soon as the group started to become in any way successful, Brian smelled money,' said Bill. 'He wanted to be a star. He was prepared to do anything that would make it happen and bring in money immediately, whereas Mick and Keith weren't into that.' Andrew Loog Oldham, however, was insistent that Mick should remain in the group.

Yet Stu's having overheard this was like a portent of his own doom. Andrew had no doubt who it was who should leave the group. The same night that Brian had signed the contract, the Rolling Stones played another live show – at Eel Pie Island just down the Thames from the Station Hotel, the second show of a weekly Wednesday night residency. That evening Andrew Loog Oldham announced to the rest of the group, in the absence of Stu, that Stu could no longer be a member of the Stones. The piano-player, with his prognathous jaw and paternal air, didn't 'look right', he decreed. He instead suggested that Stu should play on the group's records and become their road manager. Stu did not know about this plot against him.

Brian and Keith returned together to Edith Grove from Eel Pie Island. Keith told Phelge that they would have to let Stu know that he was no longer a group member. When Stu finally came round to the flat two days later, he was told how his particular land lay. And he agreed to stay on as road manager. All along Brian had promised Stu that he was a sixth of the group. Stu, Phelge thought, seemed on the verge of tears. According to Bill Wyman, Stu now became extremely bitter towards Brian Jones: '. . . the tensions between group members began to increase. Brian's relationship with Mick blossomed temporarily, but there was an underlying feeling that ruthless determination was replacing idealism,' considered Bill. 'I thought that the "sacking" was a strange way to repay Stu's incredible loyalty.'

In June, the Rolling Stones released their first single, a relatively tepid version of Chuck Berry's 'Come On'. Plugging the record on their first *Thank Your Lucky Stars* television appearance, on 13 July 1963, the Rolling Stones had left the studio and charged the length of England to play at the Alcove Club in Middlesbrough, two hundred and fifty miles to the north. Also on the bill in that tough northeastern city were the Hollies, a group from Manchester they had never previously heard of who were the headlining act. The immense harmonic competence of the Hollies unnerved Brian, as he explained on the Stones' return to Edith Grove, ready for their regular two Sunday shows in London. From now on the Stones worked on their harmonies. Hence the additions of the songs 'Fortune Teller' and 'Poison Ivy' to their sets, which Brian – still functioning as musical director – found worked well with the group singing various parts.

On 14 September, the band was given their second slot on *Thank Your Lucky Stars*. As the programme was by now recorded and broadcast from Birmingham, they were also able to fit in two gigs at separate venues in Britain's second city on the same day as they performed on the television show. After the shows Mick and Keith were the only group members to drive back in Andrew's car. 'Who could realize, at this early stage, that the splitting of the group in that way would mark our future?' reflected Bill Wyman. 'Keith and Mick were quite prepared to go along with anything Andrew said,' said Ian Stewart. 'They fed off each other. We had very little contact with them in those days. Edicts would just be issued from the Oldham office.'

The days at 102 Edith Grove were virtually over. At the end of September 1963, the twelve-month lease on the flat ran out. Mick and Keith immediately moved into a place in Mapesbury Road, off Shoot-up Hill in Willesden but sufficiently near the more salubrious-sounding West Hampstead for Mick and Keith to claim that was the area in which they lived. Brian went to stay with Linda Lawrence at her parents' house in Windsor, twelve miles outside London. Her parents may have had cause to regret their free-thinking welcome: Brian's extraordinary fecundity clearly unabated, Linda was soon pregnant. A son, Julian Brian, would be born to Linda Lawrence on 23 July 1964.

By locking himself away outside London, Brian Jones had made a further tactical blunder, removing himself from the centre of power within the Rolling Stones. His timing was off: concerned that the Stones were little more than a high-end covers group, Andrew Loog Oldham was urging Mick and Keith to write their own material. Their co-manager knew he needed a songwriting partnership in the group to push the Stones to the top. He also was aware that Brian Jones, the blues crusader, was too concerned with musical integrity to be bothered about this. 'Andrew knew he had to bring Mick and Keith together. His problem here was in breaking Keith's natural musical partnership with Brian: from the beginning, as the two guitarists, they had interlinked their lines and worked really well together,' explained Bill.

Almost as soon as Mick and Keith had left Edith Grove for their flat in Mapesbury Road, Andrew Loog Oldham had also moved in with them. Now he had the Dartford pair under his eye. Andrew's constant physical presence in the lives of Mick and Keith split the Rolling Stones into two factions. As the team of Jagger, Richards and Oldham began to draw apart from the others in the group, Mick and Keith would travel to gigs with Andrew in his car, while the rest of the group would be driven by Stu in the van.

That autumn Andrew Loog Oldham secured the Rolling Stones a support slot on a tour that the Everly Brothers were headlining; the fact that Bo Diddley was also on the bill was a further bonus that certainly did not go amiss. The tour was colossally successful for the Stones, climaxing at the Hammersmith Odeon where, playing on home ground, they had a formidable reception. The Everlys had paper cups thrown at them.

Unfortunately for Brian Jones, it was during these dates that the rest of the group learned Brian was being paid an extra £5 a week for being leader of the group. He had also expressed a desire to stay in more expensive hotels than the rest of the Stones. 'He had this arrangement with Easton,' Keith said, 'that as leader of the band he was entitled to this extra payment. Everybody freaked out. That was the beginning of the decline of Brian. We said, "Fuck you."'

Anxious for a new song, the Stones had covered a Lennon-McCartney tune, 'I Wanna Be Your Man', for their second single, released in November 1963. But the success of the Liverpudlian songwriting team had fired the ambitions of Mick Jagger and Keith Richards – and motivated the mind of Andrew Loog Oldham. The first fruits of Mick and Keith's efforts to emulate Lennon and McCartney were essayed at Regent Sound on 20 and 21 November. The Stones recorded demos of six songs written by the pair at Mapesbury Road. They included 'That Girl Belongs to Yesterday', which soon became a hit when recorded by Gene Pitney. Tucked in at the end of the sessions was another song, 'Sure I Do', one of two numbers demoed by the Stones that bore the credit 'B. Jones'. No other artist, however, picked up Brian's song.

At the end of January the Stones went back to Regent Sound to record 'Not Fade Away'. Armed with glasses of Scotch and Coke, the group transformed the session into a party. Buddy Holly's 'Not Fade Away' had a Bo Diddley-like arrangement – the Stones took it and emphasized that beat, with Keith on acoustic guitar, Brian on harmonica and Stu on piano. Alan Clarke and Graham Nash of the Hollies, whose crafted harmonies had inspired the Stones to import something similar into their own sound, were on back-up vocals, and Phil Spector, the most revered of record producers, was shaking maracas. With Mick Jagger, Spector also came up with 'Little by Little', the B-side, a song they dashed off at the session, which was credited to Phelge-Spector. Spector's presence certainly added sharper focus to both songs; although Andrew Loog Oldham was nominally at the production helm, the Stones essentially had their third single, a blast of high-end energy, produced by the most visionary pop music producer of the day.

Four days after recording 'Not Fade Away', with Brian Jones on the tune's distinctive harmonica parts, the Stones returned to Regent Sound studio on 25 February 1964 and recorded three more songs, including 'Good Times, Bad Times', a song which Mick and Keith had written. Brian was visibly disturbed that this was a Jagger-Richards composition. Although he was writing in Windsor, Brian never showed the rest of the group his material – his inferiority complex was too great. 'It was a pivotal moment in Regent Sound when Mick and Keith presented their first wares for the Stones to record,' said Andrew Loog Oldham in his autobiography *Stoned*.

Soon the Rolling Stones were off on their fourth tour of the UK, one that ran from 1 April to 31 May 1964. For two shows in Bristol the Stones played with the magnificent, black-leather-clad Gene Vincent. Perhaps a harbinger of coming events, Brian missed the first Bristol show.

On 26 April 1964 James Phelge went round to Mapesbury

Road, for a trip to Wembley's Empire Pool, where the Rolling Stones were performing at the annual *New Musical Express* Poll-Winners' Concert. At the flat he told Keith that Brian had complained that he and Mick wouldn't consider recording any of his songs. Keith laughed, calling out this news to Mick in the kitchen: 'Fuckin' Jonesey's been moaning to Phelge that we won't record his songs. Fuckin' typical.'

'They're fuckin' crap,' called out Mick.

'Everything he writes ends up sounding like a fuckin' hymn. They're all dirges of doom. You'd need a fuckin' Welsh choir to record 'em,' continued Keith.

In May 1964 Keith started going out with Linda Keith, a top British model. Brian's response to Keith's first proper relationship was to behave with extreme pettiness. One night on tour Keith punched him, blackening his eye, after Brian had eaten Keith's portion of chicken while the guitarist was having sex with Linda. The group took to calling Brian 'Mr Shampoo' after he announced to *Rave* magazine that he washed his hair twice a day. 'Brian was so sensitive, really. At the beginning it was a joke, because he was so sensitive about everything,' said Mick Jagger in 1971. 'When people used to go on about us being dirty, we used to laugh it off. But Brian got really hurt when people suggested he didn't wash his hair – which he did . . . I never quite understood what Brian wanted to do. He was very shy, and we didn't try and bring it out of him, properly. It wasn't a question of forcefully stifling him . . . He was very funny.'

On 1 June 1964 the Rolling Stones disembarked at New York's Idlewild airport from BOAC flight 505, their first visit to the United States. Mick was the first to step off the plane. At the airport press conference, he was asked, 'Who's the leader?' 'We are,' he responded, perhaps to Brian's surprise. 'All of us.'

On 24 October, the Rolling Stones began their second US tour at the Academy of Music in New York, with an afternoon and evening show. The next day they appeared on the *Ed Sullivan Show*, performing 'Time Is on My Side', their first substantial US hit, co-written by Mick and Keith. The third date on this second US tour gave the Stones more national television exposure: an appearance on the *T.A.M.I.* ('Teenage Awards Music International') *Show*, shot at Santa Monica Civic Auditorium in southern California. Although there was a balance of white acts – the Beach Boys, Jan & Dean, Lesley Gore, Gerry and the Pacemakers and Billy J. Kramer and the Dakotas – the Stones found themselves topping the bill with a five-song set over a host of their heroes: Marvin Gaye, Smokey Robinson and the Miracles, Chuck Berry, and – most of all – James Brown and the Famous Flames. During the two days of rehearsals, Brian Jones and James Brown built a friendship – later Mick and Keith would both become good friends with him. Mick, meanwhile, assiduously studied the foot movements of the Godfather of Soul.

A week after the second Stones album appeared in the British shops at the end of January 1965, the Stones began a tour of Australia, New Zealand and the Far East. On the way to Australia they stopped in Los Angeles, where time had been booked at RCA Studios in Hollywood. There they recorded two new Mick and Keith songs: 'The Last Time' and 'Play with Fire'.

In Sydney the Stones played to 35,000 people in seven nights. There had been a shift in onstage roles: although until now the back-up singers had been Bill and Brian, Andrew Loog Oldham was pushing Keith to sing with Mick, wishing to promote them as a double-act.

In the late winter of 1965, the Stones played another UK tour. The final date, at Romford ABC, was marked by an incident milked by Andrew for maximum publicity. Returning from this Essex show to nearby London at 11.30 that night, Mick, Brian and Bill were refused permission to use a toilet in the Francis Service Petrol Station in East Ham. 'Get off my forecourt,' said the attendant. 'Get off my foreskin,' replied Brian. About ten yards up an adjacent side-road, the trio's micturitions were splashed about a nearby wall.

Just over three months later, on 1 July, a private summons was issued against the three members of the Stones, alleging 'insulting behaviour' at the East Ham filling station. At the court hearing, on 22 July, each of them was found guilty of this charge and fined £5, with 15 guineas costs. The next day's *Daily Mirror* reported the case: 'Wyman asked if he could go to the lavatory, but was refused. A mechanic, Mr Charles Keeley, asked Jagger to get the group off the forecourt of the garage. He brushed him aside, saying, "We will piss anywhere, man." This was taken up by the group as a chant as one of them danced. Wyman, Jagger and Jones were seen to urinate against a wall of the garage.' Across the country, schoolboys mimicked their chant as they urinated in inappropriate locations.

On 14 September 1965 the Rolling Stones played the Circus Kronebau in Munich, where Brian Jones first met Anita Pallenberg. They spent the night together, with Brian in tears for most of their time together over the way he claimed he was being treated by Mick and Keith.

The Stones' new photographer, Gered Mankowitz, went with the group on their next, 48-date, US tour. Gered had a great time, enjoying an unprecedented creative burst. In this concentrated period with the group, the photographer was able to clearly observe the group's various members, especially Brian, who drew considerable attention to himself through his actions. 'The general atmosphere was pretty good. But it was there that Brian began to show serious oddness in his behaviour. He did a few very strange things. I saw him nearly bottle somebody in a club, for no reason other than that the guy was being persistent and an irritating pest, wanting a piece of Brian. And Brian just completely blew his top and smashed a bottle and was stopped from bottling this guy. That was a nasty incident that showed a side and an aggression that came as a bit of a surprise. I think it was in

New York, because the way the tour was organized, we had no social life anywhere else at all. They used to fly out after the show, and travel through the night, and arrive at places at three or four in the morning. So there were no fans, no groupies, no partying, no fun. It was only in some of the major cities, where perhaps we were based for two or three days, that there was some fun and some sex and some drugs and some rock 'n' roll going on.

'For most of the time it was hard graft and a rather dreary routine. So this incident with Brian was in a club, and it might have been New York and it might have been Nashville. We were in Nashville for two or three quite good nights. Brian disappeared. He got out of a limousine in a traffic jam and just disappeared. And they carried on without him and announced that he was ill. And he reappeared two or three nights later. I never really understood what went on. But there was clearly something about Brian that was odd and strange, and he was having a lot of struggles.

'I don't think I felt the band were judgmental about Brian. They were just affected. They'd find themselves without him. And they had to do a show, and this was at a point in their career when everything really counted. If one member of the group is seriously dysfunctional, the impact on everybody else is . . . he's putting everybody on the line. I remember Stu grabbing him once in the wings as he came off and lifting him off the ground, and telling him that he was letting everybody down, not just himself.

'During this nine-week tour, I began to see this other side of Brian. In Florida they broke for a couple of days. Anita Pallenberg joined Brian there, and then left after a couple of days. But he invited me up to his room, and he said, "I've got two tabs of acid left, and I wonder if you would like to have one." I said, "No, I'm not interested in acid, thank you very much." So he said, "Oh, okay. I'll tell you what: you take both of them and I'll write down everything you say." He was really out there, Brian. He was experimenting, he was ahead of them, he was freaking. In New York he was hanging out with Bob Dylan: that was the tour when there were the famous lost tapes when they were hanging out in his room. He introduced me to Bob Dylan. And then there was a tremendous power failure black-out and their idea of laying down a few tracks never happened. And they just got completely out of it. As everybody did that night. Brian was showing the character faults that he clearly had.

'He could be very interesting. He was capable of being incredibly charming and incredibly polite. Beautifully mannered. But then he'd turn, and he could be incredibly unpleasant. Very cliquey: he'd whisper in front of you, he and Anita would whisper. He loved to have the feeling that he had one over on you: that he knew something that you didn't know. And there was something weaselly about him that made him difficult.

'However, the band seemed to forgive him his transgressions very, very quickly. It wasn't like an irritating sore.

Although I wasn't privy to business meetings and discussions, and I don't know whether there were moments when they all got together and had terrible screaming matches. But certainly the feeling was that they forgave him, and that everybody was trying to work together. And when it all worked, it was fantastic. I think that was what was holding everything together. When it all gelled, it was so good – and Brian was such a crucial and integral part of that. Brian had this huge fan base, and his fans were more focused. And it made it more important to try and live with his oddness. But the seeds were being sown.

'And the other thing that happened, which I think caused terrible problems for Brian, was that Mick and Keith were writing. And Brian couldn't. People who were intimate with that whole group have confirmed to me that Brian couldn't write. He was an excellent musician, a very versatile musician, a natural and instinctive musician, and a huge and crucial part of the Rolling Stones, but not being able to write was a big, big problem for him. And that he must have known even if he couldn't really comprehend it or deal with it. He must have know that Mick and Keith writing, Mick singing, and Keith basically being the lead guitar meant he couldn't maintain his position of being the leader of the band. And I guess that was really important to him, that status.

'I think it's a real myth that Brian was plotted against. I honestly don't believe that's the case. I think that Brian sowed the seeds for his demise. And that he was responsible for it. Andrew instinctively knew that Mick and Keith were the soul of the band – although musically Charlie and Bill were the roots. And Brian was marginalized. Brian was this freaky, blond bomber. And played up to that. Perhaps he was pushed into that role more simply by what was going on.'

In many ways Brian created the template for the British musician who adopts a 'rock 'n' roll lifestyle', with all its inbuilt self-destructive potential. 'He was certainly ahead of everyone in terms of drugs and drink and possibly sex,' said Mankowitz. 'Mick and Keith had to write quite a lot, when they got a chance, because they were recording the *Aftermath* album at the end of this tour, at RCA studios in Hollywood. It was very exciting, because it was so new and different. But an awful lot of it was laborious and dreary, and not a great rock 'n' roll life at all.'

At the beginning of 1966, however, the public face of the Rolling Stones remained that of Brian Jones. Brian's image as the smug, flaxen-haired fop dominated photographs of the group and in live shows held the audience's attention. Despite Mick's reindeer-like onstage prancing, Brian – one minute still and silent, the next a smirking satyr – simply oozed moody charisma, even though his considerable talent increasingly seemed to have been reduced to little more than an engine for expressing such histrionic glamour. His curiously waddling form notwithstanding, Brian looked fantastic. He was the personification of rebellious, dandified decadence, and therefore the personification of the Rolling Stones. In a group sold as definitively 'longhaired', 'Mr Shampoo' was the only member who really was.

Despite the fact that the group were now utterly dependent on their increasingly original and catchy songs, to the fans Mick and especially Keith were mere also-rans next to Brian. This was a fact of which the pair were only too aware. The majority of the record-buying public had no inkling of the increasingly tempestuous internal politics within the Stones and, apart from the vocals and drums, hadn't a clue as to who contributed what to the group's sound and arrangements.

Now, in Anita Pallenberg, the group's founder had also scored a definitive piece of 'luxury crumpet', a status symbol 'bird' whom he was already beginning to discover was at least his match. Half German, half Italian, Anita seemed unutterably exotic to the boy from Cheltenham, as well as to the boys from Dartford. She had worked with the Living Theatre, a long established, New York-based experimental theatre group; whilst in New York, she had had a long relationship with the postmodernist Italian painter Mario Schifano. As long as their relationship lasted, Brian Jones and Anita Pallenberg were the Number One Beautiful Couple in Europe. No matter that Brian – asthmatic, unfit, and increasingly unhinged by his drug and alcohol intake – had spent his first night with Anita sobbing paranoically over the way he said he was treated by Mick and Keith. As 'top-notch totty', rather to Mick's chagrin, Anita left his own girlfriend Chrissie

Shrimpton, sister of supermodel Jean Shrimpton, in the starting blocks. For his own part, Keith's relationship with Linda Keith was virtually on the rocks: Linda's fondness not only for marijuana, but increasingly for the downer prescription drug Mandrax and now heroin – which Keith had so far resisted – had placed strains on their relationship that seemed impossible to resolve.

Meanwhile, Brian's sexual indiscretions were catching up with him. A *News of the World* banner headline trumpeted on 16 January 1966: THE GIRL WHO LOVED A ROLLING STONE, a story detailing his desertion of Pat Andrews and their son Mark. Finally Pat Andrews was given a paternity order, with the magistrate ordering Brian Jones to pay £2.50 a week – the maximum award permissible – towards Mark's upkeep.

Most days when he was in London during the spring and summer months of 1966, Keith Richards would walk the three or so miles from a flat he had rented on his own in St John's Wood – where he had been pressured by the landlords to ensure fans made less noise – across Hyde Park to 1 Courtfield Road, behind Gloucester Road tube station. There Anita Pallenberg had bought a flat, into which Brian had moved. Keith's problems with Linda had led to him feeling very much alone, and now he bonded again with Brian, as they had in the days when the two of them had been left alone in Edith Grove as Mick continued his studies at the LSE.

Despite the fact that for the group's audience Keith Richards remained almost entirely overshadowed by Brian Jones, the boy from Cheltenham for now at least was seemingly his best friend. The intriguing high priestess aspects of Anita, who was rarely without a bag containing tarot cards, and occasionally the odd bone, held more than a small attraction for Keith. For Keith the intimacy of what became near to a triangular relationship had positive consequences. By osmosis he picked up elements of Brian's ineffable dress sense, transforming his appearance. Soon he would also take Brian's girlfriend.

Christopher Gibbs, a fashionable Chelsea art and antiques dealer, had insisted to Anita that she must buy the Courtfield Road flat, which only had one room and a set of stairs leading to a minstrel's gallery that formed a bedroom of sorts. Gibbs had stressed how extraordinary the place could be made to look if money was spent on it. Almost inevitably, in this drug- and ego-befuddled household, the necessary forward-planning had never taken place. The interior of the residence resembled a much more expensive version of the post-adolescent chaos of the flat in nearby Edith Grove. Mick, exhausted from the constant squabbling with Chrissie, hardly ever ventured over to 1 Courtfield Road. The atmosphere of grime and unwashed dishes was something he found distinctly unsavoury; and he could not avoid picking up on a palpably unhealthy sexual tension that seemed to sit thickly in the air along with the fumes of best quality hashish. For some of those louche aristocrats who loved to hang out with dandy pop stars, however, 1 Courtfield Road became the epicentre of their world. Tara Browne, the Guinness heir, would often be round at the flat, staying up half the night talking with the two Stones and Anita before disappearing home in his Lotus Elan.

Christopher Gibbs was a central figure in a social milieu into which Mick, Keith and Brian had slipped with ease and which seemed to them to be daringly sophisticated. This was a world that now included such locations as Mrs Beaton's Tent, a restaurant in Frith Street in Soho, run by an Australian called Michael Stafford, that became a favourite of the set. The arty world into which Mick, Keith and Brian had been drawn was sexually ambiguous, and often outright gay.

Anita introduced first Brian, then Keith and Mick, to Robert Fraser, a gay Old Etonian art dealer who was always on the cusp of the newest scenes. After having lived in New York with Mario Schifano for six months, Anita considered herself au fait with the Manhattan art world and therefore that of Europe. Through bohemian figures like John Dunbar, the heroin-addicted husband of Marianne Faithfull, and Barry Miles (known simply as Miles), who together ran the distinctly underground Indica Gallery and bookshop in Southampton Row, the Beatles had already fallen under Fraser's spell. Now it was the turn of the Stones to take on Robert Fraser as their taste guru, although Mick usually claimed not to have the necessary money to buy any of the works Fraser offered him.

Robert Fraser also introduced Brian and Anita to the cosmic

experience of LSD, the first person in London either of them knew who had taken acid. 'I was just used to hash,' said Anita, 'but Brian and I one night at his place took this trip, went home and started to hallucinate.' Soon Keith also discovered the secret of lysergic acid.

A friend of Robert Fraser was 'Spanish' Tony Sanchez, a photographer. He was such a fan of drugs that he could always come up with large quantities of the highest quality. As a man who could always be relied on to deliver the goods, Tony Sanchez soon became an indispensable part of Keith's circle. 'Like me, Keith was young and impressionable, and he had always been content to follow where Brian led,' said Spanish Tony. 'He turned Keith on to acid, and they were drawn together.'

Keith half-moved into 1 Courtfield Road, crashing on the couch or floor, aware of the sensuous and sometimes strange sounds floating down from the gallery above as Brian and Anita made love. As Anita had done to him, Brian turned his fellow Rolling Stone on to LSD, drawing them together, accentuating the endless musical improvisation in which they indulged. The axis shifted in the Stones again as it had done briefly at Edith Grove. Mick was regarded as the 'straight', because he hadn't done acid, and confessed to being frightened of it. To further get his goat, Brian and Keith began to call him by his surname, which had the desired effect of really winding Mick up. At the same time Brian's natural paranoia, exacerbated by his daily ingestion of drugs, made him extremely fearful of the evident close relationship and affection between Keith and Anita.

That the Rolling Stones had a strong creative wind behind them was proved irrefutably in April 1966 with the release of *Aftermath*. This extraordinary LP came as the climax of a golden period of Stones' music, and Brian Jones was a crucial element of the sound, whose immediacy, clarity and distinctiveness could not be replicated by any other acts of the time. The clarity of production on these tracks is extraordinary, and the unique, fresh sound of *Aftermath*, the first album by the group to feature only Jagger-Richards compositions, can largely be attributed to Brian Jones's startlingly original arrangements. The record's instrumental line-up includes lutes, harpsichord, dulcimer, marimbas, sitar and bells – all played by Brian. If not capable of writing such songs as were on the album, Brian knew how to embellish them, enhancing them subtly with his esoteric instruments.

Brian also had his own, exclusive scene. In 1966 Alice Pollock and Sir Mark Palmer launched the English Boy model agency, 'to change the image of British manhood and put the boy, as opposed to the girl, on the magazine cover in the future,' said Palmer. Brian and Anita were on their books but never appeared in a shoot. Now Brian and Anita began to resemble the same person, Anita's hair being cut in exactly the same androgynous pageboy style as Brian's. For Germany's *Stern* magazine, they did agree to pose for a set of photographs. Except that the ones they submitted featured Brian in an SS uniform, crushing a doll beneath his feet; next to the toy, Anita cringed, trembling. Rejected by the magazine, the pictures all the same leaked out, appearing in the British press. 'It was naughty! But what the hell! He looked good in an SS uniform!' uttered Anita, years later.[22]

On 26 May 1966 all the Stones shared a box at Bob Dylan's concert at the Royal Albert Hall. Earlier that evening they had performed a new single, 'Paint it Black', on *Top of the Pops*, which went out on the BBC at seven in the evening. Legendarily, Dylan shocked his folkie devotees when the already mythical troubadour returned for the second half of the show with his backing group the Hawks, soon to become the Band, and launched into the electric phase of his career.

Following the show, Brian and Keith went to Blaise's nightclub, a few hundred yards away in nearby Queensgate, where Dylan later arrived. Nervously, Keith had approached him. With a sardonic sneer, Dylan looked straight through him and let fly: 'I could write "Satisfaction", but you couldn't write "Mr Tambourine Man".' Drunk, Keith took a swing at Dylan, and a short melee ensued. Dylan returned to his hotel, followed by Brian and Keith. Brian was steering his Rolls Royce, intent on having another pop – Dylan slipped away from them. (Brian had purchased a personalized number plate for his luxury transport: DD 666. It was as though he was thumbing his nose at the deity.)

*

In the summer of 1966, Linda Lawrence appeared on the doorstep at Courtfield Road, accompanied by Julian, their son, and her mother. Keeping them away from partying revellers, including an excessively out-of-it Keith Richards, Brian took them up to his bedroom. After some two hours, they left, Brian visibly in a disturbed emotional state.

Following a summer tour of the United States, the Rolling Stones went on holiday. At the suggestion of Christopher Gibbs, Brian and Anita headed for Morocco. There, during one of their several fights, Brian broke his hand on a hotel bedroom wall when he took a swing at her.

This meant that when the group had to make a hurried flight to New York on 9 September to unexpectedly perform their next single, 'Have You Seen Your Mother, Baby' on the *Ed Sullivan Show*, along with 'Paint it Black' and 'Lady Jane', only Mick's vocals were live. The group mimed to pre-recorded backing tracks. Brian, whose bandaged hand was clearly visible, had played the sitar that dominated 'Paint it Black' as well as the dulcimer on 'Lady Jane'.

On 12 September, the Stones shot a promotional film in New York for 'Have You Seen Your Mother, Baby', in which the group appeared in drag, dressed like thirty-year-old women in the wartime 1940s. The same theme was employed in all publicity for the record, and 'Molly' Richards and 'Sarah' Jagger adorned the single's poster, to great controversy. In the same image Brian, dressed in a World War II WREN's uniform, wears his customary visage of stoned arrogance. Might he have appeared more modest if he had been aware that he would never again tour the United States with the Rolling Stones?

The end of the summer of 1966 was a pivotal time in the emotional lives of both Mick and Keith. To the consternation of Brian, who a few months previously had seized control of the awkward triangular relationship between himself, Keith and Mick, the Stones singer now began to hang out at Courtfield Road with Keith. The guitarist was beginning to acknowledge that he had smouldering feelings for Anita, a flame that burned brighter when he discovered precisely how Brian had hurt his hand. His innate psychic abilities heightened – and confused – by his drug intake, Brian was perpetually anxious that something was going on between Anita and Keith.

By now, moreover, it was hard not to pick up on the tension between Brian and Anita. When Brian ran into Ronni Money, the wife of his friend Zoot Money, the keyboardist and bandleader, in the Scotch of St James nightclub, Anita peremptorily ordered, 'I don't want you talking to this slag!' Brian's response was to punch her on the nose and tell her never to speak of Ronni in such a manner.

The 18th of December 1966 brought a major trauma that affected London's chic young set to such an extent that it earned mention in one of the new songs being worked on by the Beatles. Brian's good friend Tara Browne was killed in a car crash. He drove his Lotus Elan, the most chic of sports cars, straight into a parked truck in Redcliffe Gardens in nearby Earls Court. With him was his girlfriend Suki Potier. She was utterly distraught, and Brian provided personal care to her on a daily basis. 'He gave me a shoulder to cry on and he picked up the pieces and made me feel a woman again,' said Suki. Later, Brian would have a relationship with her: on and off, the pair dated for approximately two years.

Anita, meanwhile, had been cast in the lead role in a film being made by German director Volker Schlöndorff. It was called *A Degree of Murder*, the story of a girl who accidentally kills her boyfriend with his own gun as he attempts to beat her. Shooting was set to start at the beginning of 1967 and Brian was taken on to write the score. He moved to Munich, staying with Anita in Schlöndorff's apartment for the duration of the filming. The director had taken Brian on for the role, not simply as a sop to Anita:[23] 'I liked Brian and trusted him. You could feel that he had a lot of creativity. He was a poet, an *enfant terrible* it's true, but he was very much in touch with his time and he was also very much in love with Anita, the only actress in the movie – and its soul. She was bound to inspire him. I know he loved her, and I think she loved him. She was certainly in love with his lifestyle.' On the soundtrack Brian drew on his by now familiar panoply of instrumentation: sitar, organ, dulcimer, harmonica, autoharp, flute, piano, violin, banjo and saxophone. Later brought in by Brian to add further textural instrumentation were Yardbirds guitarist Jimmy Page, renowned session pianist Nicky Hopkins and Small Faces drummer Kenney Jones.

In London, where Volker Schlöndorff followed Brian to get him to complete the score, the director felt he had become much more moody, an air of permanent upset hanging over him. 'There was obviously tension within the Stones too. It was very clear that Brian wanted more profile or he would go his own way.'

While the director had become fond of Brian, he was struck by his barely concealed paradoxes. 'Brian was extremely likeable . . . Yet he wouldn't often allow you to like him . . . There was also something definitely devilish about Brian. He'd sense your weakness with incredible intuition and, if the mood took him, he'd exploit it. On the other hand, he could turn around and be incredibly nice to you. I liked Brian, but he was a complicated guy.'[24]

It wouldn't have seemed like a new year if the Rolling Stones had not begun 1967 with more of their by now habitual controversy. On Friday 13 January they released a new single, 'Let's Spend the Night Together' – a title which seemed a little obvious, immature and humourless in its efforts to create media uproar. Although perfectly catchy, a tiredness also lay at the heart of the tune, with the suggestion that the cod-naughty lyrics were chosen to boost its rather uninspired melody and riffs. No doubt precisely as the group hoped, various American radio stations immediately banned the song, thereby only enhancing its word-of-mouth reputation. The B-side was 'Ruby Tuesday', a Keith composition about Linda Keith, featuring Brian on flute. In the United States, 'Ruby Tuesday' began to be promoted more and more, until it became a number 1 record. In Britain 'Let's Spend the Night Together' remained the A-side, however, and the Stones plugged it on 22 January on the *Sunday Night at the London Palladium* ITV programme. This was a variety show with an enormous mass-market audience that the Beatles had always exploited to the maximum.

When the Stones arrived at the Palladium, behind Oxford Circus, matters did not kick off especially auspiciously. Keith and Brian turned up together, tripping on LSD, and Brian immediately placed a large water-pipe on top of the piano. Such gestures were considered radical in those times.

The London Palladium date was not only intended to plug the single. Two days before it, the Stones had released yet another new album, *Between the Buttons*, the fruits of August sessions in Los Angeles. It was the first album that the Stones had recorded with a conceptual approach. In Britain's *NME*, longstanding Stones supporter Roy Carr gave it a very bad review. There was no getting away from it – it was a weak album, the songs sounding like outtakes from the *Aftermath* sessions.

But in America it received a largely ecstatic response. The cover of the album was another picture by Gered Mankowitz:

an archetypal shot of the group hunched up in their overcoats against the early morning chill, taken on Primrose Hill in north London after an all-night recording session.

There was another significant factor about that Gered Mankowitz shot: on the cover picture for *Out of Our Heads*, which Mankowitz had also taken, Brian was right up at the front of the group. Sixteen months later, for the insubstantial, confused *Between the Buttons* album, he was right at the back, like an afterthought that was fading away.

On 5 February 1967, the *News of the World* ran an article in which it alleged that the Stones' singer had taken LSD at the London home of the Moody Blues. In the article a pair of reporters described how they had met 'Mick Jagger' at Blaise's night club in South Kensington. While there he had taken six Benzedrine amphetamine tablets and brandished a lump of hash. He was also said, highly implausibly, to have admitted to having first taken LSD while on the road with Bo Diddley and Little Richard. 'I don't go much on it now the cats (fans) have taken it up. It'll just get a dirty name.'

It wasn't Mick, of course; it was Brian, seeing straight through the reporters and sending them up in his customarily supercilious manner. This didn't especially help Mick, and proved even more damaging for Brian, for whom the small episode in a nightclub would ultimately have disastrous consequences, both inside and outside the group.

The next day a writ for libel was served by Mick Jagger on

the *News of the World*. As a consequence the Sunday newspaper put even more reporters onto investigating Mick's drug habits.

Now matters began to gather pace. David Schneiderman, a self-styled 'acid king' whom Keith and Brian had met in New York on the Stones' last US tour, arrived in London. He brought with him, he said, a suitcase full of top-grade LSD. Keith and Brian were out of town, having flown to Munich to watch Anita filming in *A Degree of Murder*.

When Keith returned on Friday 10 February, and learned Schneiderman was in town with his bag of goodies, he suggested a select group should go down to Redlands, a country house in East Sussex he had recently purchased, to sample these wares. The Beatles were invited, but only George Harrison and Patti Boyd could make it. Tired from working on the Schlöndorff soundtrack, Brian and Anita were late. Brian called Keith to apologize, at the very moment that police burst into Redlands. 'Don't bother, Brian: we've all just been busted!' Keith told him over the phone.

Like an executioner's axe, the full force of the British establishment was hovering over the collective neck of the Rolling Stones. Accordingly, assorted members of the cast decided to leave the UK, with Morocco as their chosen destination.

Attempting to create a smokescreen around their eventual destination, Keith, Brian and Anita flew to Paris, checking into the George V hotel. Tom Keylock, who worked for the

Stones, took the ferry and drove to the French capital in Keith's Bentley with its black-tinted windows.

Bombing through the countryside south of Paris Brian was aware of an almost palpable psychic bond between his girlfriend and Keith. Attempting to anaesthetize himself to this in the only way he knew how, he passed the first day's journey by pouring copious quantities of French cognac down his throat and chain-smoking joints, each containing enormous amounts of hashish. By the time they were fifty miles out of Toulouse, this intake, as well as the sexual vibes in the car, had caught up on Brian, and he could hardly breathe. Was it an asthma attack? Or something more serious? No one seemed to know. Whatever the cause, he was admitted to the Centre Hospitalier d'Albi outside Toulouse.

At Brian's insistence, the other occupants of the Bentley left him there, continuing on their way through the Pyrenees into Spain. Anita ignored a telegram sent by Brian, asking her to meet him from hospital. In Valencia Keith and Anita spent the night together, but agreed to treat it as a passing whim. Finally, after Anita had spent four more nights with Keith in Marbella, she flew up to Toulouse to meet Brian on Sunday 5 March. Five days later the couple flew back to London for Brian to undergo further medical tests.

On 9 March, Marianne Faithfull – who had replaced Chrissie Shrimpton in Mick Jagger's affections – flew from Naples to Tangier to meet up with Mick. In Tangier the Stones' party took over the entire tenth floor of the Hotel

Minzah. The artist Brion Gysin was in the city and came by to hang out with them. On 15 March Brian and Anita finally arrived in Tangier. That night, after they had been tripping, Brian and Anita began to argue yet again. After Anita had taken sleeping tablets and locked herself in her bedroom, Brian left and picked up a pair of tattooed Berber whores. After bringing them back to the hotel, he tried to persuade Anita to have group sex with them, smashing up the room and beating her when she refused. She fled to Keith's room and spent the night with him. The next day Anita sat in a canvas swing by the deep end of the pool, her gaze held by Keith in the water.

That evening they learned that a plane-load of Fleet Street's finest was on its way to Tangier to track down the party. Immediately, they made off to Marrakech.

In Marrakech, they checked into the Sadi Hotel. 'We're all in Marrakech,' Keith said. 'Cecil Beaton's there, Robert Fraser, Brion Gysin, Mick, and the air's like heavy, lots of people doing acid. I'm feeling guilty.'

'They were a strange group,' wrote Cecil Beaton, the photographer, in his diary. 'The three Stones: Brian Jones and his girlfriend Anita Pallenberg – dirty white face, dirty blackened eyes, dirty canary drops of yellow hair, barbaric jewelry – Keith R. in 18th century suit, long black velvet coat and tightest pants, and of course, Mick Jagger. He is sexy, but completely sexless . . . None of them is willing to talk, except in spasms. No one could make up their minds what to do, or when.'

The next day Brion Gysin was persuaded to take Brian to the nearby Atlas Mountains, to hear the celebrated pipe sounds of the Master Musicians of Jajouka.

As soon as he had gone, Keith bundled Anita into his car and they drove back to Tangier. Everyone else also left, leaving a shocked, hurt Brian to pay the bill for the entire party. Keith and Anita caught a ferry to Spain.

The couple only drove as far as Madrid, where they took a plane to London. There, Keith and Anita went immediately to the crash pad that Keith still kept in St John's Wood, the scene of his dying relationship with Linda Keith.

Brian flew to Paris to briefly stay with Donald Cammell, the society painter who would shortly co-direct *Performance*, arriving on his doorstep drunk, with his customarily elegant clothes in tatters. Then, in deep emotional pain, he returned to London. He drove over to the flat in St John's Wood and when Keith opened the door, he collapsed on the carpet in front of him, beseeching Anita to return. This was not to be the last such occasion. For a long time Brian refused to accept that Anita had left him, just as he had refused to accept that he was no longer 'leader of the Rolling Stones'. 'He never forgave me,' said Keith. 'I don't blame him.'

Anita's leaving Brian for Keith Richards was devastating to him and Brian's father believed the shock of this altered the entire course of his life. 'He changed suddenly and alarmingly from a bright, enthusiastic young man to a quiet and morose and inward-looking young man,' said Lewis Jones in 1971. 'In our opinion he was never the same boy again. I've always been concerned that that was the turning-point in his life.'

The day Brian returned from Paris, the *Daily Mirror* reported that Mick and Keith were to be charged for offences against the drug laws: Mick for illegal possession of amphetamines, and Keith for 'premises', which found the owner or landlord of any property in which there was illegal drug consumption to be as guilty as those partaking of the particular substance.

A week after Brian had finally returned from Morocco on 18 March 1967, the Rolling Stones began a three-week European tour, opening in Malmo in Sweden. After Sweden, the group raced through four dates in Germany: in Bremen, Cologne, Dortmund and Hamburg. Anita Pallenberg, whom Brian had met in Germany, had gone off with the guy who stood on the other side of Mick Jagger onstage. So it was an uneasy Brian who embarked with the group on this tour, while Keith was conscious all the time of Brian's bitter resentment. 'Mr Shampoo', however, was unaware that at this stage Anita, who had gone to Italy for another film part, in Roger Vadim's sexual science-fiction fantasy *Barbarella,* had not in fact committed herself to Keith – although she had committed to leaving Brian. Just to add to the atmosphere of confusion, despite having apparently won Anita, Keith began an affair with a German model called Uschi Obermaier, who accompanied him to the quartet of German shows. This seemed only to rub Brian's face even deeper into the dirt of his depression, a personal shame that would have been magnified a thousand times if he had appreciated this was the last time that he would tour with the Stones.

In mid-May Keith and Anita flew to Cannes for the annual film festival. *A Degree of Murder* was Germany's official entry that year. As Brian had composed the musical soundtrack, he also arrived in the south of France, checking into the same hotel as Keith and Anita. The first night he was there, Brian tried to persuade Anita to go back to him, as Keith waited patiently in his room.

At 4 p.m. on 22 June 1967, around the same time as Mick and Keith – having elected for trial by jury – were leaving court at West Sussex Quarter Sessions, Brian was busted for possession of cannabis at the flat in Courtfield Road. With him was a friend, 24-year-old Prince Stanislaus 'Stash' Klossowski de Rola. The pair appeared the next morning at West London Magistrates, where Brian also elected for trial by jury. Ever a worrier, Brian was to be driven literally sick by these events.

On 15 June Mick and Keith added vocals to 'All You Need Is Love', the Beatles' next single. When it was released on 7 July, the B-side – 'Baby You're a Rich Man' – featured Brian playing soprano saxophone. The day after the recording at Abbey Road, Keith and Anita flew to Paris. Mick, Marianne, and Marianne's son Nicholas and his nanny went to Tangier.

Brian, however, flew to northern California, accompanied by Stones' manager Andrew Loog Oldham, for the weekend of 16 to 18 June. His destination was Monterey Pop, south of San Francisco. This was the first of the 'Love Generation' mass festivals, at which Brian arrived in the Mamas and Papas' private plane, and where Brian introduced the set by his friend Jimi Hendrix. The event, at which drug consumption was blatant, marked a significant cultural shift: the symbolic inauguration of 'rock music' as a creative entity – and marketing force.

Brian's presence at Monterey indicated that – unlike the rest of the Rolling Stones – he was as in touch with the zeitgeist as when he had decided to form a blues group. So moved was Brian by the festival's spirit that he gave a rare interview, to *Beat* magazine. 'I just came away for a few days and it's so nice to get on someone else's scene. It's a very beautiful scene happening here,' he told the reporter, saying he regretted the other Stones had not also come to California with him. 'We record practically all the time as the Beatles do. We just got about a week off so I came over here with Andrew. The others have sort of split to various places, I think, I'm not quite sure. But nobody seemed to get it together to come over here. I wish they had 'cause they have missed a very nice scene.'

In the lace-encrusted wrap he wore at the festival, Brian looked like a mediaeval English monarch – apart from the can of Budweiser that was permanently in his hand. Hanging at Monterey with Nico, singer with emerging act the Velvet

Underground, earned them the rubric of the King and Queen of Monterey Pop.

'A lot of people have been sort of critical of this kind of happening in this country. The uptight people,' the *Beat* interviewer said to him.

'They're frightened of trouble but I don't expect any trouble, do you?' considered Brian. 'It has been wonderful. I have been walking freely amongst everybody. Yesterday I was walking through and joining rings of kids and fans. You know I've never had a chance to do that much before. People are very nice here. I like it.'

Brian also revealed how he'd been spending his time: 'I did a Beatles' session the other night, actually. On soprano saxophone, of all things. I've taken up playing reeds again. I used to play reed instruments. I bought a soprano saxophone the other day and ever since I have been doing sessions on it. There are soprano saxophones on the Stones' records, future Beatle records. You know, it's a funny thing – you get hold of something and put it on everyone's records. It's great. There's a very nice recording scene going on right now in London.'

Of Monterey Pop itself, Brian Jones seemed to sense its far-reaching effect, giving a glimpse of his abiding political idealism: 'I would like to see these affairs become a regular part of young community life because I think these people here – from what I've seen so far – are acting as a community. They have the community spirit, the community feeling. I haven't seen any signs of any trouble or enmity. It's very nice. People are showing each other around and it's very beautiful. I'm glad I came. I'll have lots of nice things to say when I get back home.'[25]

On 13 September, Keith, Brian, Charlie Watts and Bill Wyman arrived in New York to shoot the sleeve shot for *Their Satanic Majesties Request*. At immigration Keith was taken to one side and questioned for thirty minutes over the drugs trial. Then he was ordered to report to immigration offices in Manhattan the next day. As Brian's case had not yet come to trial in Britain, he sailed through immigration. Mick Jagger, sporting the newly de rigueur mutton chop sideburns, arrived in New York on a later flight and went through an almost identical experience to Keith. While the Stones were in New York there was a climactic management meeting with Allen Klein. On 20 September, there was an announcement that Andrew Loog Oldham was being replaced as the Stones' manager by Klein.

Brian, however, continued to disintegrate. He had spent ten days at the Priory in London on his return from Monterey. London was awash with rumours that he was about to leave the group. All the same, whatever state he was in he was working at Olympic Studios in west London with the Stones. After sessions on 5, 6 and 7 September, he had flown to Marbella in the south of Spain with Suki Poitier, the Portuguese-born former girlfriend of Tara Browne who had been with the Guinness heir in his fatal car smash the previous December. He returned to the Spanish resort with

Suki, a doppelganger for Anita Pallenberg, on 20 October for several days. Brian needed to rest up: his court case was set for the end of the month.

On 30 October 1967 he appeared in court. He was shaky and wan despite his faint tan, a consequence as much as anything of his previous night's excesses with Jimi Hendrix at a Moody Blues concert. His voice trembled as he pleaded guilty to possession of cannabis and allowing it to be smoked at his flat. After a short trial, Brian was given a nine-month prison term, an extraordinarily heavy sentence. He was taken off to Wormwood Scrubs, where Keith had been briefly incarcerated. As soon as he arrived at the 'Scrubs', the 'screws' threatened 'Mr Shampoo' with the haircut they said he was about to have. A demonstration in the Kings Road by about fifty hippies led to the arrest of eight people, one of whom was Chris Jagger, Mick's brother. After an application for an appeal was successful the next morning, Brian Jones was released from prison on bail of £750.

Allen Klein felt obliged to issue a statement: 'There is absolutely no question of bringing in a replacement for Brian.'

Brian's appeal was set for 12 December and Mick attended the court hearing. A trio of psychiatrists described Brian as 'an extremely frightened young man'. The sentence was set aside, and Brian was given three years' probation and fined the maximum of £1,000. Two days later, still in a state of apparent ongoing nervous breakdown, Brian collapsed at his new Belgravia apartment and was taken to the nearby St

George's Hospital at Hyde Park Corner. He discharged himself the same night.

Now the undisputed leader of the Stones, Mick Jagger called a press conference. 'There's a tour coming up,' he began, although this was news to everyone around the group. 'There are obvious difficulties, one of them is with Brian, who can't leave the country.' Although there were rumours that Jimmy Page would leave the Yardbirds to replace Brian in the Rolling Stones, the group insisted they were without foundation and that they could continue as a four-piece until Brian had sorted out his problems.

At least Brian's appeal served as lateral publicity for the Stones' new album, which was released in the United Kingdom on 8 December. In the United States, where it had been released twelve days previously, *Satanic Majesties* had already sold over $2 million worth of copies. In Britain, however, the long-player was widely dismissed – especially by John Lennon, who considered it yet another Stones' rip-off of the Beatles (of *Sgt. Pepper* in this particular case).

Their tails between their legs from the critical trouncing they had received at home, Mick, Keith and Brian quit the country for Christmas. With Stash de Rola along for the ride, Brian headed for Ceylon with another new girlfriend – none other than Linda Keith. It was as though he was bound in an inescapable psychic prison with Keith Richards and Anita Pallenberg.

*

During March 1968 the Stones were again at Olympic Studios, recording what would become *Beggars Banquet*. The subject of film was high on the group's agenda. The television director Michael Lindsay-Hogg, a close friend of Mick, was hired to make a promotional clip for a new single, 'Jumpin' Jack Flash'. Some of the recording of the album that became *Beggars Banquet* was shot by Jean-Luc Godard, doyen of French New Wave cinema directors, as the backdrop for his movie *One Plus One*. As well as capturing the isolation of Brian Jones, strumming a guitar that was unconnected to the control room, Godard also caught on film the evening when Anita Pallenberg joined Keith, Brian and Suki Poitier to chant the backing vocals to 'Sympathy for the Devil'. Lurking in a corner of the frame was a well-dressed man with a sardonic and sadistic sneer attached permanently to his upper lip. This was James Fox, an actor friend of Mick. In May it had been announced that he would play opposite the Rolling Stones singer in a film entitled *Performance*, to be directed by Donald Cammell.

That same month, on 12 May 1968, the Rolling Stones made a surprise appearance at the close of the *NME* Poll-Winners' Concert at Wembley Empire Pool, performing 'Jumpin' Jack Flash' and 'Satisfaction'. The 10,000-strong audience went berserk at this first stage appearance in Britain in almost two years. Although he was of course unaware of this, the show marked the last concert appearance by Brian Jones anywhere.

Life still seemed to be running out of control for the founder of the Rolling Stones. A week later, on 20 May, he was busted yet again, at the third-floor flat he had rented on the Kings Road, above Alice Pollock and Ossie Clark's shop Quorum, from which he would order floral shirts by the dozen.[26]

After failing to wake Brian at just after seven in the morning, the police had climbed into the flat through a window to find him on the phone, calling his solicitor. A small brown lump of what appeared to be hash was found in a drawer. Appearing that morning at Marlborough Street Magistrates Court, Brian was remanded for three weeks on bail of £1,000 while the substance was analysed.

A week later, on 27 May, saw the release of 'Jumpin' Jack Flash', a record whose superficially naive simplicity turned both in and out on itself until it achieved epic proportions – until the mid-1970s the character of Jumpin' Jack Flash became like an alter-ego for Mick Jagger. The Rolling Stones' fourteenth British single, it sold almost 100,000 copies in three days, going straight to number one. It stayed there for three weeks, the group's first UK number one since 'Paint it Black' in May 1966. In the USA it was in the top spot for a week. After the shocks of the previous year, it seemed the group were once again on an upward path.

Early in June 1968, at Sarum Chase in Hampstead, north London, Michael Joseph – better known at the time for his corporate photography – shot a series of Hogarthian portraits for what would become the inner sleeve of the *Beggars Banquet* album. Joseph noted that Brian was extremely nervy. He was worried about the consequences of his pending court appearance, scheduled for 11 June. Perhaps this is an explanation for his appearance, like that of a deranged hobbit. 'Brian was upset at having been busted but he had a dog to play with,' said the photographer. One of the rooms had been given a mediaeval appearance; on a banqueting table was an entire roasted pig. It is a picture taken from this series that was used on the album's inner gatefold. Keith is leaning across the table with a fork and stuffing an apple into Mick's mouth, while Brian sprawls in a chair at the end of the table, as an Irish setter leaps up on him.

Mick Jagger spent August 1968 filming in London, working on *Performance*, co-directed by Nicholas Roeg and Donald Cammell; Anita Pallenberg had been cast opposite him. Although he had given the film's script a cursory reading Mick initially had accepted Donald Cammell's vision that all he needed to do was play himself. Vacationing with Marianne Faithfull in Ireland prior to the shoot, however, he quickly saw that his character of Turner bore only a superficial resemblance to himself. Marianne Faithfull, steeped in the ways of thespians, provided the solution – to play Turner as a cross between Brian Jones and Keith Richards: 'Brian with his self-torment and paranoia and Keith with strength and cool.' Although Mick Jagger accepted her advice, undercurrents of himself inevitably leaked into the part. But not so much that they shifted the balance. There was, however, a consequence that Marianne had not considered. 'What I hadn't anticipated,' she later realized, 'was that Mick, by playing Brian and Keith, would be playing two people who were extremely attractive to Anita and who were in turn obsessed with her.' For the future of the Rolling Stones, and the relationship between Mick and Keith, the repercussions would linger for the rest of their careers – especially when it became widely believed that Mick had actually had penetrative intercourse with Anita during the filming of one of the film's several sex scenes.

Having temporarily moved into Redlands during this period, Brian had bought his own house in the country, Cotchford Farm, near Hartfield in Sussex. It was the former home of A.A. Milne, the writer of the Winnie-the-Pooh books, and it boasted a full-size swimming-pool in the garden. On 26 September Brian's drug case was heard in court, with both Mick and Keith attending to give him moral support. Although Brian was found guilty, he escaped with a fine and a severe warning. Mick was learning how to play the guitar, with lessons from Eric Clapton. Did he imagine there might soon be a position to fill in the Rolling Stones?

On 4 December, a launch party for the release of *Beggars Banquet* was held at Kensington's Gore Hotel. A seven-course Elizabethan banquet was served. After the meal, Mick picked up a foam custard pie and thrust it into Brian's face. Masochistically, Brian seemed to delight in this, as though it proved he was still part of the group.

Especially in the United States, *Beggars Banquet* was very well received critically, almost with a breath of relief that the Stones had weathered their various storms and were back on form. The return to their blues and rock roots served them well, as did Jimmy Miller's crisp and juicy production. 'We were just coming out of *Satanic Majesties*. Mick was making movies, everything was on the point of dispersal. I had nicked Brian's old lady. It was a mess. And Jimmy pulled *Beggars Banquet* out of all that,' Keith told *Crawdaddy!* magazine in 1975.

In fact, several of the ten songs on the album were relatively nondescript and time shows the record to be patchy. However, it contained a number of bona fide classics, notably its opener, the infamous but fantastic 'Sympathy for the Devil', 'Street Fighting Man', inspired by Mick's participation in the Grosvenor Square anti-Vietnam War riot, and the extraordinary 'Stray Cat Blues', almost an ode to paedophilia with its line '*I don't care if you're 15 years old*'. Brian provided graceful slide guitar on the beautiful slow blues 'No Expectations'. This was to be his last significant contribution to the group, like a reprise of his slide sound on Slim Harpo's 'I'm a King Bee' on the group's first album.

However, the breadth of the album, coupled with Jimmy Miller's experience in producing such specifically 'album' acts as Traffic and Spooky Tooth, marked *Beggars Banquet* as the

Stones' first 'rock' LP. They had successfully made the transition into the next stage of their career.

It was not an evolution in which Brian Jones would participate, however. On 30 May 1969 Mick Taylor, a guitarist with John Mayall's Bluesbreakers, was invited to come to Olympic. The next day he recorded 'Honky Tonk Women' with the Rolling Stones, Jimmy Miller adding the sound of the cowbell that gave the record its utterly distinctive sound. Brian had not been told about the recording session.

Early in the morning of Saturday 7 June Keith crashed his Mercedes eight miles from Redlands. Although the car was written off on the tree he hit, Keith was unhurt, but Anita broke a collarbone. The day after the crash, Keith and Mick, along with Charlie, drove down to the country. Already, at Mick's request, Alexis Korner had been down to Cotchford Farm to let Brian know how worried the group were about him. Now the three Stones themselves had gone down to see Brian at his new house. They discussed their differences over the direction of the group's music, and Brian agreed he couldn't carry on in the Stones. 'What we were trying to say was a very difficult thing,' Keith admitted to the American writer Stanley Boothe. 'After all, Brian was the guy that kicked Stu out of the band. In a way it's like the script starts to take shape after this. And the guy that kicked Stu out of the band is the first one to crack.'[27]

Brian was stepping out of the fray, it was announced, so the group could tour the USA. With two drug busts, Brian wouldn't have a chance of getting a US work visa. In this argument Mick was conveniently overlooking a pending drug case hanging over himself. Through Les Perrin, their publicist, Mick made a formal statement: 'The only solution to our problem was for Brian to leave us. He wants to play music which is more his own rather than always playing ours. We have decided that it is best for him to be free to follow his own inclinations. We have parted on the best of terms. We will continue to be friends and we're certainly going to meet socially in future. There's no question of us breaking up a friendship. Friendships like ours just don't break up like that.'

Like many children of the age, Marianne Faithfull was big on throwing the I Ching, the ancient Chinese oracle. Concerned about Brian while she was with Mick one night, she threw three coins the requisite six times and came up with the hexagram whose explanation was: Death by Water. Both she and Mick felt extremely concerned by this prediction. At Mick's urging, Marianne threw the oracle once again. And came up with precisely the same reading. Mick's cynical facade fell away. Deeply concerned, he phoned Brian, who touched by this attention – immediately suggested that Mick and Marianne come down to have dinner with him at Redlands, where he was briefly staying while building work was completed on his new home.

At Redlands they found Brian with Suki Poitier. Mick, however, suddenly changed from being the caring human being. When the meal that Brian and Suki had cooked was served up, he turned up his nose at it, confiding in Marianne that he couldn't eat 'this shit'. He demanded to go out to a restaurant, 'mortally offending Brian'. Brian, however, was in no state to go out, and Mick and Marianne left him and Suki at Redlands while they went out to eat.

Returning, they found Brian in a furious rage at their behaviour. This anger culminated in a physical fight between him and Mick which climaxed when Brian fell in the moat that ran around Redlands. Aghast, Mick leapt in after him, intent on saving Brian's life . . . to discover that the water was only three feet deep.

At least the stoned absurdity of the situation brought solace to Marianne: 'I thought death by water must be a symbolic message. What a relief!'

Two weeks later, on 3 July 1969, Brian died by drowning.

At his new home of Cotchford Farm Brian Jones had insisted that no one could have any drugs with them. This was a new phase of his life and he wanted nothing about the place that might bring the police down on him again. He substituted his fondness for all manner of narcotics, however, with copious amounts of wine.

On the evening of Wednesday 2 July 1969, Brian was at Cotchford Farm with a new Swedish girlfriend, Anna Wohlin. Frank Thorogood, a builder who had been working on the house, was also present, along with his girlfriend Jenny Lawson. Towards midnight Brian and Thorogood, both of whom were quite drunk, decided to take a swim in the outdoor pool. Thorogood, who had had to help Brian onto the diving board, soon gave up swimming, pulled himself out of the pool, and returned to the house.

Just after midnight, he returned to the pool. Brian was lying on the bottom of the deep end, face down. After he had been pulled out, Anna Wohlin, a trained nurse, tried to give him mouth-to-mouth resuscitation. Meanwhile, Jenny Lawson called a doctor. By the time he arrived, 27-year-old Brian Jones was dead. A watery end for the Piscean, who for years had been slowly evaporating through the fire of the Leonine Mick Jagger and the Sagittarian Keith Richards.

For years rumours circulated that Brian had been murdered. Except that, as Keith put it to *Rolling Stone* two years later, who would have wanted to kill him? Wasn't it more a case, as he suggested, that no one was really looking after Brian? 'Everyone knew what Brian was like, especially at a party. Maybe he did just go in for a swim and have an asthma attack. I never saw Brian have an attack although I know he was asthmatic. He was a good swimmer. He was a better swimmer than anybody else around me. He could dive off rocks straight into the sea. He was really easing back from the whole drugs thing. He wasn't hitting them like he had been, he wasn't hitting anything like he had. Maybe the combination of things, it's one of those things I just can't find out. We were completely shocked. He was a goddamn good swimmer and it's just very hard to believe he could have died in a swimming pool.'

The news flabbergasted the Rolling Stones. They had a free

concert scheduled in London's Hyde Park the following Saturday, 5 July. On the evening of 3 July they were booked to appear on *Top of the Pops*, to perform 'Honky Tonk Women'. In a dazed state they appeared on the television programme and afterwards went to their offices in Maddox Street. Tearfully, Charlie suggested they should perform the Hyde Park show as a tribute to Brian.

Unusually, Mick had stage fright before the Hyde Park concert and was suffering from psychosomatic laryngitis. 'He told friends he was terrified of taking the stage for this concert,' said Bill.

With Brian no longer there to steal his sartorial thunder, however, Mick was certainly the centre of attention, a picture of androgyny. Above his white bell-bottoms, he was wearing what appeared to be a white frilly dress, especially designed for the occasion. Around his neck was a studded black leather choker. His face was made up with rouge, lipstick and eyeshadow. His jet-black hair was longer even than Marianne's. Was he a man? Was he a woman? Was he a transvestite? Would you let your son marry a Rolling Stone? Dangling down onto Mick's chest at a level with his hair was a wooden crucifix, a visible talisman of protection for this bisexual shaman, but a symbol that seemed at odds with Mick's first words. They were extraordinarily, incongruously banal and clearly covered a cascade of awkwardness and confusion: 'We're gonna have a good time. All right?'

After a moment he addressed the matter at hand: 'Now listen . . . cool it for a minute. I really would like to say something about Brian. About how we feel about him just goin' when we didn't expect it.'

He announced that he was going to read something by Shelley. Mick's slurred enunciation made many of the audience at first believe it to be a poem by 'Che', the revolutionary leader. Then he proceeded to read first stanza 39 and then stanza 52 from Shelley's *Adonaïs*:

Peace, peace! He is not dead, he doth not sleep!
He hath awakened from the dream of life.
'Tis we who, lost in stormy visions, keep
With phantoms an unprofitable strife,
And in mad trance strike with our spirit's knife
Invulnerable nothings! *We* decay
Like corpses in a charnel. Fear and grief
Convulse us and consume us day by day
And cold hopes swarm like worms within our living clay.

And then:

The One remains, the many change and pass.
Heaven's light for ever shines, earth's shadows fly;
Life, like a dome of many-coloured glass
Stains the white radiance of Eternity
Until Death tramples it to fragments. – Die,
If thou wouldst be that which thou dost seek!

Before the group could plunge into the opening riff of 'Honky Tonk Women', several cardboard boxes were emptied into the air: hundreds of white butterflies rose above the stage. Yet it became apparent that, rather fittingly, this tribute to the memory of Brian Jones was somewhat flawed. The long, hot hours imprisoned in the cardboard boxes had led to the deaths of most of the creatures, and only a small percentage escaped their prisons. For the entirety of their set, Mick and the Stones felt the corpses of desiccated butterflies scrunching beneath their feet as they moved about the stage. Thus did they enact their tribute to Brian, founder of the Rolling Stones.

JIMI HENDRIX

'I am Electric Religion'

Lucille Jeter Hendrix, Jimi Hendrix's mother, was a 17-year-old schoolgirl when he was born, on 27 November 1942. By this time, Al Hendrix[1] – her 23-year-old husband – had been called up to serve in the US army, a private in the country's war effort. Lucille and Al had married on 31 March 1942, after learning that Lucille was pregnant. Both were from backgrounds of extreme poverty. On each side there were ancestors who were slaves, slave-owners and Cherokees; Jimi was at least one-eighth Cherokee – when Jimi would play cowboys and Indians games as a child, he was always the Indian.

Al, Jimi's father, had moved to Seattle from Vancouver, Canada, his place of birth. He had travelled 120 miles south to Washington State, in search of employment and opportunities to meet black women, rare in Vancouver. The local black community were suspicious of his motives and his Canadian roots. A deformity didn't help matters: Al had six fingers on each hand, and superstition regarding such abnormalities was common. Al's adamant insistence that Jimi should switch from his natural left-handedness may well have been informed by this experience – later he would even try to make Jimi play guitar right-handed. 'My dad thought everything left-handed was from the devil,' Leon Hendrix, Jimi's younger brother, told the writer Charles Cross.[2] Al would come to insist that music itself was 'the devil's business'.[3]

When Al was drafted three days after their marriage, Lucille was still at high school, her parents both on welfare. She quit school and, despite being underage, the pregnant teenager took a job as a waitress in a bar, the Bucket of Blood. During low points in her job, she took to singing to the customers. Strikingly beautiful but definitively wild, Lucille would become the archetype for the frequently unstable women to whom Jimi would later be drawn – 'electric ladies', as he came to call them.

With Al Hendrix away in the army, Lucille spent much of her time living in rooming houses, having relationships with other men even while pregnant, notably with one John Page. When her son was born, Lucille named him Johnny Allen Hendrix – there was a suggestion that the boy's name was influenced by that of her lover, and unfounded whispers that Page might even be the father. Page took Lucille 200 miles south to Portland in Oregon, where she was hospitalised after her lover beat her. John Page was then sentenced to five years' imprisonment under the Mann Act for taking Lucille over the state border at the age of seventeen. (After serving his time, Page reappeared in Lucille's life in 1948, allegedly keen to pimp her as a prostitute. In a street-fight, Al boxed him out of their lives.) There were rumours that Lucille was neglecting her baby son, so Jimi was moved to Berkeley, California, and the home of a family friend, Mrs Champ, who had a young daughter named Celestine.

So who exactly was Jimi's mother? The ruptured spleen, cirrhosis of the liver and hepatitis that eventually did for Lucille at thirty-three, a testament to her lifestyle, painfully illustrated what she considered her priorities. Lucille Jeter was a wild girl – hardly a woman – of the night, devoted to having a good time. Before she had lived out enough of her fantasies she had found herself pregnant by Al Hendrix at the age of seventeen – a baby having a baby. She was too young to have a child, especially as a woman who loved liquor and staying up all night dancing and smooching with men – not that she let being pregnant with Jimi get in the way of her devotion to having a good time. She was an erratic, dysfunctional party girl and a largely absent mother, but she became Jimi's first female archetype, the template for his understanding of women. From a very young age, Jimi started to have some very bruising experiences.

As Jimi later recalled, 'Dad was level-headed and religious, but my mother used to like having a good time and dressing up. She used to drink a lot and didn't take care of herself, but she was a groovy mother. There were family troubles between my mother and father. They used to break up all the time and I always had to be ready to go tippy-toeing off to Canada. My brother and I used to go to different homes. I stayed mostly at my aunt's and grandmother's.

'My grandmother's a full-blooded Indian, that's all. I used to spend a lot of time on her reservation in British Columbia. There's a lot of them on the reservation, man, and it was really terrible. Every single house is the same, and it's not even a house, it's like a hut . . .

'Yeah, my grandma is full-blooded Cherokee. She used to tell me beautiful Indian stories, and the kids at school would laugh when I wore the shawls and poncho things she made . . . There's a lot of people in Seattle that have Indian mixed in them. It's just another part of our family: that's all.'[4]

When Al was discharged from the army in September 1945, he took his son from Berkeley, California back to Seattle, where they moved into Lucille's sister Delores's apartment in the first racially integrated housing project in the United States.

This was the first time that Jimi had had a male figure in his life; for his part, his father had decided to divorce Lucille. But when she turned up at their home one day, Al was taken aback by the beautiful woman his schoolgirl bride had become: there was a strong physical attraction between them and they decided to try and keep their marriage together. The pair of them remained heavy drinkers, booze often worsening Al's temper. Accordingly, Delores asked them to move, and

Al found a room in a cheap hotel, which he paid for with his work at a slaughterhouse. He also legally changed his son's name to James Marshall Hendrix. Jimi, though, 'would never answer to James', according to his brother Leon. 'When we lived in the projects, there was a field house where every Saturday, if you brought a nickel, you could watch fifteen minutes of Buster Crabbe in *Flash Gordon*. So one day he came home, put a cape on and said, "My name is Buster." We've been calling him Buster all our lives.'[5]

As is the case with many black families in the United States, Jimi's upbringing had its religious side. In the Pentecostal church attended by his father he observed and began to take part in the spiritual dancing and music, the songs of praise that were forever being changed and rearranged. His father being the proud owner of a classic record collection, at home Jimi's life was lived out to a soundtrack of the blues: from Elmore James and Muddy Waters to Howlin' Wolf and B.B. King.

Taking employment as a merchant seaman, Al embarked on a boat to Japan. When he returned, months later, Lucille had been evicted from the hotel for non-payment of the rent.

By 1947, Jimi's mother and father had been given an apartment in another housing project. It was so tiny that Jimi (now commonly known as 'Buster') would sleep in a cupboard, where he would hide whenever his parents argued. At one point Lucille even moved out for a month and lived with a Filipino man. Increasingly withdrawn, Jimi developed a slight stutter, for which he would be teased when he started school. The stutter lasted all his life. Like many lonely kids, he also created an imaginary friend, whom he called Sessa; he was his constant companion.

Despite her errant ways and the earlier accusations of neglect, when Lucille was at home she was extremely loving, affectionate and friendly towards her son.

That year, Lucille became pregnant again. The fractious relationship between Jimi's parents calmed down. On 13 January 1948, Leon Hendrix was born, a healthy second son. By the end of the year, another boy had been born. Joseph Allen Hendrix had double rows of teeth, a club foot, a cleft palate and one leg shorter than the other. Each parent tried to blame the other for these abnormalities.

Nervous of the expense involved in caring for his third son, Al began to emotionally withdraw. His latest job as a janitor, secured when he returned from sea, meant they had little money, and his sons were consistently undernourished. For a time, all three boys were sent to live with Al's mother in Vancouver. On returning to Seattle, Jimi lived for a time with Delores.

A sister was born in 1950; she was blind from birth. A second sister was born the next year, and she also had health problems. Both these girls were put into foster care.

In late 1951, Lucille finally left Al, these tragic children weighing heavily on all concerned. In the subsequent divorce, Al was given custody of his sons. This was something of a technicality as they continued to be raised by their grandmothers and aunts. The exception was Joseph, who was made a ward of the state, a heartbreaking separation for the ten-year-old Jimi and a further rendering asunder of his family. This, as Al and Lucille both knew, was the only way their three-year-old son could receive the expensive medical treatment he needed.

In 1954, Leon was removed from under Al's wing and put into foster care – the squalid conditions in which the boys lived with their father had come to the attention of the social services. Jimi had been looking after Leon at home, cooking food for his younger brother from a very early age. Fortuitously, Leon was lodged nearby, and the two brothers still saw each other daily. Buster came close to himself moving into Leon's foster home, spending much time there.

At other times he would be with his aunt Dorothy.[6] 'Doortee', as he called her, had nine children, and Jimi was frequently over at her place, going to church with them on Sundays. A tirelessly conscientious mother, she worked two jobs to keep her children together, sleeping on the couch. These children noted the Hendrix boy's extreme sensitivity, and his tendency to break into tears. 'I'm going to leave here, and I'm going to go far, far away. I'm going to be rich and famous, and everyone here will be jealous.' With considerable prescience, Jimi declaimed these words to his stable, upstanding aunt, perhaps because he could trust 'Doortee' with his inner belief.[7]

Roaming the streets for much of the time, Jimi exposed himself to danger. Years later, he told a girl that some time around his early teens he had been sexually assaulted by a man – a man in uniform, he said – a traumatic experience. His early life was clearly one of constant suffering: so bad were the living conditions at his father's house that in 1955 there were further efforts to place him in care also. Al Hendrix managed to broker a compromise, lodging Jimi for a time in the nearby home of Al's brother Frank. Frank's wife, Pearl, was a 'strong African American matriarchal figure', according to Charles Cross.[8]

A quiet child who gradually revealed an imagination of startling originality, Jimi knew how to listen. He learned to speak only when he had something to say, which would often be encapsulated in just one sentence he would drop into a conversation. Meanwhile, the errant ways of Jimi's mother were driving his father nuts. Lucille continued to make erratic entries and exits into and out of his sons' lives, distractions from Al's best efforts at establishing some order for them. Lucille's demeanour hardly displayed her as a dependable role model.

'My dad was very strict and taught me that I must respect my elders always. I couldn't speak unless I was spoken to first by grown-ups. So I've always been very quiet. But I saw a lot of things. I used to be really lonely. I used to bring a stray dog home every night till my pa didn't let me.'[9]

Trying to keep his boys on the straight and narrow, bringing them up the best way he knew for them to survive, Al Hendrix soldiered on, redoubling his efforts to imbue his boys with various cardinal virtues: politeness and generosity, for example. In their turn, however, his sons felt aggrieved that their father made them work as labourers on various projects for no pay. 'Dad was a gardener and he'd once been an electrician. We had to carry stones and cement all day and he pocketed the money.'[10] All Al was trying to do, however, was ensure that, most of the time at least, there would be food on the table. But a lot of the time they were poverty-stricken and close to starving. Yet in his father's assiduous efforts to raise his boys almost certainly lay the source of the older Jimi's stamina, courtesy, and strange tranquillity.

By the time he reached his teens, Jimi had discovered the primal magic of early rock 'n' roll and R'n'B, and had begun to learn the guitar by practising along to the hot tunes of the day. Before he had an instrument of his own, he played with a broom handle. Then he attached a piece of wood to a large cigar box. But that was later.

The teenage Jimi Hendrix was a great fan of Elvis Presley. On 1 September 1957 he went to see Elvis play at Seattle's Sick's Stadium. This was a chance for the fourteen-year-old boy to see the king of rock 'n' roll in his prime, on his last tour for over ten years. Presley was at the peak of his fame, and his tour through the Pacific Northwest that week included a series of intense fan rioting. Jimi couldn't help but absorb some of the more notable ingredients of Presley's success: his wild stage antics – the impact of which wouldn't be repeated until he took to the stage a decade later – and the fact that Elvis inspired awe by crossing racial boundaries with music.

That same year, Little Richard (who had had a big hit with a song whose title was the same as Jimi's mother's name – 'Lucille') came to Seattle to see his mother, who lived in the city. During a tour of Australia, Little Richard had decided that he should henceforth do only the Lord's work and had flown back to the States. His mother had a place just round the corner from Jimi and his younger brother Leon, and she knew the boys were just nuts about music. So she sent round Little Richard, in penitent mood, to see them in his Cadillac. The brothers were bemused.

An old bluesman lived nearby. Jimi would go and watch him play, sitting out on his stoop of a hot summer evening. He observed how he ran his fingers over the frets, transported by the music despite his age and the oppression lines on his face as he pulled the country blues tunes from deep within him.

Despite his hard life, about Jimi there was always a strange sense of certainty, of knowing the unknown. As he developed his fondness for reading, Jimi discovered that these sensations and vibrations of the strange, angular, and poetic took form and shape in the science fiction that he came to love. Flash Gordon remained Jimi's favourite science fiction character. At school in Seattle this nervous pupil, whose stuttering exposed his sensitivity, painted pictures of life on Jupiter, the planet that astrologers see as a harbinger of good fortune.

'At school I used to write poetry a lot and then I was really happy. My poems were mostly about flowers and nature and people wearing robes. I wanted to be an actor or a painter. I particularly liked to paint scenes on other planets, "Summer Afternoon on Venus", and stuff like that. The idea of space travel excited me more than anything else.

'They said I used to be late all the time, but I was getting As and Bs. The real reason was I had a girlfriend in the art class and we used to hold hands all the time. The art teacher didn't dig that at all. She was very prejudiced. She said, "Mr Hendrix, I'll see you in the cloakroom in three seconds, please." In the cloakroom she said, "What do you mean, talking to that white woman like that?" I said, "What are you, jealous?" She started crying and I got thrown out. I cry easy.'[11]

It was in September 1957, the same month that he had seen Elvis Presley, that Jimi met Carmen Goudy, who would become his first girlfriend. He would need this female figure in his life, for in February 1958 his mother died of a ruptured spleen, exacerbated by cirrhosis of the liver and hepatitis. Al Hendrix would not allow his eldest son to attend the funeral, provoking bitter resentment in the boy and permanently affecting his relationship with his father. Other relatives were also horrified by Al's bad decision. (Later Al confessed to not having had the money to get his boys to the service.) Jimi became extremely withdrawn and hypersensitive. He began to live each day as it came, never planning for the future.

'In his own internal world,' wrote Charles Cross, 'Jimi

began to idealize the mother he had lost, and Lucille increasingly became the subject of the poems and embryonic songs he'd begun writing that spring.'[12] To Jimi's boyish obsession with science fiction and space, he added a new fascination with angels. 'Mama became an angel to him,' Leon said. 'He told me he was sure she was an angel, and she was following us around.'[13]

'One of these days, I'm going to astral project myself up into the skies. I'll be going to the stars and the moon. I want to fly and see what's up there. I want to go up to the sky, from star to star,' Jimi told his aunt Delores the spring that his mother passed away.[14]

Lucille came back to Jimi in dreams; after one he wrote the song 'Angel'. Often thought of as a love song, 'Angel' in fact revealed Jimi's fantasy of his angelic mother returning to earth to collect her son. On some of the early demos for that song, Jimi sang the line 'And she said little boy . . .'

In the song 'Belly-button Window', Jimi was speaking at a spiritual level, with great objectivity, to both his parents. In an extraordinary conceit, Jimi recalled how this earthly existence appeared to him as an embryo in his mother's womb, looking out of her 'belly-button window'. He asked if his parents really wanted him around; if they didn't, he said, he vowed not to return to earth ever again.

'There's some dream I had when I was real little, like my mother being carried away on these camels, and it was a big caravan and you can see the shade, the leaf patterns across her face – you know how the sun shines through a tree, well these were green and yellow shadows. And she's saying, "Well, I won't be seeing you too much anymore, you know, so I'll see you", and about two years after that she died . . . there's some dreams you never forget.'[15]

Friends observed that Al resorted to physical violence with his boys, hitting and strapping his son. Even when Jimi was aged eighteen, Al was still whipping him with his leather belt. All the same, in the spring of 1959, Al finally bought his sixteen-year-old son an electric guitar, a white Supro Ozark, which he paid for on hire purchase.

The instrument was given to him relatively late for someone who would become a master of his craft. In some ways the guitar was a substitute for Lucille, his prodigal mother. The death of his mother marked a watershed: from then on Jimi's true love became his guitar, and during the summer vacation of 1959 he began to work with a variety of bands in his home town. 'Tall, Cool One' by The Fabulous Wailers, a local group who were highly revered, was the first tune Jimi learned to play. He was impressed with a tenor-sax player called Big Jay McNeely, who played his instrument lying on his back, and consequently Jimi tried to make his guitar sound like a saxophone. He played with the Velvetones, who performed jazz, blues and R'n'B, and various other Seattle groups.

One night his guitar was stolen from a club. When he started playing with the Rockin' Kings, formed by a high school friend, the other members clubbed together to buy him a replacement, a white Danelectro Silvertone which came with a matching amp and cost $49.95. The Rockin' Kings showed promise, even claiming second place in the All State Band of the Year contest in Seattle during 1960.

'I always dug string instruments and pianos, but I wanted something I could take home or anywhere . . . Then I started digging guitars. When it was time for us to play on stage I was all shaky, so I had to play behind the curtains. I just couldn't get up in front. And then you get so very discouraged. You hear different bands playing around you and the guitar player always seems like he's so much better than you are. Most people give up at this point, but it's best not to. Just keep on, just keep on. Sometimes you are going to be so frustrated you'll hate the guitar, but all of this is just a part of learning. If you stick with it you're going to be rewarded. If you're very stubborn you can make it.'[16]

Pretty soon The Rockin' Kings were playing regular gigs as far away as Vancouver, 120 miles to the north. When half the group quit, the remaining band members re-formed under the name Thomas and the Tomcats.

As a guitarist, Jimi was particularly fond of Muddy Waters, who made the first serious impact on him of any musician.

'The first guitarist I was aware of was Muddy Waters. I heard one of his records when I was a little boy and it scared me to death, because I heard all those sounds. Wow! What was that all about? It was great. I liked Muddy Waters when he had only two guitars, harmonica and bass drum. Things like "Rollin' and Tumblin'" were what I liked – that real primitive guitar sound.'[17]

As well as Muddy, supplemented by B.B. King, Elmore James and Howlin' Wolf, Jimi was soon also into Jimmy Reed, John Lee Hooker and Roscoe Gordon. He had noted, meanwhile, the way that the great bluesman Charlie Patton played his guitars behind his head. He liked hanging out at a celebrated local club, the Spanish Castle, where The Fabulous Wailers would play. Although they were an all-white group, he offered to play with them.

The pace of life for Jimi was certainly speeding up. In the autumn of 1959, Carmen Goudy now in the past, he started going out with Betty Jean Morgan. (Early in the spring of 1961 he would ask her to marry him, but neither Betty nor her parents took the proposal seriously.) Other girls came calling, but Jimi told his father to say he wasn't at home. Rather than a sign of great moral certainty, however, this was simply a reflection of Jimi's habitual shyness.

Meanwhile, on nights out with his friends, a wildness was raising its head that could cause big problems. In fact, it was beginning to look like music or jail: in May 1961 Jimi was arrested for riding in a car that had been taken without the owner's consent. Jimi said he hadn't known the car was stolen, but still spent a day locked up. Four days later he was arrested again, for riding in another stolen car, for which he spent eight days in juvenile jail. 'I was eighteen. I didn't have a cent in my pocket. I spent seven days in the cooler for taking a ride in a stolen car. But I never knew it was stolen.'[18]

He was only saved from a custodial sentence when his lawyer assured the judge that his client was considering joining the army. The sentence? Two years, suspended, but get your ass down to that recruitment office now. He did. And after basic training he went on to Paratrooper School, graduating in January 1962 to become a 'Screaming Eagle', a parachutist in the 101st Airborne.

Based at Fort Campbell in Kentucky, Jimi was able literally to float in space, at one with the cosmos until his feet hit the ground.

'When you first jump it's really outta sight . . . You're just there at the door and all of a sudden, FLOP! RUSH! For a split second a thought went through me like, You're crazy! . . . It's so personal, because once you get out there everything is so quiet. All you hear is the breeze . . . It's the most alone feeling in the world . . .Then you feel that tug on your collar . . . And so you look up and there's that big, beautiful, white mushroom above you. That's when you begin talking to yourself again, and you just say, "Thank the Lord." That was about the best thing in the army – the parachute drops. I did about twenty-five.'[19]

Back on earth at the military base he was unable to float through life so freely as when he was hanging from a parachute. The local radio stations were immersed in the blues and southern R'n'B, but Jimi's musical obsession, coupled with his introverted nature, provoked open hostility from his fellow soldiers. Comments were made by Jimi's barrack-mates when he slept with his guitar. He spent much of his free time in nearby Nashville, hanging out in the town's myriad music clubs. 'The army's really a bad scene. They wouldn't let me have anything to do with music. They tell you what you are interested in, and you don't have any choice.'[20]

Dream time was very important to Jimi, yet there was little head space for sensitive self-nurturing in the daily military routine. However, he did make one invaluable ally while in the army. Stationed at the same army camp was another soldier with musical inclinations, a bass player called Billy Cox. He and Jimi became friends and started playing together, forming a group called The King Kasuals. They played not only the service lounges but also off-base clubs. This was the only part of his army life in which Jimi could find fulfilment. Cox had decided to quit the force and become a full-time musician. Jimi decided to do the same.

To get out of the army, Jimi pretended to be homosexual, telling the base psychiatrist that he had sexual fantasies about men in his barracks, and that he had become a compulsive masturbator – he was even caught masturbating, almost certainly a deliberate ploy. The story he later gave out, that he had broken an ankle on a parachute jump and was therefore invalided out of the army, was utterly untrue.

'One morning I found myself standing outside the gate of Fort Campbell on the Tennessee-Kentucky border with my little duffle bag and three or four hundred dollars in my pocket. I was going back to Seattle, which was a long way away. But there was this girl I was kinda hung up on.'[21]

Waiting in Clarksville, Tennessee, while Billy Cox served his final three months in the army, Jimi became involved with a woman called Joyce and moved into her apartment. He wrote to Betty Jean, saying he wouldn't be returning to Seattle. Soon he was involved with a string of girls. It was now that Jimi began to practise intensively on his guitar. On occasion he would also purchase illegal amphetamines – the first time he had used drugs.

Then Jimi and bass player Billy Cox moved to Nashville, keeping The King Kasuals going. Johnny Jones of the Imperials became a major influence, essentially because he was the best guitar player in Nashville. The King Kasuals began touring the 'chitlin' circuit, the black showbusiness network of southern bars, theatres and clubs. 'Chitlin' is a corruption of chitterling – pigs' intestines, the cheapest meat, a staple of soul food. And they were considered cheap meat, these acts playing the circuit: it was an uncomfortable hand-to-mouth existence in The King Kasuals. Like many of the other guitarists playing these same southern venues, as well as those anxious to grab a crowd's attention in the sweaty clubs of Southside Chicago, Jimi would play his guitar behind his back or pick his guitar strings with his teeth, emulating such 'chitlin' circuit staples as T-Bone Walker. (Such instrumental acrobatics had their origins in the performances of African musicians, talking drummers who would play with their instruments behind their backs or standing on their heads, for example.)

'I started a group called the Kasuals with a fellow who played funky, funky bass [Billy Cox]. It was pretty tough at first. I was often in a situation where I didn't know where my next meal was coming from.

'I used to have a childhood ambition to stand on my own feet, without being afraid to get hit in the face if I went into a white restaurant and ordered a white steak. But normally I just didn't think along these lines. I had more important things to do – like playing guitar.

'I like Robert Johnson. He's so cool. That sort of music gets the message over and comes through so easily.

'There used to be cats playing behind their heads or playing with their teeth or elbows . . . Some cat tried to get me to play behind my head because I would never move too much. I said, "Oh man, who wants to do all that junk?" . . . The idea of playing guitar with my teeth came to me in a town in Tennessee. Down there you have to play with your teeth or else you get shot.'[22]

In the winter of 1962 Jimi moved up to Vancouver, where he had a regular gig with a local band called The Vancouvers (featuring as lead vocalist one Tommie Chong, later to become half of the comedy duo, Cheech and Chong).

Jimi returned south at the start of 1963. In Atlanta, in need of musicians, Little Richard, who had reconsidered his promise to the Lord to give up rock 'n' roll, hired half the band with whom Jimi was then working; the deal included their guitar player. Jimi would remain with Little Richard for a considerable time, playing not only live dates but also on studio sessions. Although Richard's finest moments had come in the preceding decade, he inevitably influenced the young guitarist; the singer's flamboyance and sheer stage presence made a significant impression.

'He wouldn't let us wear frilly shirts on stage. Once me and Glyn Wildings got some fancy shirts because we were tired of wearing the uniform. After the show, Little Richard said, "Brothers, we've got to have a meeting. I'm Little Richard and I'm the King of Rock and Rhythm and I'm the only one who's going to look pretty on stage. Glyn and Jimi, will you please turn in those shirts or else you will have to suffer the consequences of a fine." He had another meeting over my hairstyle. I said I wasn't going to cut my hair for nobody. That was another five dollar fine. If our shoelaces were two different types we'd get fined another five bucks. Everybody on the tour was brainwashed.'[23]

Soon Jimi found gigs as guitarist with both Solomon Burke and Otis Redding; in each case, after only a few days he was fired for playing too flashily. Then, when working with Motown's Marvelettes, the opening act for Curtis Mayfield, Jimi was sacked when he accidentally destroyed one of Curtis's amplifiers. He continued to use uppers.[24]

Despite his time on the road, Jimi still had no real reputation at all: he was simply another guitar player trying to scrape a living, another hired gun. But he was learning the essence of stagecraft. Gigs, however, were hard to find, although Jimi had one important fan, a friend of Ronnie Isley. Ronnie was a member of The Isley Brothers, who, a few years earlier, had smashed the charts with such hits as 'Twist and Shout' and 'Shout'. The group was looking for a guitar player and Ronnie's friend, who had seen Jimi at an audition, recommended him. The result was regular work with the Isleys, who appreciated him and – less uptight than other soul acts and R'n'B acts – even allowed Jimi to take the occasional solo spot, an invaluable experience. And, in addition to the blues that were already in his DNA, with the Isleys he now really learned the essence of soul music.

Jimi was alive with ideas about stretching the guitar to the max. Such explorations, however, had never been accommodated in his previous bands: the guitarist's function in R'n'B was to follow the singer, embellish the melody lines but never to take the limelight. But despite his rising reputation with The Isley Brothers, Jimi was still not satisfied.

'I played with The Isley Brothers for a while and they used to make me do my thing, because it made them more bucks or something . . . Most groups I was with, they didn't let me do my own thing.'[25]

He was still on tour with The Isley Brothers in January 1964 when they had dates to play in New York City. In Manhattan he quit the group and lived briefly in Harlem. 'I went to New York and won first place in the Apollo amateur contest, you know, twenty-five dollars . . . So I stayed up there, starved up there for two or three weeks. I'd get a gig once every twelfth of never. Sleeping outside between them tall tenements was hell. Rats runnin' all over your chest, cockroaches stealin' your last candy bar from your very pockets. I even tried to eat orange peel and tomato paste.'

At Manny's Music Store on 48th Street Jimi bought his first Fender, a Duosonic. In the concrete canyons of Manhattan he remained ethereal, spacy, intangible, as though he was still floating suspended on that magical parachute. Soon he met a nineteen-year-old girl called Lithofayne Pridgeon – or Fayne, as she was known.

In mid-May 1964 Jimi played on Don Covay's 'Mercy Mercy', the first record he appeared on that made the US pop Top 40. He also made a pilgrimage to meet Steve Cropper, co-writer and guitarist on the soul classic 'Green Onions'.

Then Jimi took a job working for the mysteriously magical Sam Cooke, the king of R'n'B, with whom he stayed almost until the singer's death in December 1964. Back on the road he continued playing behind soul and R'n'B acts. He found an ally in the Chicago bluesman Tommy Tucker, who had hit the charts with his song 'High-Heel Sneakers', and appreciated his guitar-playing and ambition.

Back in Nashville he discovered a kinship with Steve Cropper and then with Albert King, another left-handed guitar player. Out on the package-tour circuit, he finally met and received instruction from B.B. King, a hero.

Playing again with Little Richard's Upsetters band, Jimi decided to quit the tour once it reached Los Angeles. Encountering local rock 'n' roll visionary Kim Fowley there, Jimi informed him that his music was 'science fiction rock 'n' roll'.[26]

While in LA, he encountered a hip black musician called Arthur Lee, then in the process of forming the group Love. Lee needed a guitarist to record a song of his for a single, 'My Diary', sung by Rosa Lee Brooks. Jimi's guitar work on the single was distinctive, mistaken by some for Curtis Mayfield. And despite having given his notice to Little Richard, the pompadoured one requested Jimi's licks on his next single, 'Don't Know What You've Got But It's Got Me' (unfortunately destined to be the first Little Richard single to fail to make the charts).

On New Year's Eve 1964, in Los Angeles, Jimi finally met Rosa Lee Brooks at a show by The Ike Turner Revue – he joined up with Ike Turner's outfit for a time before returning to Little Richard.

Back with Little Richard a third time for a spring tour, things came to a head when they hit New York in April 1965. Three dismal dates at the Paramount Theatre culminated in Little Richard being thrown off the bill. Meanwhile, Jimi managed to miss the tour bus to Washington DC the next morning and was himself canned from the backing group.

It was the proverbial blessing in disguise. In New York Jimi's ambitions were properly focused by the music exploding out of the city. Jimi stayed in Harlem with Fayne Pridgeon or in cheap hotels around sleazy Times Square. Joining up again with The Isley Brothers, he played a one-month New Jersey beach-town residency with them. In Harlem he was confronted by the extraordinary sounds of the latest jazz. Jimi became a big fan of Roland Kirk and Ornette Coleman – especially of the Coleman album *Something Else!!!!* – and John Coltrane.

Such work offered new sonic possibilities for Jimi's own music, a point of departure from his R'n'B roots. His day-to-day playing, however, was less artistically daring. In October 1965, in the lobby of the Hotel America, Jimi met Curtis Knight. Knight had a group called The Squires, who Jimi joined, getting the chance to play the featured star guitar player. Jimi worked with Knight for the next eight months. During that time he also did a 58-show tour with Joey Dee and The Starlighters, hit-makers with 'Peppermint Twist' and house band at the Peppermint Lounge. A racially integrated group, Joey Dee and The Starlighters would play to largely white crowds of up to 10,000.

'Nowadays people don't want you to sing good. They want you to sing sloppy and have a good beat to your songs. That's what angle I'm going to shoot for.'[27]

In Manhattan Jimi began a relationship with Diana Carpenter, a 16-year-old prostitute. She got pregnant by him.[28] He then began a relationship with his first white girlfriend, Carol Shiroky, also a prostitute. In May 1966 he met an English girl called Linda Keith. She was the girlfriend of Rolling Stone Keith Richards, which greatly impressed Jimi. She even lent him one of Keith Richards' guitars.

Then he met Richie Havens, another distinctive black performer, whose set included Bob Dylan's 'Just Like a Woman'. He told Jimi about clubs in Greenwich Village like the Café Wha?, where Jimi would later play his first show with Randy California and Jeff 'Skunk' Baxter.[29]

Jimi moved downtown to Greenwich Village, where he was influenced even more by the lyrical innovations of Bob Dylan that had changed the vocabulary of popular music. *Highway 61 Revisited* was a significant influence, and he began to adopt a look like that of a black Dylan, his hair in particular taking on a look not dissimilar to the singer's. Linda Keith turned Jimi on to Bob Dylan's masterly new album *Blonde on Blonde*, and he spent the last of his food money on buying it.

In 1966, following his last R'n'B sideman gig with the saxophonist King Curtis, Jimi formed his own band and elected to sing for the first time. Away from the rigid confines of working as a background musician, he shaped a new blueprint for the future. His group was called Jimmy James and the Blue Flames and they had a regular spot at the Cafe Wha? in Greenwich Village. Among other tunes Jimi played was a version of Tim Rose's 'Hey Joe'. Word soon spread about this extraordinary black guitarist who even played with his teeth. It was unlike anything else, a glorious noise that challenged all notions of electric music.

When Linda Keith took Rolling Stones manager Andrew Loog Oldham down to the Cafe Wha? to watch Jimi, he didn't get it. However, when she took along Chas Chandler, the bassist from The Animals, Chandler understood it immediately. Overwhelmed by the sheer vivacity of Hendrix's performance ('I thought immediately he was the best guitarist I'd ever seen'[30]), Chandler offered Jimi a management contract and invited him to London. The breakthrough had come.

But really Jimi Hendrix came to England because he had no place else to go. He had no doubts whatsoever about his own abilities – the only problem was in getting other people to recognise them. There he had been, stuck in Manhattan, playing low funky clubs for no money at all, and all of a sudden Chas Chandler served notice that he recognised his talent. The action was happening in England at this time. And here came Chas saying let's go to England. Why the hell not?

On 24 September 1966, the quiet dynamic force that was Jimi Hendrix arrived in London. On the first-class Pan Am flight from New York, he and Chas Chandler had put their heads together and come up with the idea of changing his name from Jimmy to Jimi.

On arriving in London, they stopped off on the way from the airport at Zoot Money's house in Fulham, where the guitarist Andy Summers – a member of Money's Big Roll Band who was later guitarist in The Police – rented a room. 'I was friends with Chas Chandler who had sort of "discovered" him and brought him over. I remember him calling me and telling me he's got this amazing guy. The first time I actually saw him was at Blaises in the Cromwell Road. It was a club that we all used to go to and I walked in and there he was onstage playing with Brian Auger. At the time, of course, it was amazing. He had a white Strat and as I walked in he had it in his mouth and he had a huge Afro and he had on a sort of buckskin jacket with fringes that were to the floor . . . Yeah, it was intense and it was really great. It kind of turned all the guitarists in London upside down at the time. Yeah, I remember when it all started up.'[31]

Also present at the house in Fulham was a twenty-year-old girl called Kathy Etchingham. The next night Kathy watched Jimi play at the Scotch of St James club. She went back to his hotel with him. They would become an established item. 'It happened straightaway,' she said. 'Here was this man: different, funny, coy – even about his own playing.'[32] But Jimi displayed another side of himself: violent when his jealousy was aroused.[33] Expecting another woman to run out of his life as his mother had done, he once attacked Kathy when she was making a phone call: imagining she was talking to another man, he grabbed the phone and beat her around the head with it. (Although he considered it acceptable for him to have sex with groupies backstage even when she was around.) 'People often saw Jimi on stage looking incredibly intense and serious,' she said. 'And suddenly this smile would come across his face, almost a laugh, for no apparent reason. Well, I remember that very well, sitting on the bed or the floor at home in Brook Street [where they rented a flat[34]]. Sometimes, he would play a riff for hours, until he had it just right. Then this great smile would creep across his face or he'd throw his head back and laugh. Those were the moments he had got it right for himself, not for anyone else.'

Chas Chandler introduced Jimi Hendrix to hip England. Following an impromptu jam with Cream at a show at the Regent Street Polytechnic, Jimi became a rising star in London. With his loose velvet clothing and electric hair, he looked as though he was bringing messages from Mars – which he possibly was.

The first priority was to form a group. Within a month Jimi Hendrix had found drummer Mitch Mitchell, formerly with the celebrated Georgie Fame's Blue Flames – the same name, of course, as Jimi's New York band. It was almost like divine providence: Mitch Mitchell, at heart a jazz player, was to prove the only drummer with whom Jimi would have a complete artistic empathy. A great love and respect developed between the two musicians. Not only could Mitch keep up with Jimi's outlandish musical thinking, but Jimi would even listen when Mitch, as stubborn and musically violent as Jimi, disagreed with what the guitarist was trying to do. Jimi, who would intimidate almost all other musicians with whom he played, was unable to have the same effect on Mitch.

Guitarist turned bass player Noel Redding was also taken

on, and The Jimi Hendrix Experience were officially formed on 6 October 1966.

'I was sacked from Georgie Fame's Blue Flames on a Monday,' remembered Mitch Mitchell in 1971.[35] 'Then on the Tuesday John Gunnell mentioned to me that Chas Chandler and Jimi Hendrix, a friend of his, were over here, and would I care to go and have a play. There was Noel and he'd never played a bass in his life, not ever, with his two tiny 15-watt amps. Hendrix arrived in like a Humphrey Bogart raincoat and his Stratocaster with two little Burns amps. We just proceeded to play and I found out that they had already auditioned something like thirty drummers. We just played over various rhythms and that was that. Hendrix said, "Okay, I will see you around." Chas said there was a gig in Paris the next week with Johnny Halliday and asked if we fancied doing it. So we said okay and spent three days rehearsing. Then off we went and that was how it started. There was complete freedom in what we played, it was like escaping from jail.'[36]

The following week The Jimi Hendrix Experience played a four-date French tour supporting Johnny Halliday, the Gallic Elvis.

On 23 October, the band recorded their first two songs, 'Hey Joe' and 'Stone Free', at London's De Lane Lea Studios. The record was cut as an independent production and Chas Chandler went in search of a record deal. Incredibly, he was rejected by a number of companies before The Who manager

Kit Lambert signed the Experience to his new Track Records, distributed through Polydor.

When the single was released at the very end of 1966, The Jimi Hendrix Experience almost immediately became the hottest new group in Britain. 'Hey Joe', the Tim Rose tune which Chas Chandler had heard Jimi play in New York's Cafe Wha?, was an explosion of primal sound and new rhythmic possibilities. The song had been a US pop hit for The Leaves, but Jimi slowed the pace of the number, slurring the vocal while hitting that rich guitar tone that came to distinguish his work. 'Underground rock' had just been born, and the record set the Experience up as the standard-bearers for this new musical movement.

In the UK 'Hey Joe' was released on 16 December 1966, coinciding with the group's debut on the second-to-last edition of the influential television show *Ready Steady Go!*. By February 1967, the record had reached number four in the charts. Its successor, 'Purple Haze', got to number three. Although this second single did not seem as instantly commercial as 'Hey Joe', it was a stronger showcase for Jimi's talents – not only had Jimi written the song, but it showed how he could be both lead and rhythm player at the same time. The psychedelic jolt of Jimi's guitar work on 'Purple Haze' was to become his most identifiable sonic trademark. Jimi was assisted in this by sound experimentalist Roger Mayer, an acoustician for the Admiralty but also a specialist in sound-shifting gadgets for guitarists, whom he had met at a show in Chislehurst on 27 January 1967. When 'Purple Haze' was recorded at London's Olympic Sound Studio on 3 February, Jimi Hendrix used Mayer's octave-divider invention for his overdub solo. 'We started from the premise that music was a mission, not a competition,' said Roger Mayer. 'That the basis was the blues, but that the framework of the blues was too tight. We'd talk first about what he wanted the emotion of the song to be. What's the vision? He would talk in colours and my job was to give him the electronic palette which would engineer those colours so he could paint the canvas.'[37]

'The Wind Cries Mary', the group's third hit, was a beautiful, plaintive ballad, written for Kathy Etchingham when she had stormed out of their home after an argument ('Mary' was her middle name). The trio's debut album, *Are You Experienced?,* was number two to the Beatles' *Sgt. Pepper* through the summer of 1967. 'Hendrix was a magpie,' said the journalist Keith Altham. 'He would take from blues, jazz – only Coltrane could play in that way – and Dylan was the greatest influence. But he'd listen to Mozart, he'd read sci-fi and Asimov and it would all go through his head and come out as Jimi Hendrix. Then there was just the dexterity – he was left-handed, but I remember people throwing him a right-handed guitar and Hendrix picking it up and playing it upside down.'[38]

The time had come to introduce the United States to The Jimi Hendrix Experience. Word of the band's British success had percolated across the Atlantic and Warner Brothers snapped up the US record deal.

In June the group travelled to California to play at the Monterey International Pop Festival. This was a vast open-air concert, a celebration of the burgeoning alternative culture and focus of the Summer of Love, the first such festival. The bill included The Grateful Dead, Jefferson Airplane, Electric Flag, The Byrds, Ravi Shankar, Quicksilver Messenger Service, Country Joe and the Fish, The Steve Miller Band, Buffalo Springfield, Big Brother and the Holding Company, The Mamas and the Papas, Otis Redding and, from Britain, The Who and The Jimi Hendrix Experience.

Jimi's appearance at the festival came courtesy of an important testimonial: that of Paul McCartney, one of the festival's 'board of governors'. In 1967 there could be no more credible recommendation, except possibly for an onstage introduction to the act by Jimi's new friend Brian Jones – which duly took place. The group's performance climaxed when, in a now celebrated moment, Jimi torched his guitar with lighter fluid as they played 'Wild Thing', a phenomenal, powerhouse version of a pop song previously associated with the British group The Troggs. The performance of this tune, as documented in D.A. Pennebaker's film of the festival, is one of the great moments in the history of rock – even though its effect is thoroughly calculated: 'Make sure you've got plenty of film in your camera,' Jim advised photographer Jim Marshall before he went on stage.[39] More than anything, it was this show, culminating in the performance of 'Wild Thing' that broke Jimi in the United States. Jimi Hendrix walked out on to the stage unknown and left it a legend.

When Jimi set his guitar alight at Monterey he was simply taking those chitlin circuit musical histrionics to their most logical extremity. Not only was Jimi a master musician, but he was also a supreme entertainer, capable of holding an audience in the palm of his hand. In time this particular ability of Jimi's would come to haunt him: he became deeply concerned that audiences were coming only to watch him, rather than listen to his music.

Following their US debut at Monterey, The Jimi Hendrix Experience became the hottest new act in the world. Jimi and the group, fuelled by adrenaline-fired energy, were flung into a maelstrom of concerts, recording, promotion and travel.

In Los Angeles in July 1967, Jimi met Devon Wilson, a gorgeous, intelligent 'super-groupie' but also, like so many of Jimi's lovers, a former prostitute with drug problems. For the next three years, she was one of Jimi's regular girlfriends. Like Lucille, his mother, Devon was another very damaged woman.

In southern California Jimi also began going out with Carmen Borrero, a stunning blonde Puerto Rican and former Playboy bunny he had met when she was waitressing at the Whiskey a Go Go on Sunset Strip. In a drunken fit of jealousy, which was becoming something of a familiar pattern, he threw a vodka bottle at her, hitting her above the eye. The wound required stitching up. Alcohol would tip him over the edge, as it had done his parents.

Despite offers from the hippest promoters, Jimi's co-manager, Mike Jeffery, made a curious decision: he booked the band as support act on a tour by The Monkees, the manufactured group who could not have been further in spirit from The Jimi Hendrix Experience. When the dates started it was clear a mistake had been made. Eight days into the tour, The Jimi Hendrix Experience made their excuses (blaming comments from the right-wing Daughters of the American Revolution) and left. After a hastily arranged schedule of showcase concerts, including a week at San Francisco's Fillmore West, Jimi Hendrix and the group returned to Britain in late August.

A new single, 'The Burning of the Midnight Lamp', was released. A song of extraordinary beauty and power, it had the strongest, most insidious melody of all the group's releases up until then. And on 1 December 1967, towards the end of their second British tour (the band's first as headline act), The Jimi Hendrix Experience released a new album. *Axis: Bold as Love* was looser than *Are You Experienced?*. A more melodic, meditative album, it featured songs like 'Little Wing', a song about Jimi's mother, 'If Six Was Nine', 'Castles Made of Sand' and 'Spanish Castle Magic'.

In Tin Pan Alley's tradition of expecting a fast pay-off from pop, *Axis: Bold as Love* was released just before Christmas 1967, a rapid follow-up to *Are You Experienced?*. The record was an enormous seller, but cutting-edge cultural parameters had overtaken the thinking of the men in the music business. As the concept of 'rock' took hold, albums become the central pillars of the new underground. In interviews Jimi emphasised how his latest LP was designed to be listened to in stereo: along with their rivals Cream and Steve Winwood's new group, Traffic, The Jimi Hendrix Experience were one of the first acts perceived by fans as specifically part of this newly dominant format.

In Sweden, in January 1968, Jimi was fined after smashing up his hotel room; and he met – and deflowered – Eva Sundquist.

By February 1968, the group was back in the United States, headlining arenas and theatres. *Are You Experienced?* had sold over a million copies there, and the newly-released *Axis* was rising in the top 40.

The Jimi Hendrix Experience were one of the biggest concert draws in the US, and Jimi made a triumphant return to Seattle when they played at the Center Arena on 12 February. Al Hendrix was in the middle of the front row. It was seven years since Jimi had been back to his home town. Scheduled to appear the next morning at his former high school's assembly, he was hung-over when he arrived there, unable to play the promised show. He revealed to Ernestine Benson that he had to take a pill to sleep and a pill to perform.[40] Ernestine thought Jimi seemed as lost as ever. After Otis Redding, Jimi was the first black sex symbol in the USA: unsurprisingly, in Chicago he famously encountered the 'Plaster Casters of Chicago'.

When the tour ended a few weeks later, Jimi Hendrix lingered in New York. His restless creativity was becoming frustrated inside the rigid trio line-up of the Experience; he wanted to play with other musicians and pitch his ideas in other directions. For Jimi, of course, America was home. For Redding and Mitchell it was but a place to tour and visit. At the height of its success, the winning formula behind The Jimi Hendrix Experience began to dissipate.

Sessions for the new album were fixed at the Record Plant in New York. Although simply credited to The Jimi Hendrix Experience, the eventual album, *Electric Ladyland*, also included contributions from Jack Casady of Jefferson Airplane, Al Kooper, Buddy Miles and, from Traffic, Steve Winwood, Dave Mason and Chris Wood.

Jimi spent much of the year travelling with Mitchell and Redding between Europe and the United States, fulfilling a tortuous schedule of live dates and studio sessions. Jimi also took plenty of time out to jam with other musicians, playing a whole number of ad hoc club sessions with bands and musicians such as Electric Flag, Eric Clapton, Larry Coryell and Jeff Beck. He also spent a considerable time with drummer Buddy Miles, whom he had first met on an Isley Brothers/ Wilson Pickett double-header some years before. Through all the changes, music remained Jimi's fundamental priority. He even sat in with jazz great Roland Kirk at London's Ronnie

Scott's Club, an indication of his increasing fascination with jazz.

On 18 October 1968 'All Along the Watchtower' was issued as a single. Although it was a Bob Dylan song, Hendrix's version was definitive, an epic performance which came as the prelude to the *Electric Ladyland* LP, released the following week. This double album, recorded in both Britain and the United States, represented an extraordinary moment of creativity. It burned with energy, high on ambition and experimentation. *Electric Ladyland* included the near fifteen-minute groove of 'Voodoo Chile' together with its five-minute little sister 'Voodoo Child (slight return)'. It also featured 'Crosstown Traffic', 'Have You Ever Been (to Electric Ladyland)' and, of course, 'All Along the Watchtower'. *Electric Ladyland* established Jimi Hendrix as one of popular music's supreme artists. Not only was he the consummate guitarist of his age, but his unique approach to stage presentation and to music and lyric-writing seemed truly from another world. The soundscapes he created reflected his inner consciousness, the totality of his experience in this and other imagined lives.

Electric Ladyland gave Jimi Hendrix his only number one album in America and, despite the band's internal politics, the Experience were nevertheless the top-grossing act on the US concert circuit. The start of 1969, however, was spent in Britain and Europe. Early in 1969, in Dusseldorf, Jimi met Monika Danneman, a blonde ice-skating instructor. She stayed with him for several days. On 24 February 1969 The

Jimi Hendrix Experience gave their last British performance at London's Royal Albert Hall.

In the middle of March Jimi flew to Manhattan for a month's recording and shows. At first he hung out with Devon Wilson. By now Devon was into cocaine and heroin, and she turned Jimi on to the two drugs. Before Kathy Etchingham arrived from London, Devon vacated the hotel suite. All the same, his London girlfriend was shocked by Jimi's entourage: in her eyes, they were prostitutes and drug dealers. When one of the latter produced a briefcase of cocaine – and a gun – she decided to return to London. This move marked the end of Kathy's relationship with Jimi.

Then came the band's final North American tour, distinguished by Jimi being busted for possession of heroin and hashish when arriving in Toronto on 3 May 1969. In court he eventually beat the charge, claiming the drugs had been put into his bag by fans without his knowledge. The tour ended at the Denver Pop Festival on 29 June, the Experience's last show together. Jimi's restless creativity was consumed by new ambitions. At the height of the band's success, its winning formula was feeling suffocating: The Jimi Hendrix Experience imploded. And Jimi cut off his hair.

By 1969 Jimi Hendrix didn't want to know about burning his guitar or putting on onstage displays of gymnastics: listen to the motherfucker or leave the hall. And so people did start to listen. Critically, however, there was a downside: the phenomenon of Jimi Hendrix was out of favour; he was considered possibly burnt out.

The frictions in the Experience were proving too much. Noel Redding quit the trio and went back to England. Mitch Mitchell also left the band but soon returned to take his place among the pool of musicians Jimi Hendrix was assembling. Jimi, meanwhile, had contacted his old army friend Billy Cox and persuaded him to leave Nashville. Cox's solid, more funky bass style was to be a crucial part of Jimi's new music.

'I'm not sure how I feel about the Experience now. I died a thousand times in that group and was born again. But after a while you have to get yourself straightened out. Maybe we could have gone on but what would have been the point of that, what would it have been good for? It's a ghost now – it's dead, like back pages in a diary. I'm into new things and I want to think about tomorrow, not yesterday.'[41]

In a little less than eighteen months The Jimi Hendrix Experience had released three of the most epochal albums in contemporary music. This burst of creative energy triggered many of the songs that had lain dormant in Jimi's creative psyche ever since he started to express the musical ideas bubbling within him.

A new level had now been reached, however. The public had woken up to him – now he could start dreaming. And there were many more works within him that required a more studied approach than what up until now had essentially been a primal outpouring of art. Financially secure beyond his wildest dreams, Jimi now turned his attention to these larger concepts. He had had ideas for working with orchestras, employing great soundscapes and soundwashes to summon up the music within his head. Unable to read and write musical scores, however, he would scribble out an arrangement in longhand: 'at this point the guitar plays three notes . . .'[42] If he didn't write out new compositions in this way, the only means to prevent them vanishing into the ether was to rush into the studio and immediately record them. All the same, Jimi began to feel frustrated about his lack of orthodox musical training, and planned in the near future to learn to write music formally. He needed to start expanding and expressing all the ideas that he had.

Music that went even beyond jazz was now at the forefront of Jimi's mind. 'I hear sounds in my head and if I don't get them together, then no one will,' he said.[43] Around the same time Jimi was introduced to the producer Alan Douglas, who soon became a close friend. Through the course of the year they worked on various projects, including the soon-to-be-unveiled musical collective the Band of Gypsys.

'We're making our music in electric church music,' Jimi once explained to a writer for the *East Village Other*, '– a new kind of Bible, a Bible you can carry in your hearts, one that will give you a physical feeling . . . [Rock] is more than music, it's like church, like a foundation for the lost or potentially lost.[44]

'You hypnotize people to where they go right back to their

natural state, which is pure positive – like in childhood when you got natural highs. That is why the name "electric church" flashes in and out.[45]

'When I get up on stage – well, that's my whole life. That's my religion. I am electric religion.'[46]

Thus resolved within himself, the songwriting of Jimi Hendrix became even more extraordinary. Many of his songs until now had had a linear structure – although highly achieved and beautiful as they were in their own right. Jimi would refer to tunes like 'Purple Haze' or 'Crosstown Traffic' as his 'cartoon songs'. Works like the new 'Cherokee Mist', however, were constructed almost on classical lines, built around progressions and movements. Even earlier songs like 'Castles Made of Sand', with its musical evolution and reprises, suggested the complexities that were to come.

'1983, a Merman I Should Turn to Be', meanwhile, was another indication that here we were dealing with a master composer. Apart from its extraordinary subject matter – not many songs had previously had lyrics about living underwater – it was a musically inspired composition, with Jimi exploring musical places you would not think would be available within the structure of the song. And the lyrical subject matter of '1983' was in many ways as unique as the song's musical context. Science fiction truly inspired Jimi: who always had one foot in this world and one in the next.

In songs like 'Third Stone from the Sun' there was real wit in his words: Jimi returned to earth and the most intelligent life forms he found there were chickens. Where does this shit come from? Not, certainly, from the acid he would regularly ingest – Jimi wouldn't be taken places by acid; he'd tell the acid where to take him. No, Jimi's poetic thinking was harnessed to a mind naturally attuned to science fiction. He was bored beyond belief by the mundane aspects of life. Which is why he would constantly run to his beloved guitars.

The rush of ideas never stopped, never let up. In mid-conversation his eyes would all of a sudden rise upwards as he spaced out on the latest creative flash that had shot through him. The ideas were impossible to control and never gave him a break. All the time, he was thinking about his music – new songs, new ideas. Sometimes this inability to stop the flow of creativity became nerve-racking, draining.

Alan Douglas's jazz connections provided fresh avenues of musical exploration. It was through Douglas that one of the most intriguing projects was proposed: a Jimi Hendrix/Miles Davis album. Alas, the idea foundered because of Miles's financial demands.

In July 1969, accompanied by Stella Douglas, Alan's wife, and others, Jimi Hendrix went to Morocco for nine days, the only holiday he ever had. While in Morocco an elderly woman gave him a tarot reading – the Death card came up, freaking Jimi out.

On 6 August 1969, Jimi flew back to New York, via Paris's

Charles de Gaulle airport. Running into Brigitte Bardot while in transit, he went AWOL with her for two days.

In August 1969, for a $32,000 fee, Jimi Hendrix appeared at the Woodstock Music and Art Fair in upstate New York, playing with the Band of Gypsys, a loose pool of musicians. 'We decided to change the whole thing around and call it Gypsy Sun and Rainbows,' Jimi announced on stage. 'For short it is nothing but a Band of Gypsys.' Hendrix's Band of Gypsys featured Mitch Mitchell, Billy Cox and rhythm guitarist Larry Lee, with Juma Sultan and Jerry Velez on percussion.

Woodstock was the biggest celebration of the counterculture, billed as three days of peace and music. The organisers had reckoned on an audience of 100,000 people; in the event nearly 500,000 turned up. The massive logistical problems, amplified by dramatic and torrential rainfall, meant the festival overran disastrously.

It was intended that Jimi would go on stage at eleven o'clock on Sunday night and close the festival. In the manner of all things at Woodstock, however, he was interminably delayed. In the end, however, it seemed that in this endless procrastination about when Jimi would appear on stage there was some form of divine plan. By the time he stepped out onto the boards at 7.30 on the Monday morning, the spectacle was extraordinary. The sun was rising; contrasted against it, the festival site looked and smelled like a war zone.

Jimi was unveiling his new line-up for the first time, and the show was initially ragged. He had not felt well as he waited for his slot finally to arrive. But then he hit 'The Star-Spangled Banner'. The Band of Gypsys' impressionistic interpretation of the American national anthem was like the manifesto of the new time they were ushering in, ripping up the anthem's traditional values and reshaping them with Utopian passion. It seemed as though a coup had taken place in humanity's collective soul. This wordless performance, delivered at the height of America's civil rights unrest and Vietnam War turmoil, was a compelling and eloquent statement. The new music that followed on for the rest of the set revealed itself as magical, floating, clearly inspired from on high. Jimi became a pure poet of his instrument. 'I have plans that are unbelievable,' he had promised.[47]

'With the Experience there was more room for ego-tripping. All I had to blast off the stage was the drummer and the bass player. Now I want to step back and let other things come forward.

'Woodstock was groovy. The non-violence, the very true brand of music, the acceptance of the crowd, how they had to sleep in the mud and the rain and get hassled by this and that. There's so many scores you can add up on this thing. If you added them all up you'd feel like a king. I'd like for everybody to see this kind of festival, see how everybody mixed together in harmony.'[48]

Jimi hung out in New York. He took an apartment downtown, on the edge of the Village, on Sixth Avenue and West 12th Street. At the Record Plant he made a block booking, although he rarely arrived to work there much before midnight. In the evenings he would turn up at Alan Douglas's house and listen to his stories about Charlie Mingus and Art Blakey and Coltrane and Miles. Douglas was producing The Last Poets, perhaps the first rap record, and Jimi was fascinated by this, even recording with Jalal, the group's leader.

Jimi flew Carmen Borrero over to NYC from Los Angeles. She moved into the West 12th Street apartment with him and they spent Christmas together. But again Jimi attacked her with a bottle while drunk, the spectre of Lucille ever present.

On New Year's Eve 1969, the Band of Gypsys played the Fillmore East in New York. The group was now a trio, with Buddy Miles and Billy Cox featuring in an all-black line-up. The shows (the group also played on New Year's Day) were recorded, resulting in the Band of Gypsys' album, released the following April. The LP included an exceptional performance of Hendrix's strident anti-war song 'Machine Gun'. 'That first set was really tight. It was scary. Buddy's going to do most of the singing from now on. I'd rather just play.'[49]

On 28 January the Band of Gypsys headlined a benefit concert for the Vietnam Moratorium Committee at New York's Madison Square Garden. Hendrix, however, had to leave the stage after two numbers, a victim of illness. The show was, coincidentally, the last performance by this line-up.

Through the summer months of 1970, Hendrix played the 'Cry of Love' tour in America as a part of a trio. His rhythm section had now stabilised: Mitch Mitchell had replaced Buddy Miles and Billy Cox was on bass. This US tour began at the Los Angeles Forum on 25 April. Among the dates were appearances at Berkeley, Rainbow Bridge in Hawaii and the Atlanta Pop Festival, as well as a 4 May benefit in New York for acid guru Timothy Leary. This line-up of the Band of Gypsys – still frequently billed as The Jimi Hendrix Experience – was burning, Mitchell and Cox proving to be Jimi's finest rhythm section. Never intimidated by Jimi, as other drummers often were, Mitch drove the group, as Billy Cox fed Jimi bass lines. And Jimi's guitar playing was extraordinary.

'When I was in Hawaii I saw a beautiful thing . . . a miracle. There were lots of rings around the moon and the rings were all women's faces. I wish I could tell someone about it.'[50]

Jimi Hendrix was also working overtime in the recording studio. He was planning another double album, to be called *First Rays of the New Rising Sun*, which was to be a reflection of the profound musical level he was working at – part of it was released posthumously as *The Cry of Love*. He was also starting to write music for a big band, 'a new form of classical music'.[51]

The idea for Jimi to have his own studio had been percolating since 1968, in essence because of his habit of block-booking the Record Plant at peak rates. Jamming in the studio was not a cost-effective exercise at the best of times and Jimi's recording expenses mounted at a simply astronomical rate. Plans for the new studio, Electric Lady, were drawn up in conjunction with Jimi's long-time recording associate

Eddie Kramer. Electric Lady was planned as a state-of-the-art facility – red carpeting, curved white walls, a floating ceiling with a remote-controlled theatrical lighting system plus film projection suite.

'There is one thing I hate about studios and that is the impersonality of them. They are cold and blank and within a few minutes I lose all drive and inspiration. Electric Lady is different. It has been built with great atmosphere so it makes people feel like they are recording at home. I want it to be an oasis for all the rock musicians in New York.

'I'm working on my own album which will have about twenty tracks on it. It will be a double set again and some tracks are getting very long. But, you see, our music doesn't pertain to one thing. You don't have to be singing about love all the time in order to give love.'[52]

At the same time, Jimi and Alan Douglas were planning a jazz collaboration with the great arranger Gil Evans, whose work in the late 1950s and early 1960s with Miles Davis yielded some of the landmark albums of contemporary music. They agreed to embark on the project once Jimi had returned from his European tour in the late summer. It was to be called *Voodoo Child Plays the Blues*, and it was intended that Jimi would stand up in front of an orchestra and play, as Miles Davis had done so effectively with Evans on *Sketches of Spain* and *Miles Ahead*.

On 26 August 1970, the night before he was set to fly to London to play at the Isle of Wight festival, the Electric Lady

Studios opened in Manhattan, at 52 West 8th Street. Retiring from the throng of the opening party inside, Jimi came upon a young singer-songwriter sitting out on the building's stoop – Patti Smith. 'Out came Jimi and sat next to me. And he was so full of ideas; the different sounds he was going to create in this studio, wider landscapes, experiments with musicians and new soundscapes. All he had to do was get over back to England, play the festival and get back to work.'[53]

Jimi and the Cry of Love band arrived in England for their only UK date, headlining at the Isle of Wight Festival on 30 August, an event soured by tensions and bad weather. By the time the Cry of Love band hit the stage, it was Monday morning, the early hours of 31 August.

In London Jimi had met Kirsten Nefer, a 24-year-old Danish model, and he took her to the Isle of Wight with him. In Denmark he asked her to marry him. But in London on 12 September that old pattern reasserted itself: he lost it with Kirsten, shaking her in a jealous rage. She left the hotel and called him over the next few days but heard nothing back. This was because Monika Danneman had reappeared the day she left.

The Isle of Wight was followed by a week of European concerts during which Billy Cox was handed a drink spiked with LSD. He had a traumatically bad reaction and the group's final dates were scrapped. Jimi brought Cox back to London, where he could recover away from the pressures of touring.

'I'm thinking of the days when people will be able to

have this little room, a total audio-visual environment type of thing. So that you can go in there and lay back and the whole thing just blossoms with colour and sound. Like a reflection room. You can just go in and jingle out your nerves. It would be incredible if you could produce music so perfect that it would filter through you like rays and ultimately cure.

'I want to wake up in the morning and just roll out of my bed into an indoor pool, swim to the breakfast table, come up for air and maybe get a drink of orange juice and . . . you know . . . a shave. Is that luxurious? I was thinking about a tent, maybe overhanging a mountain stream.'[54]

Jimi Hendrix stayed in London with Monika Danneman at her rooms at the Samarkand hotel in Lansdowne Crescent in Notting Hill, yards from Ladbroke Grove. Two days before Jimi died, Monika Danneman was bloodied in a catfight with Devon Wilson, who had flown to London to see him. All the same, Jimi did the social rounds and jammed with Eric Burdon and War at Ronnie Scott's Club.

'I am planning a world tour and this will be either before or after Christmas. There are lots of places we want to play. I want to go to Japan and Australia. We really want to come back to England and do one big concert at each of the major cities.'[55]

On the night of Thursday 17 September, Jimi took some sleeping pills so he could sleep through the next day and leave London the following Monday.

Early the next morning Monika Danneman noticed Jimi

had vomited during the night. He seemed to be breathing normally, however, and she felt no reason to panic. A little later she tried to wake him but Jimi remained unconscious. This time Monika Danneman was really alarmed. After first phoning Eric Burdon for advice, she called an ambulance.

On 18 September 1970 Jimi's soul reunited with the cosmos and with his troublesome mother, Lucille. His last and greatest trip.

'My goal is to be one with the music. I just dedicate my whole life to this art . . . Something new has got to come, and Jimi Hendrix will be there. I attribute my success to God. It all comes from God. I go by message. I'm really a messenger from God. My name is nothing but a distraction. Forget my name. Remember it only as a handshake.'[56]

JANIS JOPLIN

'I'll kill anyone who tries to stop my success'

On Saturday 3 October 1970, Bobby Womack received a phone call at his Los Angeles home.[1] It was from Janis Joplin, who was recording in the city at Sunset Sound studios. 'Everybody tells me they have recorded at least one of your songs,' she told the great soul singer and songwriter. 'I just want to say I've recorded one. Can you bring me a song?'

At first Womack was not convinced the call was from her. To reassure him, she put her producer, Paul Rothchild, on the line.

Bobby Womack drove over to Sunset Sound. 'She was a real fruit-cake: she had every piece of fruit on her hat,' Womack recalled.[2] She was also holding a small bell. 'Play your songs,' she instructed him, 'and every time I don't like something I will ring it.'

The first tune that Womack played for her was one called 'Trust Me'. Janis didn't ring the bell. 'I love it, that's the song. Bobby, we got one.'

For the next couple of hours, Bobby played her all the

other songs he had brought down. After each of these numbers – or even before they had been completed – Janis would ring her bell. Eventually she told him that she had never intended to sing more than one of his tunes, and had already established that it would be 'Trust Me'.

Then she asked him to stick around and play on the song, which she intended to record immediately. 'We showed "Trust Me" to her outfit, The Full Tilt Boogie Band, cut it and wrapped it up.'[3]

Womack noted that throughout this time at the studio, Janis Joplin seemed depressed and tearful. He heard her on the phone, speaking with her latest boyfriend, Seth Morgan; he wouldn't come to Los Angeles to visit her, Womack overheard, unless she sent him some money. 'I heard her scream into the phone, "You always want money from me, that's all you want."'[4] Bobby Womack put his comforting arms around the distressed singer. But his actions, he felt, were to no avail: Janis had been hitting the Southern Comfort. 'I'd only met her that day, but I could see the girl's life was in turmoil, a whole mess of trouble.'[5]

Because she had been drinking, Janis decided to leave her Porsche in the studio's parking lot; could Bobby Womack give her a ride to where she was staying, at the nearby Landmark Hotel?

Womack led her to his new Mercedes 600.

Janis was extremely impressed. 'How'd you get a car like this?' she asked him.

'From writing songs for people like you,' came Bobby Womack's direct answer.

As they drove towards her hotel on Franklin Avenue, a couple of lines suddenly slipped out of Janis's mouth: 'Oh Lord, won't you buy me a Mercedes Benz / My friends all drive Porsches, I must make amends . . .'

Insisting that the soul maestro turn his vehicle around and return to the studio, they headed back to Sunset Sound, Janis completing writing the song en route.

The Full Tilt Boogie Band had already departed, and Paul Rothchild himself was readying to leave. Janis Joplin persuaded him otherwise. With Womack on electric guitar and Janis on acoustic, they quickly put the number down on tape.

Again, they left the studio. Now it was around midnight.

Back at the Landmark Hotel, they headed for Janis's room, number 105.

Sitting there, talking, listening to Bobby Womack's *Lookin' for a Love* album – which she had asked him to bring in to the hotel from his Mercedes – Janis told him that she wanted to cross over to black audiences. 'I don't want to be Tina Turner. I want to be Janis Joplin and I want to go out on the black side of town and be able to sing and show those people that I used to sing for drinks in New Orleans . . . You take me to the ghetto and I'll take you to the white side of town,' she proposed.

Then Janis began to open up, revealing her myriad insecurities, telling Womack how kids at her school would call her ugly and that now they viewed her as a freak; all she wanted, she said, was to be loved. 'I understood how vulnerable she had become,' he recalled.[6]

Bobby Womack felt that they might end up having sex. But instead the subject of drugs raised its head. Why did she do heroin? he asked her. 'She told me she became a user to bury all her thoughts and deaden her from the world. "Because it lays me back."'[7]

But then she took a call. Her smack connection was on his way over, and Womack had better leave.

They hugged, and Bobby Womack left the Landmark.

Apart from her heroin dealer, the soul legend was the last person to see Janis Joplin alive.

Janis Joplin was born in Port Arthur, Texas, on 19 January 1943, to Dorothy (née East), a 30-year-old registrar at a business college, and her husband, 33-year-old Seth Ward Joplin, an engineer at Texaco (in its heyday, Port Arthur was considered to be the 'oil capital of the world'). Both were supporters of the Republican Party. Janis had two younger siblings, Michael and Laura. The family attended the Church of Christ, and would say grace before each meal.

In the Lone Star State in the 1930s, people would describe Janis Joplin's mother, Dorothy, as 'the Lily Pons of Texas', because of her splendid operatic soprano. Dorothy also adored the music of Cole Porter. 'She sang at any opportunity, which in Amarillo [where she had been raised] meant church, weddings, and the Kiwanis club,' wrote Laura, her second daughter.[8]

Both parents were driven by intellectual concerns, Janis's cigarette-smoking flapper mother a fan of Dostoevsky and Tolstoy. Her father, Seth, would smoke still-legal marijuana and make bathtub gin:[9] hard-drinking was part of Texan culture. (At university in Austin Janis would later write a song called 'What Good Can Drinking Do?' in which she described how she might drink all night, but 'still feel blue'.[10]

As a very young child, Janis was taught to play the piano by her mother, busking along to nursery rhymes. Over such a choice of material, however, her father took offence – only the music of Frederic Chopin was good enough for him. Before she was six, the piano had been sold. (Seth had a private reason for this: Dorothy had had a thyroid operation that irrevocably changed the sound of her voice, effectively spoiling it, a flaw emphasized when she would sing with Janis around the piano.)

Port Arthur was an inland port, linked by a 20-mile canal to the Gulf of Mexico. Only four feet above sea level, and distinctly provincial, although known for its excellent schools, the city had a population of 57,000 people. Semi-tropical, during autumn it had a pronounced rainy season. 'What's happening never happens there. It's all drive-in movies and Coke stands on the corner, and anyone with ambition like me leaves as soon as they can or they're taken over, repressed, and cut down,' Janis said later.[11] What Janis was omitting from her memory of her hometown was that it had a wild underbelly, catering to the various needs of the merchant sailors who worked on the oil tankers. For such characters, whorehouses were the principal social centres; the establishment run by one Marcella Chadwell was the most celebrated, but there were others with sizable reputations, such as Grace's Wood Yard. Once Janis and some girlfriends stole a construction sign and stuck it in front of Grace's; it read, 'Men at Work'.[12] For non-participants in such a world, however, many of whom did not realize such institutions even existed, redneck Port Arthur was suffocatingly straitlaced. (In 1961 these brothels were shut down, and the town cleaned up.)

Janis Lyn Joplin's birth was slightly premature, three weeks prior to her expected date. With a broad, intelligent forehead and curly blonde hair, the young girl was clearly spirited and sensitive.

Despite his orthodox employment, and his taking against nursery rhymes, Seth encouraged his wife's cultural aspirations for their children. All the kids would be taken on weekly trips to the local public library – learning was understood to be at a premium. Janis herself demonstrated a real talent for art, with innate drawing abilities.

Early in her teens she had a summer job, working as an intern at the local library when she was 14, momentarily becoming a local celebrity. That she was doing the artwork for the institution's posters, a series illustrating *The Wizard of Oz*, was picked up by the local press: The *Port Arthur News* photographed her in front of one of her illustrations. Beneath the headline 'Library Job Brings Out Teenager's Versatility', Janis Joplin was quoted in the article: 'It gives me a chance to practice art and at the same time to do something worthwhile for the community.'[13] (Later in her teens Janis was very much a painter, taking up oils.) What the newspaper article did not mention was that, according to her classmate David W. McFadden, 'she had a reputation for going out behind the public library on school nights to make out with boys.'[14] Later she would comment in interviews on how she had been ostracized at high school. 'Janis Joplin got a category all to herself: slut,' said her classmate James Ray Guidry.[15] As a member of the First Christian Church choir, she had a reputation for letting boys feel her up after practice was over. 'If you want to make out, take Janis Joplin home,' remembered another member of the choir, the Reverend Darrell Evans.[16] It could be said, of course, that in right-wing, neurotically conventional Port Arthur, Janis Joplin was simply more courageous than others of her own age: two decades later, her behaviour would have been seen as almost conventional.

All the same, at Thomas Jefferson High School, she worked on her high school literary magazine, the *Driftwood*, both writing and illustrating. She also wrote for the *Sea Breeze*, the school paper. This was one of the few areas at the school where she felt she fitted in.

Indeed, at that time much of her life seemed consumed by teenage angst. In Texas you could acquire a driving licence at the age of fifteen, which offered a measure of independence. But after crashing her father's car and failing to halt at a stop sign, her sister felt 'Janis was crushed, embarrassed, frustrated, and upset that she had failed so miserably. It was just another sign that she didn't measure up to the standards of the world.' [17]

After the publication of Jack Kerouac's *On the Road* in 1957, Janis and her gang idolized the very notion of Dean Moriarty and the Beats. As though to assert her bohemian approach to life she started a relationship with one Rooney Paul, an *American Graffiti*-style rocker with ducktailed, greased-back hair and a black leather jacket, a quintessential Leader of the Pack; to add to his authenticity, he worked at a local drive-in cinema. Although they were only boy- and girlfriend for a brief period, they continued to be friends throughout high school.

During this time, Janis Joplin got into the poetry of Lawrence Ferlinghetti and Allen Ginsberg's *Howl,* but also the widely popular pulp crime fiction of Mickey Spillane. Meanwhile, through a friend, Janis was turned on to such black blues singers as Leadbelly, Odetta and, especially, Bessie Smith, known in the early 1920s as the 'Empress of the Blues', and legendary for her drinking. When she was herself a star, Janis Joplin paid for a headstone for Bessie Smith's unmarked grave; Smith had died after a car accident, having been refused admission to a Southern white hospital. It was by studying Smith's vocals that Janis taught herself to sing the blues.

Unsurprisingly for a city in the southern United States, Port Arthur had a large black community. This was distinctly separated from the rest of the city, however. When Janis spoke up for the oppressed black minority – 'Society's treatment of the black person is wrong! They are people like you and me.'[18] – she was derided locally as a 'nigger lover' and fellow students would spit on her.

In 1958 Janis and her friends would cross the nearby state border into Vinton, Louisiana, where the drinking age was 18, despite the fact that she had not yet reached even that age. On 26 January 1960, she drove with some male friends the 260 miles to New Orleans in Louisiana to listen to music. There, they barhopped, listening to a number of acts. Again, she had borrowed her father's car – saying she would be visiting a friend in Port Arthur – and had a further minor collision. This alerted Louisiana police to the fact that she was underage, and travelling with older boys. The grim spectre of the Mann Act reared its head, with its implications of statutory rape charges – despite the fact that this trip had all been Janis's idea. Janis's mother had to stand up for the good characters of all involved; only then did the Louisiana police release them from custody.

However, this trip across the state line was the occasion for considerable tension within the family home. It also turned Janis Joplin into a figure of gossip at her high school. 'Our parents,' wrote her sister, Laura,[19] 'saw Janis damaging her reputation, a thing so important and nebulous that a girl was supposed to do anything to keep it pure.' Janis's maternal grandfather had been indiscreet about his own affairs, which had troubled Dorothy Joplin and worried her about the course on which her daughter seemed to be set. The more liberal Seth Joplin gave his eldest daughter more support. But all the same both parents agreed to send her for counselling.

All that Janis Joplin was really doing was simply searching for people with whom she could empathize. Aged 17, Janis went to Lamar State College of Technology in Beaumont, Texas, 30 miles from Port Arthur, where she majored in art. Her favourite artist was Amedeo Modigliani, almost the personification of the bohemian artist. She was extremely impressed that he had spent much of his life drinking and smoking hashish, ignoring the fact that this was largely to mask his tuberculosis.

However, she soon realized that Lamar State College, which had a large engineering faculty for prospective oil industry workers, was not the place for her. Janis left and enrolled at Port Arthur Business College, where her mother worked as a registrar, to learn clerical skills.

That year, 1961, Janis started playing music with her friend Patti McQueen. Employing her father's reel-to-reel tape recorder, she attempted for the first time to put her voice onto tape: she was unimpressed with the results.[20]

Janis's parents were equally unimpressed with the gang she ran with at that age. Her mother's two sisters, Barbara and Mimi, lived in Los Angeles. Between them they came up with a scheme: to move Janis to Los Angeles, where she could be under the eye of her aunts, while experiencing the city's burgeoning art scene.[21] That summer, Janis set off on a Greyhound bus on the 1,600 mile-journey to the southern Californian city. She moved into an artist's cottage at the rear of Mimi's Brentwood home, more usually used by Mimi's husband, Harry, also a painter.

Soon, however, Janis moved to stay with Mimi's sister Barbara. Something of a freethinker,[22] Barbara's day would often begin with a male friend coming over at 10 a.m. to kick-start the day with a martini; and the cocktail hour would begin at Barbara's at 4 p.m. Janis was impressed with such a lifestyle, so opposite to what she had known with her parents; possibly Barbara was not the best of role models.

Then Janis discovered the Los Angeles beatnik suburb of Venice. By 1961 this multi-racial, beachfront district had become rather tricky. The area was past its creative peak, which had been signalled in Lawrence Lipton's book *The Holy Barbarians*, the apotheosis of the world of the Beats.[23] By now, it was somewhat rundown. Drugs were available, largely marijuana, but also, to some extent, heroin. Janis found an apartment in the district, and took employment at a local branch of the Bank of America. At night she would hang out at the Venice West Café. 'She had a reputation of being really smart and really nice. We thought of her as benignly bisexual – she had both a girlfriend and a boyfriend,' said Anna Hull, who knew her then.[24]

The Gas House was the most famous – or infamous – coffee house in Venice. While hanging out at the Gas House, Janis Joplin learned of the existence of San Francisco's North Beach arts scene. Despite offers of bus fare from her aunts, Janis hitchhiked the 400 miles to San Francisco. In the City Lights bookstore she encountered the proprietor, poet and painter Lawrence Ferlinghetti, whose poetry had so impressed her and who had been the proprietor of the store since 1955. The following year he had published Allen Ginsberg's *Howl*, which Janis also adored, and been arrested for obscenity.

Just before Christmas 1961, Janis returned to Port Arthur. On New Year's Eve she went with her friend and mentor Jim Langdon to a local club and sang one song with a small jazz band. After her tune, the band leader uttered, 'Enough.' He had not been expecting Janis's gruff tones.[25]

While working the evening shift waitressing in the restaurant of a local bowling alley, Janis revealed the core of rebellion that persisted within her: 'I want to want the white house with the picket fence covered with climbing roses, but I don't,' she admitted.[26]

By now Janis was drinking heavily, often in nearby Louisiana bars.[27] On one drunken evening at Patti and Dave McQueen's apartment, Patti and Janis kissed each other on the mouth, shocking each other. But nothing further ever occurred between them.

*

In 1962 Janis enrolled as an art student at the University of Texas in Austin, 250 miles from Port Arthur.

This was at the beginning of legally-ordained racial integration, when segregated bathroom facilities were removed from the institution. Yet Janis and her friends called themselves 'the Ghetto crowd', an attempt by this bohemian intellectual set to be deliberately confrontational and challenging of authority. 'I wish I was black because black people have more emotion,' she confided while in Austin.[28] She would wear a Second World War flying jacket, often inside out, later tearing off its sleeves to accommodate the Texan heat. The word 'fuck' was omnipresent in her vocabulary, used deliberately provocatively.

After only having been in Austin for four weeks, Janis Joplin found herself featured in the *Summer Texan*, the college newspaper: '"Jivey" is what Janis calls herself, not "Beat". She leads a life that is enviably unrestrained . . . She doesn't bother to get her hair set every week, or to wear the latest feminine fashion aids, and when she feels like singing, she sings in a vibrant alto voice.'[29] The article also revealed that she would sometimes go about her day 'shoeless'.

Another, more alternative, local paper was the *Texas Ranger*, edited by the cartoonist Gilbert Shelton, later the creator of the *Fabulous Furry Freak Brothers*.

Later she went out with another editor from the *Texas Ranger*, Bill Killen. He liked to take girls to graveyards in his hearse.[30] When he read her an article about LSD making people want to jump out of windows, Janis immediately expressed an interest in trying the drug. All the same, while going out with Bill, Janis changed her look, wearing high heels and pretty dresses.[31] A perpetual scourge of youthful relationships blighted their love, however: Janis lived in a lodging house, and Bill was constantly shifting digs, which meant they had almost nowhere to be alone together.

Everyone on campus seemed to drink a lot. Janis was also partial to smoking grass – in some measure because it was illegal – and experimented with peyote, which was still legal, and available at a local garden centre.

While in Austin, she had what in retrospect can be seen as a life-changing experience: she fell in love with Bob Dylan's first album, believing folk music to be society's saving grace. Around this time she also took up the autoharp.

In fact, her love of Dylan and folk simply marked her out as a rider of the zeitgeist: when, for example, a former University of Texas alumnus called Chet Helms passed through in August that year, he was astonished at the wealth of folk music in the city. This showed how Austin was in tune with the spirit of the times; across the nation the folk scene was in full bloom, and Peter, Paul and Mary were a national concert draw, earning $7,500 per show.

A Texan, Helms was now living in San Francisco, where, he assured Janis, there was now a music scene that hinged around a folk rock sound. Moreover, he assured her, she could really do something with her singing voice in the northern

Californian city. To save money for her move there, Janis began shoplifting her food.[32]

Finally, midway through January 1963, with considerable trepidation,[33] Janis Joplin hitchhiked to San Francisco with Chet Helms, a trek in which they spent 50 hours on the road.

The centre of the San Francisco scene which Chet Helms had described remained Lawrence Ferlinghetti's City Lights Pocket Book Shop. But by the time Janis arrived in San Francisco's North Beach, the energy of this exciting world was starting to ebb. All along, it had been fuelled by coffee and Benzedrine. At the Coffee Gallery in North Beach, Janis would frequently sing. Among the other musicians regularly playing there was shaven-headed guitarist James Gurley, later to join Janis in Big Brother and the Holding Company. Another future member of the group, guitarist Sam Andrew, played jazz at the same venue.

At the Coffee Gallery Janis met and befriended Linda Gottfried, a 19-year-old Los Angeleno, who, down in the dumps, had been advised to visit the venue and watch Janis Joplin. Similar spirits, they clicked, and Linda moved into the basement of the house on Sacramento Street where Janis was living. To get about the hilly city, Janis acquired a Vespa motor scooter.

That year, 1963, Janis Joplin took part in a broadcast by a local radio show, with Peter Albin, a country-blues guitarist.

*

During the summer of 1963, Janis hitchhiked to New York to check out Greenwich Village, the home of the Beat Movement.

In New York,[34] she took a job as a keypunch operator – as her parents had hoped, that spell at Port Arthur technical college had stood her in good stead.

Methedrine was extremely popular in New York City that year; Janis dabbled in the drug, but hardly to the extent she did later. She moved into an apartment on the rundown Lower East Side, and began performing in Manhattan, singing in a gay bar.

Having purchased a British Morris Minor convertible, a stylish classic of the marque, she drove back to San Francisco, via Port Arthur. In her hometown Janis presented her sister, Laura, with her old six-string guitar; in New York she had bought her own twelve-string instrument. The two sisters spent a night playing together, before Janis headed off on the highway to San Francisco, dropping in on friends in Austin along the way.

Not long after Janis returned to San Francisco, the United States was stricken by a national crisis: on 22 November 1963 President John F. Kennedy was shot dead in Dallas, Texas. This helped fuel Janis's belief that Texas was beyond hope.

On 2 July 1964, however, the Civil Rights Act was passed by Congress, a landmark piece of legislation that outlawed major forms of discrimination against racial, ethnic, national and religious minorities, and women. And notwithstanding

Janis's misgivings about her home state, the Civil Rights Act was driven by a Texan President, Lyndon Baines Johnson, who had succeeded Kennedy.

All along, Janis had been very moved by the civil rights struggle and appalled by racism, a legacy of what she had witnessed growing up in Port Arthur. She told Linda Gottfried[35] that she was 'the first black-white person'. In saying this she was not merely uttering fashionable liberal words. She had looked into and examined all aspects of this controversial subject; at the instigation of her father, every Thursday Janis would purchase the latest edition of *Time* magazine and study the issues of the day.

Throughout 1964 Janis Joplin, in tandem with Linda Gottfried, started a regular consumption of speed. By the end of the year she had an amphetamine habit; she began to shoot up and was involved in small-scale dealing to pay for this. And there was worse: occasionally she would use heroin to help herself come down from the speed.

Soon Janis briefly fell in love with another Methedrine-head. But his usage was such that he ended up in a clinic for those suffering from addiction-related mental health problems. Visiting him in hospital, where he was recovering, drove home to Janis Joplin the reality of her own drug dependency. By now she weighed only 88 pounds: 'One day I woke up and realized I was going to die.'[36]

She had decided, however, that she would marry this man. She announced this when she returned to Port Arthur in May

1965. Her sister, Laura, was surprised that Janis went out and bought new dresses with long sleeves. To wear in the hot Texan summer? Janis, of course, was trying to hide the needle tracks on her arms.

Yet it seemed that in returning to her hometown Janis Joplin had turned a corner. She wanted to go back to college, she declared, to study sociology. She signed up at Lamar Tech and worked hard.

Then, relatively cleaned up, her boyfriend from San Francisco followed her to Port Arthur and asked her father for her hand in marriage. Afterwards he returned to his family in Detroit, to put his affairs in order, as it were.

Unfortunately, back in San Francisco, Linda Gottfried encountered Janis's fiancé's wife, who was visibly pregnant.

The man never returned from Detroit. Janis was heartbroken. 'She had tried to marry and live the straight life, but not even that would work for her. Why can't it work for me? she thought, over and over and over,' wrote her sister.[37]

As though personifying the adage that what does not kill you can only make you stronger, through the early months of 1966 – and despite her pronouncement to her parents that she would make her future in sociology – Janis began singing in clubs in Port Arthur, as well, occasionally, as those in Houston and Austin. Among those she played with in Austin was the future master-songwriter Guy Clark. She played a benefit at the 11th Door Club in Austin on 13 March for Teodar Jackson, a sick blind musician. In the

Austin American-Statesman, Jim Langdon, her old friend, wrote: 'The most exciting portion of the program may well have been created late in the second half of the show by Port Arthur blues singer Janis Joplin – the only female performer on the bill – who literally electrified her audience with her powerful, soul-searching blues presentation.' At the time the disciplined and impressive breathy tones of Joan Baez were the benchmark for women singers. Janis did not sound like that – at all.

Then from an unexpected angle came an opportunity. Local Austin band The 13th Floor Elevators were looking for a singer, a possible – and appealing – gig for Janis. But Chet Helms, the self-styled 'cultural curator' who was frequently in touch with Janis, said there might be an opening with another outfit in San Francisco. This was Big Brother and the Holding Company, whose members already included her friends Peter Albin, Sam Andrew and James Gurley. The band had got together at the end of 1965 in the basement of a Victorian mansion house owned by Albin's uncle at 1090 Page Street in San Francisco's slum area of Haight-Ashbury. Guitarist Albin was also the singer, and their first show had been at the Open Theater in Berkeley in January 1966. Sam Andrew defined their sound at that point as a 'progressive-regressive hurricane blues style'[38]. As this description suggests, they did not take themselves too seriously, sometimes taking a hotplate onstage and playing an entire number as eggs and bacon cooked on it. In part due to the dazzling, ground-breaking guitar playing of James Gurley, they quickly established a loyal local following.

It was Chet Helms, their manager, who had given the group its vaguely Orwellian name. And he was aware what Janis Joplin's vocal chops could bring to them. So, in June 1966, courtesy of a bus ticket from Helms, Janis Joplin went back to San Francisco. To her parents, she sent a profound letter of apology for having yet again not stuck to what she had promised them.

San Francisco was suddenly a very different city to the place she had left the previous year. In the brief time since she had been away from the city, it had seen the birth of the 'hippie', a twist on the word 'hipster'. This new scene was centred around the slum district of Haight-Ashbury.

In a letter to her worried parents, Janis wrote that 'the whole city had gone rock & roll'. She gave them a roll-call of the curious names adopted by the groups that had sprung up in the city since she had left: 'The Grateful Dead, The Love [sic], Jefferson Airplane, Quicksilver Messenger Service, The Leaves, The Grass Roots.' What she did not tell her parents was how the introduction of LSD had recalibrated even the atmosphere of the city, partially due to the pioneering psychedelic activities of Grateful Dead associates The Merry Pranksters, led by Ken Kesey, author of *One Flew Over the Cuckoo's Nest.*

The San Francisco scene heralded the arrival of the rock music genre – album-oriented material, as opposed to that of

45 rpm rock 'n' roll and pop. Although sometimes capable of taking itself rather too seriously, rock was ostensibly part of a new democratic 'underground' tradition, which would become interlinked with left-wing politics, symbolized by opposition to the rapidly escalating war in Vietnam. Time would show how Janis would become a central figure of this new genre.

For now Big Brother and the Holding Company seemed a natural foothold for Janis. She knew sexy guitarist James Gurley and Peter Albin from the North Beach folk scene. In fact on that North Beach scene she had also met the other two band members. On bass was Sam Andrew, also good-looking and an undoubted intellectual (he had studied linguistics and music theory), while behind the drum kit was Dave Getz, a Fulbright Fellow and artist who taught at the San Francisco Art Institute. All the members of the group were highly intelligent, ideal companions for Janis's questing intellectual spirit. She would not necessarily be the lead vocalist, frequently alternating with Peter Albin's already established role. As figureheads for Big Brother, she and Peter Albin would be rivals. Musically, however, Big Brother always had a problem: their sound was somewhat ponderous.

On 10 June 1966 Janis Joplin joined Big Brother and the Holding Company onstage for the first time. She played her own blues tune, 'Turtle Blues', as well as 'Bye Bye Baby', written by her friend Powell St John, by whom she had become pregnant at the University of Texas. The set also included such folk standards as 'Blindman' and 'I Know You Rider', the traditional woman's blues song.

Janis quickly proceeded to fall in love with buckskin-clad James Gurley, whose aura was only enhanced by the months he had spent in Mexico ingesting psilocybin mushrooms. A married man, Gurley briefly left his wife, Nancy, to live with Janis for a few weeks. Afterwards, fittingly for the time, Janis became good friends with Nancy, a former teacher at Los Angeles' progressive Summerhill School. The well-read Nancy was also a speed freak.[39]

Janis was very taken with the mores of hippie San Francisco, notably that of 'free love'. She and her friends would wander around the Haight picking up attractive men to take back to her apartment. She would also pick up attractive women. 'Singing with Big Brother was the first time I was able to make my emotions work for me. I put everything I had into the songs. I think if I hadn't gotten a chance to really sing like that, I would have destroyed myself,' she said.[40]

But how did Big Brother and the Holding Company fit into the pantheon of new San Francisco bands? 'From an audience standpoint, at the time the Airplane was more accessible,' considered Grace Slick, admittedly a singer with Jefferson Airplane. 'It was easier to identify with the people in the Airplane than The Grateful Dead or Janis, because Janis was so powerful and so different, all the emotions right out there.'[41]

At the art deco Avalon Ballroom at 1268 Sutter Street, which was run by Chet Helms, Big Brother and the Holding

Company became the regular house band. The Avalon was a rival to the city's other principal 'underground' venue, the Fillmore, run by the feisty Bill Graham. Of the two halls, the Fillmore possessed the greater cachet. Because of Big Brother's connection to Helms, however, Graham would not book them, which became a growing source of contention. The ostensibly Zen underground was full of closet careerists, and it came as no surprise when Big Brother and the Holding Company rapidly dumped Chet Helms as manager.

In the spirit of the age, Big Brother and the Holding Company decided they should live communally. They moved into a house in the town of Lagunitas in Marin County, in the North Bay Area 30 miles outside San Francisco. Nearby was The Grateful Dead's home.

For Janis Joplin her role with Big Brother and the Holding Company was also a search for self-worth. After playing a show on 12 August 1966, she – worryingly, one might feel – expressed this in a letter to her parents: 'I/we got an ovation, bigger than any other groups, for a slow blues in a minor key. Wow, I can't help it – I love it! People really treat me with deference. I'm somebody important. SIGH!!'[42] As though to prove she was utterly of her time, Janis recommended to her parents a pair of books: J.R.R. Tolkien's *The Hobbit* and his *Lord of the Rings*.

In the middle of August, Janis was approached by Paul Rothchild, the revered A&R man at Elektra Records, who would produce The Doors. Rothchild wanted to put together an English-style blues group, and had Janis play with a unit that comprised Taj Mahal, Stefan Grossman and Al Wilson, who went on to form Canned Heat (and became another member of the 27 Club). When the other members of Big Brother and the Holding Company learned of this, they were disturbed. Although nothing came of it, it would not be the last time that Janis Joplin and Paul Rothchild were connected.

At the end of August 1966, Big Brother and the Holding Company played a four-week run of shows in Chicago, at the Mother Blues venue. In the Windy City, they played five sets a night, six days a week. Although they received $1,000 a week for the first two weeks, the promoter then ran out of money; Big Brother had not been the sizable audience draw he was expecting. When he had no further money with which to pay them, Janis stole – claiming it as part of her fee – a cashmere sweater that belonged to a friend of his.

However, Chicago's Mainstream Records – who had already been turned down by Chet Helms – offered them a deal. Their first sessions, while still in Chicago, were inconclusive.

Returning to San Francisco, Big Brother played a free concert in Panhandle Park on 2 October 1966 to protest the banning of LSD in the United States. Janis's further participation extended to drinking a bottle of cheap wine – despite her initial interest, acid was never really her style.

Then Big Brother and the Holding Company were back in the studio, this time in Los Angeles. Their first single, 'Blindman', backed by 'All is Loneliness', was released to a deafeningly silent commercial response. There was, however, some critical fervour. 'This chick really can sing,' wrote Ed Denson in the *Berkeley Barb*,[43] although he added that he was as impressed by the playing of the musicians in the group.

Throughout the final months of 1966 Big Brother were busy. As well as shows at the Avalon Ballroom, where they had almost become the house band, they were now travelling around northern California to play dates, in places as far apart as the state capital of Sacramento and Santa Cruz, the pretty seaside town to the south, as well as a 'happening' at Stanford.

In December they drove 400 miles down to Los Angeles to record further songs for Mainstream. Already, Janis was being presented by the record company as the face of Big Brother. By now there had been favourable live reviews of the group in both *Newsweek* and *Time*. That month Otis Redding played at the Fillmore; using her privileged position of local superstar, Janis Joplin arrived at the venue at three in the afternoon to ensure she would be in the front row of the audience to watch the legendary soul man.

She spent the days before Christmas 1966 in Los Angeles, following a show at Santa Monica Civic Auditorium on 18 December.

On Christmas Day Big Brother played a party show, and they brought in the New Year of 1967 with 'a multi-dimensional experience of fun and good will' at Kezar Pavilion in Golden Gate Park.[44] Later in January, they played a further show in the park, co-promoted by the local Hell's Angels chapter.

On 4 January 1967 there was a 'Human Be-In' on the polo field of Golden Gate Park. Acid guru Timothy Leary spoke to the gathering; The Grateful Dead, Jefferson Airplane, Quicksilver Messenger Service and Dizzy Gillespie played.

March 1967 saw Janis Joplin move to a new apartment, back in San Francisco. Her flatmate was Linda Gravenites, the former wife of Bay Area musical legend Nick Gravenites, who had worked with Quicksilver Messenger Service. Linda was a clothes designer. She began dressing Janis in sexy hippie fashions, very different from the Earth Mother image she had previously adopted. She was also given lessons in applying make-up. 'Still faced with the problem of what to wear on stage,' Janis wrote to her mother in March 1967. 'I think I am going to have some clothes made by someone. A lot of the hippie girls sew and work from your design. Now all I have to do is design them. I'm pretty heavy again – so I want flattering things, plus they can't be too hot, plus I have to be able to move around a lot in them. I have one idea – I have an old lace curtain – very pretty that I want to use for sleeves and make some sort of simple dress to go w/them.' In that same letter Janis declared the group's dissatisfaction with Mainstream, indicating that they were intending to try to get out of the contract.[45] For the next six months Janis also took vocal lessons from a seasoned teacher, Judy Davis. Although a great singer, Janis always was more of a performer than a vocalist.

In this period she fell into a relationship with another local musician, 25-year-old Country Joe McDonald ('a Capricorn like me'[46]), leader of the highly respected Country Joe and the Fish, which lasted for approximately the next six months, their love affair finally succumbing to the demands of their respective careers.

In April 1967 Janis wrote excitedly to her mother that Paul McCartney – ('he's a Beatle') – had been to see the group play.[47] She was now on a not insubstantial wage of $100 a week. She had moved to another new apartment, at 123 Cole Street, opposite Golden Gate Park.

On 2 June 1967 *Sgt. Pepper's Lonely Hearts Club Band* was released. 16 to 18 June 1967 saw a large-scale version of the burgeoning West Coast sound, the Monterey International Pop Festival, just over 100 miles south of San Francisco. The event, with free admission, was held 'for the betterment of pop music', according to its organizers, Los Angeles music bigwig Lou Adler and John Phillips of The Mamas and Papas. On the board of musicians who recommended acts were Paul McCartney, Smokey Robinson and Paul Simon. For better or worse, the festival, which attracted 40,000 fans, was the starting point for what became known as the Summer of Love.

On the afternoon of Saturday, 17 June, Big Brother played to a tumultuous reception. However, unlike the other acts on the bill, their performance was not filmed. Julius Karpen, their new manager, had refused to permit it, on the grounds they were not being paid for this; Karpen considered the film being made of the festival to be an egregious example of 'the Man' ripping off 'the kids'. On learning of this, the ever pragmatic Big Brother and the Holding Company insisted on filming a second set of propulsive performances by Janis of set staple Big Mama Thornton's 'Ball and Chain' – during which The Mamas and Papas' Mama Cass could be seen staring wide-eyed, visibly mouthing 'Wow!' at the end of the number – and 'Combination of the Two'.

At Monterey Big Brother were introduced to Clive Davis, the revered major-domo of Columbia Records. Manager Julius Karpen and Bob Gordon, their Los Angeles-based attorney, were invited by Davis to the imminent Columbia convention. When Karpen had taken them on, Big Brother were earning $400 a show; now – without a hit record – they were pulling in $2,500 a night, an unusual turn of events.[48] By the late summer of 1967, Atlantic, Mercury and Columbia Records each wanted to sign Big Brother and the Holding Company, with offers between $50,000 and $75,000.

On the back of the publicity from Monterey, the group's eponymously titled first album, on Mainstream, rose up the US album charts, eventually peaking at number 60. Soon, however, Big Brother and the Holding Company would fall out with Julius Karpen. Their problems with him came to a head when he refused to let the band open for Jefferson Airplane and the Grateful Dead at the Hollywood Bowl, as he felt that Big Brother should have been the lead act.[49] At Monterey they had met Albert Grossman, who was legendary for his abilities as a manager and as a businessman. Originally from Chicago, Grossman managed Odetta, Peter, Paul and Mary, Richie Havens, Buddy Miles, Paul Butterfield, Mike Bloomfield, and – most significantly – Bob Dylan. In the verbal negotiations the group initially had with him, the manager insisted on an important caveat: although he would partake of marijuana and cocaine, Grossman was adamant that he would not work with anyone into heroin.

On 11 November 1967 Big Brother and the Holding Company signed a management deal with Albert Grossman. Janis felt genuine affection for him, seeming to see him as a father figure; she would refer to him as 'Uncle Albert'.

Early in 1968, however, Janis discovered she was pregnant; the father was someone with whom she had had a brief flirtation. She went to Mexico for an abortion, which left considerable physical and psychological scars.

On 17 February 1968 Big Brother and the Holding Company played their New York debut in Manhattan, at the Anderson Theater on Second Avenue in the East Village. Two days later Albert Grossman signed Big Brother and the Holding Company to Columbia Records for over $100,000, buying them out of their contract with Mainstream. In New York Big Brother stayed at the Chelsea Hotel. Janis wrote a note home to her family: 'Signed the contract on the 26th floor of the CBS Building, met the president, had a press party and got drunk.'[50] 'I tell all the performers I meet to drink Southern

Comfort because it preserves their voices. It's just an excuse for my own drinking,' she said to the Bell-Mclure Syndicate wire.[51] She wrote to her mother that New York was 'competitive and ugly'.[52]

At the instigation of Albert Grossman, Myra Friedman became Janis's publicity agent. On that first visit to New York City, Janis was interviewed for articles in *Vogue* (including a photo session with revered fashion and portrait photographer Richard Avedon), *Glamour*, the *New York Times*, *Life*, the *Village Voice*, and *New York* magazine – an exceptionally prestigious set of publications, one that definitively marked her arrival in the city.

Across America Janis was beginning to be noticed as an icon of style; the *San Francisco Examiner* featured her in its lifestyle section.

What people liked about her was that – as Nat Hentoff wrote in the *New York Times* – she was 'so intensely, joyfully' herself; in other words, Janis Joplin was the real thing.[53]

As their road manager the group took on John Cooke, the son of the illustrious BBC broadcaster Alastair Cooke. Cooke approached his task with commendable zeal, industriously organizing the band.

Regularly phenomenal on stage, Big Brother seemed to have trouble making representative records: when they played at Detroit's Grande Ballroom on 1 and 2 March 1968, the recording of their shows – intended as the possible crux of the first Columbia LP – failed to come up to scratch.

The celebrated documentary director D.A. Pennebaker, who had made the *Don't Look Back* documentary about Bob Dylan, had filmed Monterey Pop. Now he began making a movie about Janis Joplin, though it was never completed. Meanwhile, Nat Hentoff, clearly already a fan, interviewed her for the *New York Times*. 'Maybe I won't last as long as other singers, but I think you can destroy your now by worrying about tomorrow . . . We look back at our parents and see how they gave up and compromised and wound up with very little. So the kids want a lot of something now rather than a little of hardly anything spread over 70 years.'[54]

Part of the public persona that Janis expressed was the hard-drinking, hard-drugging warrior woman. But this had its downside: unable, for example, to always separate herself from her myth, by now Janis Joplin was probably an alcoholic. And booze was not her only addiction: during the Los Angeles recording sessions for their first Columbia album, *Cheap Thrills*, a bag of heroin had been found on a restaurant seat vacated by the group. When this was reported to Albert Grossman, he had flown the members to New York to give them a dressing-down about the dangers of the drug. Was he aware of the extent to which heroin was being used by the band? Although in San Francisco they were occasionally described as an 'alcodelic' band, there was little use of psychedelics; the band members' principal drug was alcohol, supplemented from time to time with heroin.

Janis, in a clear sign of insecurity, would test the extent of her friends' love for her by waltzing off, for example, with a man on whom Linda Gravenites had a large crush.[55] Yet on other occasions Janis would visit a waitress friend in San Francisco's North Beach, standing in for her and serving customers at their tables, accepting their meagre tips.[56]

However, her work would always predominate, and about this she would be highly professional. The notion behind this first LP for Columbia was that it would capture the raw sound of the Big Brother live shows. Accordingly, three tunes on the album were live recordings: 'Combination of the Two', 'I Need a Man to Love', and 'Ball and Chain', recorded at the Fillmore West. Ironically, the first words on the record are from Bill Graham, something of an adversary of the group in the time when they were managed by his rival Chet Helms. Original tunes on the LP were 'Combination of the Two', 'I Need a Man to Love', 'Turtle Blues' (the only song written entirely by Janis Joplin), and 'Oh, Sweet Mary'. Bert Bern's and Jerry Ragavoy's 'Piece of My Heart' and George Gershwin's evergreen 'Summertime' completed the record.

Finally the record was completed. Although Big Brother and the Holding Company wanted to title their first Columbia album *Sex, Dope and Cheap Thrills*, the record company would only go along with *Cheap Thrills*. They also baulked at the band's desire to have a cover picture showing the entire group naked in bed together.

A compromise was arrived at. Part of the visual accoutrements of the San Francisco scene was its poster art, and many local acts employed local artists to produce album artwork. Although Robert Crumb was not immediately associated with this genre, his subversive satire had ensured he was the most influential cartoonist of the new culture. Crumb was commissioned to create a hilarious montage of the song titles, which he completed in a single session, and for which he was paid $600. Originally intended for the back of the sleeve, his work turned into a distinctly iconic cover, an eye-catching stroke of genius. 'Janis used to come around, smoke pot, talk about the comics,' he remembered. 'She was nice.'[57]

While playing the Newport Folk Festival at the end of July, Janis met the up-and-coming Kris Kristofferson, with whom she hit it off. *Cheap Thrills* was released in August 1968, days after Big Brother had played the Columbia convention in Puerto Rico at the end of July. Within three days *Cheap Thrills* had gone gold, finally hitting number one in October. It stayed in that slot for eight weeks, the biggest-selling US LP of the year, selling almost a million copies. 'Piece of My Heart', originally recorded by Erma Franklin the previous year, was released as a single, reaching number 12, and selling over 500,000 copies.

In an article by Rasa Gustaitis for the *Los Angeles Times West* magazine, the journalist captured the essence of Janis Joplin's appeal: 'She's us. She's not a star, she's us. I've never met her but I know her. It's like, hearing her, you leave your body and you just move, man. She's just all energy. I don't know, she's all of us.'[58]

The altruistic ideology of the West Coast within Janis Joplin began to evaporate as she found herself more and more in New York.

In Manhattan people would constantly be giving her 'advice', whispering in her ear that the group was holding her back and that she would perform far better as a solo act. There were suggestions that Albert Grossman orchestrated these approaches.[59] Moreover, there were inklings that Janis was beginning to believe in her press, always a fundamental error.

It was hardly surprising, therefore, that in Manhattan at the end of the summer of 1968, Janis Joplin made an announcement to the rest of the group at the Chelsea Hotel: 'I'm leaving the band,' she said, adding, 'I'll kill anyone who tries to stop my success.'[60]

By the end of September 1968, Janis was writing to her family in Port Arthur,[61] telling them that Big Brother and the Holding Company were about to embark on their final tour, which would conclude on 7 December in Hawaii. (In fact, the Hawaii dates never took place.) She told them that she was 'going to do a thing on my own.' She needed, she said, to get 'the best musicians in the world.' 'There'll be a whole lot of pressure because of the "vibes" created by my leaving Big Brother and also by just how big I am now. So we've got to be just super when we start playing – but we will be.' She also told them of her new business structure, that she was 'now a corporation called Fantality', which would be paying all the bills. She added that Albert Grossman had told her that the next year she would make half a million dollars, and that she was already making good money. She told them that the previous week she had purchased a 1965 Porsche 356c Cabriolet – she didn't add that it had a psychedelic paint job, considered sacrilegious by car collectors – and that at the time of writing she was vacationing in Lake Tahoe.

On that final Big Brother tour she was on a high. But, unsurprisingly, this mood was not shared by the rest of the group; there was plenty of tension, both on and offstage. Eventually this stress seeped into Janis, and shows in Austin and San Antonio were cancelled when she became sick. But her health had recovered by the time of the Houston date,[62] attended by her parents and brother and sister. They were surprised when they were obliged to run for a car to whisk them away from the venue, to a rather mundane motel. Later her parents were hurt by Janis's persistent insistence to the media that as a child they had mistreated her.[63]

The final Big Brother and the Holding Company show was played on 1 December 1968, less than a year since they had signed their CBS record deal. The date was in San Francisco, where it had all begun for them.

Only 21 days later, on Saturday 21 December, in Memphis, Tennessee, Janis Joplin and her new – and under-rehearsed

– band played a 15-minute set on the bill of the Stax-Volt show, an all-black show apart from herself and her musicians. Janis had created a white soul revue-type band, replete with horns, and the concert's line-up indicated the direction in which she wished to travel.

After the date she went back to Port Arthur for Christmas.

To evade the extreme criticism – and bad vibes – she was receiving in San Francisco for having broken up Big Brother, Albert Grossman had set up the first part of Janis's first solo tour on the East Coast.

Janis was based at the Chelsea Hotel in Manhattan. Famously, she once encountered Leonard Cohen in its elevator at 3 a.m. She told him she was looking for Kris Kristofferson; the Canadian poet-songwriter said that he was searching for Lily Marlene: 'We fell into each other's arms through some divine process of elimination which makes a compassion out of indifference.'[64] Later Cohen wrote his song 'Chelsea Hotel' about their encounter. Around the same time Janis also had a brief liaison with American artist Brice Marden; after Janis passed away Marden immediately repainted his *A Mediterranean Painting*, giving it the title *For Pearl*, and dedicating it to the memory of Janis Joplin.

Janis Joplin did not always stay at the Chelsea, however. From time to time, she would be based at the equally funky Gorham Hotel on West 55th Street. Sometimes this would be while The Jeff Beck Group were also staying there, as Rod Stewart recalled in his autobiography, *Rod*: 'Janis Joplin, who was by no means a shy or retiring kind of woman, was always chasing Ronnie [Wood] and me around the place, trying to shag one or the other of us, though without success. We were terrified of her and would hide behind the pot plant in the lobby until she had gone past.'[65]

Notwithstanding the amount of time that she spent in New York, Janis disliked the city and its neurotic self-celebration. 'She hated New York,' wrote her sister.[66] 'It represented everything she didn't want to be, and contained the trappings of society that she rebelled against.'

Janis Joplin's first solo tour opened on 4 February 1969, with The Grateful Dead as opening act. It began with four sold-out shows at Manhattan's Fillmore East. Although she still hardly knew the musicians in her new band, she had let them know how things would be when on 20 January she met them in a Manhattan bar prior to rehearsals. The previous day had been her 26th birthday, and she and a girlfriend had picked up a pair of super studs, she said, and had amazing sex.[67] Instead of heading off for rehearsals, she instead got into playing pool, destroying an opponent: 'I'm the pool room wizard of the Lower East Side,' she trumpeted. Already drunk by the time they reached the rehearsal space, Janis was then ratty and irritable with her musicians, until confronted by drummer Lonnie Castille – at which point she apologized.[68]

Paul Nelson from *Rolling Stone*, which was still based in San Francisco, proprietorially loathed the New York date he attended, which Janis played wearing a shoulder-strap pant-suit, to the roaring approval of horny young men in the audience. 'Janis: The Judy Garland of Rock? by Paul Nelson', was the strapline on the 15 March edition of the magazine's front cover. High on adrenaline straight after that first show at the Fillmore, Janis had been narcissistically buzzing: 'Hey, I've never sung so great. Don't you think I'm singing better? Well, Jesus fucking Christ, I'm really better, believe me.' With such self-satisfied quotes, the critic damned her. A sounder overview had come from Frank Zappa, backstage after the show. When Sam Andrew had expressed to him that they didn't as yet have a completely distinctive sound, Zappa immediately spotted the problem: 'The band will loosen up in a while.'[69]

Janis Joplin's new musical ensemble was as yet without a name. Although The Band From Beyond was tested out, it would soon be permanently titled The Kozmic Blues Band. On lead guitar – from Big Brother – was Sam Andrew, an ally from the past. Bass player Keith Cherry worked with her at first, and was later replaced by Brad Campbell. On tenor sax was Terry Clements, and Terry Hensley was on trumpet. Essentially they were all musicians for hire, and the group ethos and camaraderie of Big Brother was utterly missing. The new guys were seasoned professionals, with far greater experience than Janis Joplin,[70] who was no longer merely boozing excessively but by now reputedly using $200 worth of heroin a day; the author of a *Playboy* profile was so taken with her that he refrained from mentioning the smack habit he had uncovered. In an interview with the *New York Times Magazine* she confessed, dismissively, that a doctor – whom she no longer attended – had told her that her liver was swollen.[71] *Newsweek* critic Hubert Saal felt obliged to note when interviewing her that Janis's breakfast on that occasion was 'an unlovely concoction apparently made of wood alcohol and chocolate syrup'. 'When I can't sing anymore,' Janis told him, 'I'll have babies.'[72]

Besides, Janis would claim to have more weighty matters on her mind. 'Being an intellectual creates a lot of questions and no answers. You can fill your life up with ideas and still go home lonely. All you really have that really matters are feelings. That's what music is to me,'[73] she told *Newsweek* in February that year.

On *The Ed Sullivan Show* on 16 March, Janis performed an interestingly diverse set of material, indicating the soul-infused direction of her new sound: the Bee Gees' 'To Love Somebody', Rodgers and Hart's 1935 tune 'Little Girl Blue', and 'Maybe' by The Chantels.

Janis seemed to be in inner turmoil, which was not alleviated by the deluge of disdain unleashed on her on the West Coast by her audience and the media: on 24 March – following a show at San Francisco's Winterland, and echoing the hostility towards her in the Bay Area – the esteemed critic Ralph Gleason wrote in the *San Francisco Chronicle* that Janis's 'new band is a drag. She should go back to Big Brother, if they'll have her.'[74] Reading the review at a newsstand, Janis was furious and hurt; she disappeared into a nearby bar and trampled all over the newspaper. Then, in an effort to alleviate her pain, she scored some smack.

In 1969 the Haight-Ashbury scene was experiencing a heroin epidemic. The drug was hardly difficult to find. After finding Janis lying on the floor one day, her skin turning purple, her friend Linda Gravenites, who adamantly disapproved of heroin, walked Janis around the neighbourhood until the early hours of the morning, almost certainly saving her life.

During April 1969 Janis Joplin embarked on a tour of Europe, starting off in Frankfurt, followed by appearances in Stockholm, Amsterdam, Copenhagen and Paris, and concluding in London. This was her first time out of North America. Janis's set list for the dates comprised 'Raise Your Hand', 'Maybe', 'Summertime', 'I Can't Turn You Loose', 'Try Just a Little Bit Harder', 'Combination of the Two', 'Piece of My Heart', 'Work Me, Lord', 'Walk Right In' and 'Ball and Chain'.

On 21 April she topped the bill at London's Royal Albert Hall, receiving an ecstatic audience response, which was mirrored in a review in *New Musical Express* by Nick Logan beneath the headline 'Standing Ovation for Janis'.

> Janis herself was superb.
>
> How such an almighty rasping then a clearly sweet voice comes from such a diminutive frame without doing her an injury I'll never know!!

> She looked like a child at her first party: a mane of unruly hair, little or no makeup, a garish blue low-cut trouser suit and a pair of golden sandals.

On this, her first visit to Europe, Janis enjoyed herself. She would visit art galleries with Bob Neuwirth, the singer/songwriter. Invited to George and Patti Harrison's for dinner, Janis soon came to the point. 'Hey, man,' she told the Beatle, 'I've been wanting to make it with you for years.'

'I don't think I'd be big enough for you,' the guitarist deadpanned, the tension of the occasion dissolving into laughter.

When Janis Joplin returned to the United States, she appeared on *The Dick Cavett Show* and was oddly disparaging about the European dates. 'They don't get down,' she complained to Cavett about European audiences, dismissing them as being too cerebral. The talk show host was clearly taken by Janis; in his autobiography he revealed that the last time he had smoked marijuana had been with her.[75]

Perhaps Janis was having trouble recalling the tremendous responses in Europe. Back in New York, there immediately had come tragic news. Nancy Gurley, the speed freak who had become friends with Janis in 1966 following the singer's affair with her husband, Big Brother guitarist James Gurley, had died of a heroin overdose. Janis and Sam Andrew commiserated with each other by themselves shooting up heroin (despite Andrew having overdosed on heroin only recently, at a party after their show at the Royal Albert Hall. He had eventually come round after being dumped in a bath of cold water).

James was subsequently charged with her murder: he had injected Nancy with the drug. After a two-year legal fight, he was sentenced to probation.

Added to The Kozmic Blues Band in June was Cornelius 'Snooky' Flowers, a black baritone saxophonist and Vietnam veteran, who disapproved of Janis's heroin intake.

Someone who took a more pragmatic approach to Janis's obvious heroin habit was Albert Grossman, her manager. In June 1969 he took out a $200,000 life insurance policy on his client, at $3,500 a year.[76]

Having moved out to the West Coast, from 16 to 26 June, Janis was in Los Angeles, working in Columbia's Hollywood studio on her first solo album, *I Got Dem Ol' Kosmic Blues Again Mama!*. Janis Joplin and the group checked into the Landmark Hotel on Franklin Avenue, round the corner from Hollywood Boulevard. (After four days there came a break in recording for an appearance at the three-day Newport Pop Festival held at Devonshire Downs in nearby Northridge, California, a suburb of Los Angeles. The outfit had also played the Atlanta Pop Festival, to 50,000 people, three weeks previously, at which Janis had sung a duet with Little Richard.)

The new songs were produced by the extremely versatile Gabriel Mekler, a classically trained pianist who had helmed albums by the hugely popular acts Steppenwolf and Three Dog Night. With Janis, Mekler also co-wrote the album's title track. Criticism of the record when it was released would hinge around the shift to a soul music sound, away from the psychedelic rock of Big Brother. Carping also arose over the alleged mercenary status of Janis's new musicians, a floating talent pool of guns-for-hire, many of whom would be replaced over the ensuing months; even former Big Brother guitarist Sam Andrews would be substituted by John Till, a former member of Ronnie Hawkins's Hawks. However, the LP would prove to be her finest piece of work, including breathtakingly fine performances of the three tunes first aired on *The Ed Sullivan Show*.

At Mekler's insistence, Janis moved out of the Landmark Hotel, to stay at his own home: he was intent on keeping her away from drugs and druggy companions.

The next month, when Janis played the Atlantic City Rock Festival, her set did not go down well; apparently averse to her new, as yet unreleased material, the audience was calling out for Big Brother songs.

On 25 July 1969, Janis Joplin and The Kozmic Blues Band played the first of two nights at Washington DC's Merriweather Post Pavilion. The first night was reviewed in the *Washington Post* by Carl Bernstein, who, five years later, would break the story of the Watergate break-in with Bob Woodward, leading to the resignation of President Richard Nixon.

Now, in the 26 July edition of the *Post*, Bernstein was highly enthusiastic: 'Janis Joplin has gotten it all back together again . . . from the first note it was a love affair between her and a wild audience of more than 5,000 . . . Joplin's seemingly steam-powered voice cooed, moaned and screamed. Janis has finally assembled a group of first-rate musicians with whom she is totally at ease and whose abilities complement the incredible range of her voice.'

Bernstein compared the enjoyment level to that created by the Beatles on their concert tours; surely there could be no higher praise. He wrote that she and the new group gave a 'musicality' to Big Brother songs that was missing from the original group.

'Perhaps,' concluded Carl Bernstein, 'Miss Joplin's new revue will put an end to the inevitable and unfair comparisons drawn between her, Big Mama Thornton, and other great female blues singers. The comparisons are a superfluous exercise. She is Janis Joplin and that is enough.'

The pair of festivals Janis and her group had played in June would soon be dwarfed by what was to follow on 16 August. The Woodstock Music and Art Fair, the largest mass celebration of the alternative values of the 1960s, took place in extreme climatic conditions over the weekend of 15–17 August 1969, at a natural amphitheatre in upstate New York. Posters for the event, on which Janis Joplin was billed as one of the headliners, promised 'Three days of Love, Peace and Music'. Organizational incompetence led to the event being declared a 'free festival', and to Governor John Rockefeller declaring a state of emergency around the entire Woodstock festival area. Ultimately, this 'Aquarian Exposition', another of the poster's claims, was a tribute to hippie capitalism: the promoters sold $1.4 million worth of tickets and paid the artists a total of $150,000, and the film of the festival transmogrified the counter-culture into mass-market box office gold.

By the afternoon of 15 August, all roads in a 25-mile radius of Woodstock being utterly blocked, the organizers summoned up 16 helicopters to bring in acts. By Friday evening, the day before Janis Joplin was due to play, the festival audience was 500,000 strong.

Hunkered down that night with many of the other acts at the nearby Holiday Inn, Janis ate a seven-course meal, washed down by champagne, and retired to her room with Vince Mitchell, a new roadie. Janis had warned Vince, however, that her lover was en route from San Francisco.[77] What she had not told Vince was that this lover was a woman, Peggy Caserta, something of a surprise for the new roadie, who had fallen for Janis.

Janis was certainly in the mood for creating controversy; at a press conference the following day, before 25 reporters, Janis openly fondled Peggy's breasts. Back in her room, she did heroin. Later she blamed the smack for her rickety performance. She had also been drinking vodka and tequila for the 10 hours she waited at the festival before going onstage.

Before her appearance at Woodstock, for which she was

paid $10,000, Janis had been invited by John Morris, one of the festival's organizers, to spend a few days at his house in the Virgin Islands. Catching up with him at the event, she extolled the virtues of this brief Caribbean sojourn: 'I fucked a lot of strangers.' Morris noted that she had a bottle in her hand. 'She had just gotten totally ripped . . . We weren't going to get a great one.'[78]

And so it was: when she finally made the stage, at two o'clock in the morning, following Creedence Clearwater Revival, Janis's onstage dancing was distinctly shaky, and although she sang fierily, on several occasions her voice cracked. But she seemed to enjoy entering into a rapport with the enormous audience, demanding to know if they were stoned enough. 'I don't mean to be preachy,' she offered, before her encore of 'Piece of My Heart', 'but music's for grooving, and if you're getting more shit than you need, you know what to do about it. Music's supposed to be different to that.'

Remaining on the site until the conclusion of the festival, happily hanging out with Grace Slick, she watched the final performance, by Jimi Hendrix, on the Monday morning, from Joe Cocker's van.

Straight after Woodstock, Janis went home to Port Arthur, enthusing about the event, somewhat to the bafflement of her parents, for whom hippie culture remained rather alien.

In *Newsweek* she was offered a platform to voice her thoughts on the cultural phenomenon of Woodstock. The festival's audience, she decreed, was 'a whole new minority group . . . There's lots and lots and lots of us, more than anybody ever thought before. We used to think of ourselves as little clumps of weirdos.'[79] Now it was apparent that what Janis first witnessed in San Francisco had swept the whole United States. Soon it would be the entire Western world.

But the dark side of the movement was rearing its head. Haight-Ashbury was awash with heroin and acid casualties; on 9 August, this grim underbelly fully revealed itself, when in the Hollywood Hills members of the Charles Manson 'family' murdered the actress Sharon Tate, the heavily pregnant wife of film director Roman Polanski.

At the behest of Albert Grossman, concerned that she would not appear in the best light, Janis Joplin's performance was not featured in either the epic, hugely triumphant movie of the festival which was released the next year, or on the equally successful triple album soundtrack. Pete Townshend, who had performed with The Who at Monterey, would have quibbled over this decision. 'She had been amazing at Monterey,' he wrote in his biography,[80] 'but tonight she wasn't at her best, due, probably, to the long delay, and probably, too, to the amount of booze and heroin she'd consumed while she waited. But even Janis on an off-night was incredible.'

Just over three weeks later, on 11 September 1969, *I Got Dem Ol' Kozmic Blues Again Mama!* hit the stores. With supreme confidence the front cover bore only a single blurred headshot image of Janis Joplin, with the record's title only on the spine. *I Got Dem Ol' Kozmic Blues Again Mama!* quickly sold over a million copies, becoming a platinum record. This was despite many US reviews that were decidedly iffy, notably in the San Francisco-based *Rolling Stone*. She certainly had an ally in the highly respected rock critic Robert Christgau, who awarded the album an A- in his *Consumer Guide Review*: 'Everyone who called Janis Joplin a great blues singer was wrong. She was, and is, a great rock singer. Anyone who has given up on Janis along the way ought to try again. She's coming on.'[81] But, its high sales notwithstanding, *I Got Dem Ol' Kozmic Blues Again Mama!* never rose higher in the US album charts than number five, hardly matching the eight weeks at number one that *Cheap Thrills* enjoyed.

Already the fate of Janis's personal copies of *Kozmic Blues* had caused her to reflect on who her friends really were. With a similar naivety to that of the Rolling Stones, who in December that year would employ them as security at the tragic Bay Area Altamont event, the San Francisco Hell's Angels had been given a respectful credit on *Cheap Thrills*. In September 1969 a bunch of this same chapter of Angels came over to Janis Joplin's San Francisco house and helped themselves to a box of LPs supplied to her by her record company. When Janis – who had just shot up – remonstrated, one of them punched her, knocking her over.

For much of the rest of the year, Janis Joplin and the Kozmic Blues Band toured throughout the United States, promoting the album. There were a couple more large-scale events: one was the Texas International Pop Festival, which ran from 30 August to 1 September at the Dallas International Motor Speedway. In September they played the New Orleans Pop Festival at Baton Rouge International Speedway in Louisiana, as well as a show at the Hollywood Bowl in Los Angeles.

For the Hollywood Bowl date Janis, again staying at the Landmark, only a few hundred yards from the venue, was with a new boyfriend. Paul Whaley was the founder of, and drummer with, Blue Cheer, a hard rock outfit who boasted they were the loudest group there had ever been. Their *Vincebus Eruptum* album had made number 11 in the US album charts. Linked by a mutual fondness for heroin and sex, their time at the Landmark alone together – indulging in both – contributed in Janis's mind to her exceptional but brief performance that evening, for which she was paid $60,000. Somehow it managed to slip the minds of both Janis and her new boyfriend that he was in fact married.

Following her show Janis managed to miss her ride out of the prestigious venue. She was obliged to walk the short distance back to the hotel, surrounded by puzzled fans. By then Whaley had departed, and Peggy Caserta helped her friend relax by performing oral sex on her.[82]

On 5 October 1969, Janis was on home turf, with a show at Winterland in San Francisco. This was road manager John Cooke's last show with her. Afterwards he quit. Part of the reason for his departure was Janis's drinking, which by now was routinely affecting her performances. In his review, local journalistic *éminence grise* Ralph Gleason again savaged her gig.

Much of the time, Janis besported herself in a Russian lynx coat that she had hustled out of Southern Comfort, for having mentioned their liquor and been photographed holding its distinctively shaped bottle in so many interviews and photo shoots.

On 26 October 1969 Janis had a run-in with a security guard at Houston Coliseum: during 'Ball and Chain', a cop had tried to get her to cool out the audience, and claimed to have been subjected to some choice language.

On 16 November 1969, Janis Joplin and the Kozmic Blues Band played at the Curtis Hixon Hall in Tampa, Florida. Rock acts were already under strong scrutiny in Florida, which seemed to be fighting a strenuous rearguard action against the counter-culture's forward march; after a 1 March 1969 concert at the Dinner Key Auditorium in Miami, The Doors' singer Jim Morrison had a warrant for his arrest for indecent exposure issued by the Dade County Police department, a case that would dog him for the rest of his time in the USA.

Now it was the turn of Janis Joplin. Following her Tampa show, she was charged with two counts of using vulgar and obscene language on stage. In fact, Janis had been speaking to the excited audience, attempting to get them to return to their seats: 'Now listen, we can't go fuck with each other because that will give them something to chop on. If we don't hurt nothing, they can't say shit.'

Before the show could end she was arrested and charged by Tampa police, taken to the station and photographed for mug shots. The full body shot indicated the time, day and year, by way of a clock and calendar on the wall behind her: 12:15 a.m., 17 November 1969. Afterwards, Janis spoke to the press:[83] 'I say anything I want onstage. I don't mind getting arrested because I've turned a lot of people on.' Ten weeks later she was fined $200, without even needing to appear in court.

There was a greater significance to both Janis Joplin and Jim Morrison having been busted in Florida for inappropriate onstage behaviour. Of all the musical figures in the American counter-culture of the late 1960s, it was these two who had emerged as the female and male figureheads – onto whom were projected the unconscious fantasies and impossible aspirations of their fans, simultaneously earning the wrath and detestation of the straight element of the desperately fragmented society that America had become. It was a weight that both were finding increasingly hard to bear.

Later that month Janis Joplin appeared at the Auditorium Hall in Chicago, and on 27 November 1969 she joined Tina Turner onstage at New York's Madison Square Garden, singing a duet with her of 'Land of a Thousand Dances' (Ike and Tina Turner were supporting the Rolling Stones). Janis went onstage completely off her face, 'so drunk, so stoned, so out of control, that she could have been an institutionalized psychotic rent by mania,' according to Myra Friedman, her own publicist.[84]

On 6 December 1969 Janis appeared on national ABC television in an edition of the *This Is Tom Jones* series. She was introduced by Jones as 'the legendary Miss Janis Joplin', and she lived up to the epithet: she sang a poignant, breathtaking version of Rodgers' and Hart's 'Little Girl Blue' – her favourite song – and Eddie Floyd's 'Raise Your Hand', a duet with Tom Jones of a steaming, show-stopping tune she regularly featured onstage.

Two weeks later, on 19 and 20 December, Janis Joplin herself topped the bill with two shows at Madison Square Garden, joined on stage by guitarists Johnny Winter – with whom her empathy was sensational – and Paul Butterfield. During the period of the shows she was reportedly 'romantically linked' with the New York Jets' star quarterback Joe Namath; although she name-checked him onstage at the Garden, however, the football player didn't show. In fact, she had already seduced him, and this mention of his name was like a groupie's boast to her audience. John Cooke, since the Winterland date no longer her road manager, went to the after-show party, and was concerned that she 'seemed in bad shape'. The Madison Square Garden shows would prove to be Janis's last ever dates with The Kozmic Blues Band.

At the instigation of Albert Grossman, Janis was given an appointment with a Manhattan physician, Dr Edmund Rothschild. Unsurprisingly, Grossman was concerned about the excessive lifestyle of his client. 'Dr Rothschild found Janis to be a bouncy, vibrant, and exciting young woman,' wrote her sister, Laura. 'She pranced into his office wearing a translucent blouse with feather boas in her hair. She told him she wanted to quit using heroin but that she didn't think of herself as a heavy narcotics user. He took a thorough oral history and did a physical exam, finding nothing unusual. He found her heroin use to be intermittent and episodic.'[85]

Dr Rothschild was at least as concerned about Janis's diet, which largely consisted of junk food and alcohol, plus handfuls of sugar products – to which consumers of heroin are often partial. Janis explained to Rothschild that she used smack to come down after shows; although there had been the aberration of Woodstock, she made it her practice never to do this most powerful – and most addictive – of all drugs before a performance. She revealed, however, that she wanted to stop using it altogether: she'd had enough of heroin. The doctor prescribed Janis a week's supply of methadone, synthetic heroin-lite that anaesthetizes junkies' withdrawal symptoms.

If Janis was embarking on a sincere period of change, the methadone might have helped. Certainly there were other indications that she was intent on removing excessive elements – and individuals – from her lifestyle. Her friend Linda Gravenites had remained in Europe following Janis's dates there in April, partly to escape the hedonistic influence of Janis's circle. Now Janis wrote to her close friend, urging her to return; she was giving up drugs and drinking, she swore, turning instead to yoga, walking, and learning the piano.

The singer's promises were sincere. Having returned to San Francisco, Janis moved into a house that she had bought across the Golden Gate Bridge in Marin County. Her new home was in a cul-de-sac in the small town of Larkspur, a suburb of San Francisco tucked away on the edge of the legendarily beautiful Mount Tamalpais, with its stunning ocean and inland views. (Ever conflicted, Janis soon started to complain about its rural isolation, driving off to bars to drink until they closed.)

Returning from London, the ardently anti-heroin Linda Gravenites came to live with Janis in Larkspur. Linda provided support in Janis's endeavours to come off smack.

The redwood house was decorated in a simple, tasteful style. At the end of December 1969 Janis Joplin had a house-warming party with 400 guests. This elegant affair gradually degenerated as many of the guests became wildly inebriated, and Janis's personal bedroom was used for the consumption of heroin by herself, Peggy Caserta and Mike Bloomfield.[86] Soon Linda Gravenites was threatening to move out unless Janis kicked the drug.

At the beginning of 1970 Janis went back onto methadone. Again, she seemed sincere about quitting smack. She made a decision to take the first four months of 1970 off, part of her effort to become clean. To further facilitate this, after turning 27 on 19 January, at the suggestion of Albert Grossman she set off with Linda Gravenites to Brazil to vacation at the annual Rio de Janeiro carnival at the end of January. Heading for San Francisco airport for her flight she handed Peggy her remaining heroin, $2,500 worth. It came close to killing her friend.[87]

On the beach in Rio Janis met David George Niehaus. George, as he was known, was an upper-middle-class boy from Cincinnati who had just spent 18 months exploring the Amazon basin. He had no interest in drugs, and helped this hippie beach-girl – as he had first believed her to be – to get over her heroin addiction.

When Linda returned to San Francisco to oversee work being done on the Larkspur house, Janis and George headed to Salvador in the northeastern Brazilian state of Bahia. With no other possibility of live entertainment in the city, they took to hanging out in the local whorehouse, where Janis sang with the in-house band. She became intrigued by the local santeria, that marriage of Catholicism and African animism.

Keen to continue his world travels, George urged Janis to go with him to Nepal. The idea of abandoning her career was anathema to her, however, and after only one of the three months she had intended to be away for, she returned to San Francisco.

Stopping in Los Angeles on the way, Janis bought $10,000 worth of heroin. Although unaware that his girlfriend had made this enormous purchase, it was impossible for George

Niehaus not to be aware that in San Francisco Janis had immediately returned to the drug. And when this new boyfriend got back from a two-day skiing trip, he was more than surprised to find her in bed with Peggy Caserta, heroin works visible. Her friends had felt that George was the most appropriate boyfriend Janis had ever had. But he left San Francisco and went off to Turkey.

'When Linda saw David Niehaus leave,' wrote Laura Joplin,[88] 'she decided that Janis would never quit dope. Linda couldn't live around heroin anymore. She was so close to Janis that she could tell her the truth. Sometimes Janis let herself hear it.' Eventually, Janis became fractious about Linda's ceaseless reminders of the harm she was doing herself, and asked her friend to move out. She did, the next day. Despite having been the instigator of this, Janis was devastated by Linda's departure, and she once again decided to give up heroin altogether. She went to counsellors and psychiatrists, but was struck by what she felt was their lack of empathy. All the same, she accepted the methadone she was offered as a heroin substitute. Then, once again at the instigation of Albert Grossman, she travelled to an addictions clinic, one that was discreetly tucked away in a corner of Mexico. Janis's personal solution to coming off heroin was to replace it with constant alcohol, drinking almost from the moment she rose.

Yet despite the continuous alcohol intake, there were suggestions that Janis Joplin was somehow still flowering and maturing, both as a vocalist and as a human being. Come what may, she was coming to comprehend that her stage persona and her day-to-day existence didn't need to be one and the same, that a separation could be made.[89] Through studying Rosicrucianism and the I Ching, which were perhaps guiding her to such an internal revelation, she was clearly drawn to the currents of mysticism popular in that era.[90]

On 4 April 1970 at the San Francisco Fillmore, she performed with Big Brother and the Holding Company, a show promoted by Bill Graham as a reunion concert. Before she went on stage she was drinking and simultaneously swallowing methadone tablets. She included a new song in the set, 'Ego Rock', which she sang as a duet with Nick Gravenites, Linda's former husband. The tune attacked Texans for the way she felt she had been treated by them as a youth. Eight days later, she appeared again with Big Brother, this time at Winterland.

That month, however, Bobby Neuwirth reintroduced her to his friend Kris Kristofferson, the handsome intellectual and former Rhodes scholar she had met in Newport, a Texan like herself. Then together they introduced Janis to 'The Great Tequila Boogie'.[91] This alcohol binge began in New York's West Village, then continued at Janis's home on the West Coast. Very quickly, she fell in love with Kristofferson. The bender lasted for three weeks, with a local tattooist setting up shop in her house, adorning many of the revellers. Among those so embellished was the actor Michael J. Pollard, who had come to prominence in the 1967 classic *Bonnie and Clyde*. By the end of this bender, Janis and Kristofferson went their separate ways, each intent on pursuing their career.[92] But Kristofferson had donated her a song, 'Me and Bobby McGee', that would become known as one of her defining numbers. 'Kris qualified as one of Janis's "mythic men" – talented, reckless, self-destructive, and unavailable,' wrote Ellis Amburn in *Pearl*, his biography of Janis.[93]

Afterwards Janis, who was about to go on the road once more, again attempted to go cold turkey on both booze and methadone. This could be a chance to save herself. In the pool room of her Larkspur house, she was putting together a new group, The Full Tilt Boogie Band, for an already booked tour. From the Kozmic Blues Band she brought guitarist John Till and bass-player Brad Campbell. From Ronnie Hawkins's band there was pianist Richard Bell. She stole Jesse Winchester's organ player Ken Pearson, and chose Clark Pierson as her drummer.[94]

The dates began with a party for the local Hell's Angels at Pepperland in San Rafael, Marin County, with Big Brother as the support act. Considering how only a few months previously, Angels had invaded her home, stolen her records, and punched her to the ground, there were those who felt Janis had been intimidated into playing the Pepperland. After her set, a teary Janis confessed to Michael J. Pollard that she had no memory whatsoever of playing it – an alcoholic's blackout.[95]

The official Full Tilt Boogie Band tour started in Gainesville, Florida, on 29 May 1970. Initially planned to last eight weeks, it soon stretched to three months. (Janis confessed to a reporter in Louisville, Kentucky on 13 June that her drinking was now so extreme that she had frequently blacked out before she reached the stage and could recall nothing of her performance.[96])

This tour included a five-day train trip – a further five-day binge, more like – through Canada, playing three concerts for $75,000. Also along for the trip were The Grateful Dead, The Band, Buddy Guy, Delaney and Bonnie, and Ian & Sylvia. Janis had a permanent hangover. Was it her alcohol intake that was causing her to frequently vomit during the journey? Or was it a sign she was back on heroin? Certainly her libido was unaffected; later she estimated that on the train journey she had 65 sexual encounters in the course of five days.[97]

Dates in Hawaii followed this Canadian sojourn. Although the band now took a few days off, on 10 July 1970 Janis flew to Austin, Texas, for her mentor Ken Threadgill's birthday party. Ken owned Threadgills, a bar where Janis used to play when she was younger, She sang before 8,000 people, performing Kris Kristofferson's 'Me and Bobby McGee' and his 'Sunday Mornin' Coming Down'.

The next day, 11 July, she was back on tour, another double bill with Big Brother, in San Diego, from where she flew back to San Francisco, buying drinks on the plane for all her Bay Area friends.

That summer Janis Joplin immersed herself in reading Nancy Milford's *Zelda*, a biography of the troubled wife of the novelist F. Scott Fitzgerald; when she appeared on *The Dick Cavett Show* again in June, she recommended the book.

In between drinks, what Janis was most interested in was the new album she was readying herself to record. She already had a title: *Pearl*, a nickname by which she was sometimes known in San Francisco, with its implied sexual double-entendre.

She also reconnected with Paul Rothchild, who had produced the hugely successful first five albums by The Doors, as well as The Paul Butterfield Blues Band, and had tried to seduce her from Big Brother in 1966. Now she was considering him as the producer of her next album. Rothchild was a well-read intellectual – as Janis considered herself to be – and his appealing rebel credentials were clear: early in the 1960s he had been briefly imprisoned after a pot bust. Initially, Rothchild was dubious: 'The last time I saw Janis she was a junkie. She couldn't focus on her art,' he wavered.[98] At the San Diego Full Tilt Boogie Band show on 11 July, however, Rothchild had been in the wings. 'She was singing and I was enraptured because I was listening to one of the most brilliant vocalists I ever heard in classical, pop, or jazz music . . . I went, "Oh! My God!" All of the woman was revealed. The vessel of Janis vanished.'[99]

Theoretically, under the terms of her contract, Janis Joplin should only have recorded at Columbia's own studio in Los Angeles. A compromise was struck with the label, however, and it was agreed that she and Rothchild would work together on her new album at Sunset Sound at 6650 Sunset Boulevard in Hollywood. When Rothchild had asked Janis what she would like to be in later life, her reply had been immediate: 'The greatest blues singer in the world.'[100]

Paul Rothchild taught her to get in touch with the voice she had used in church when she was ten years old, and to develop it into a full, passionate and dramatic instrument. Untutored as she was in many of music's subtleties, Janis hugely appreciated the thoughtful input of the producer.

On 12 August 1970 Janis Joplin and The Full Tilt Boogie Band performed at Harvard Stadium before a 40,000-strong audience. Perhaps in light of the incident in Tampa, Florida, there was a heavy police presence.[101] It would prove to be her last-ever public performance.

The next day Janis flew to Port Arthur to her tenth annual high school reunion. Why did she do this? It was to prove a point to her former fellow classmates, which she had emphasized on that June's *Dick Cavett Show*: 'They laughed me out of class, out of town, and out of the state – so I'm going home.'[102]

Just prior to that high school reunion, however, Janis had again appeared on the *Cavett Show*. This time she was visibly drunk.

Her return for the high school reunion was a cause of controversy at home. Although Janis had been making the effort to distinguish between her personal and professional personae, they seemed once again to have become blended together, especially on this occasion. 'The caricature of the woman who was known as Janis Joplin had even affected her relationships in the family. Janis was very clever in getting press attention and slinging out one-liners that cried, "Headline." But the quotes had changed people's views of her,' wrote her sister.[103] Janis had again insisted in press interviews, for example, that her parents had made her leave home when she was fourteen – which was simply not true.

There seemed little celebration by her parents of the prodigal daughter; at one point they left to attend a wedding, Janis accompanying them.[104]

She attended the wedding wearing – as her sister described it – 'San Francisco rock clothes'.[105] When Laura questioned her as to why she was wearing feathers in her hair, Janis became irritable. 'Stay out of other people's business,' she barked, angry at this reinvention of herself being questioned.[106]

In Port Arthur there was a press conference at the Goodhue Hotel, at which Janis was asked, 'What do you think you've got in common with your classmates of 1960 besides the fact that you were classmates?'[107]

'There's always a point of communication for people,' she obliquely replied. 'You must get down to human level and discard the accent or the dress or whatever. We've still got things to talk about. We've just got different kinds of experiences. They've got kids, I ain't got kids. I wear feathers, they don't wear feathers. See, we have a lot of common ground. We can talk about birds,' she said, making a bad joke.

At the reunion itself, she received few accolades. 'In honour of having come the greatest distance to this reunion, the committee wanted to give Janis a tire,' joked the event's master of ceremonies, equally badly.

Rather than stick around for the dance afterwards, Janis headed into town, where Jerry Lee Lewis was playing a show. After the Killer had made what Janis deemed an inappropriate remark about her looks, Janis punched him in the face. Jerry Lee hit her back.[108]

When she left Port Arthur, she asked her sister to come and stay with her that Christmas at Larkspur.[109]

Back in San Francisco Janis Joplin began a relationship and fell in love with Seth Morgan, a handsome motorbike-riding Berkeley student and a trust fund recipient, who was the son of the heir to the Ivory Soap fortune. He was six years younger than Janis and – like her – bisexual. In 1964 his alcoholic mother had died, drinking herself to death; clearly there was a connection between the female archetype represented by Janis and his mother. Seth Morgan was also a coke dealer, using his earnings to pay for his own heroin habit.[110] He had met Janis when he delivered cocaine to her house, and had also physically threatened Peggy Caserta over money she owed him for cocaine. (Later Morgan continued his heroin habit, pimped his wife, served time for armed robbery, and wrote the best-selling *Homeboy* before dying in a motorcycle crash in 1990. Janis certainly could pick them.)

All the same, they made plans for a wedding, on a Caribbean liner, and Janis had her attorney draw up a prenuptial agreement.

Before such arrangements could be finalized in September Janis Joplin drove to Los Angeles in her psychedelic Porsche to record with Paul Rothchild; the producer was also a Porsche owner, and the pair would race their vehicles against each other along Sunset Boulevard. Seth Morgan stayed at Janis's Larkspur home, from time to time flying down to LA, where he was present at eight of the recording sessions.

At Sunset Sound, where James Taylor was in an adjacent studio as he made his *Sweet Baby James* album, Janis was putting down some strong music. Jerry Ragavoy had written a new tune for her, 'I'm Going to Rock 'n' Roll Heaven'. Meanwhile, Nick Gravenites had composed 'Buried Alive in the Blues'. The dark poetry of these titles hardly needs emphasizing.

But in Los Angeles Janis once again started doing heroin, justifying it to Morgan as a necessary part of her creativity, claiming she would stop using it when the new album was completed. 'Several people,' wrote her sister,[111] 'knew or guessed that Janis was using heroin, because her behaviour would change. The strange truth was that when she did heroin, she turned into a hazy little girl. She lost the vibrant energy that was the persona of Janis Joplin . . . When she was straight, her intellect bloomed; she knew what she wanted and she knew ahead of time what the people around her wanted.'

On 18 September 1970 grim news came from London: 27-year-old Jimi Hendrix had died, his end incorrectly attributed to an overdose of drugs. 'I can't go out this year because he was a bigger star,' came Janis's alleged response to the tragic event.

While Janis Joplin was in Los Angeles, Doors singer Jim Morrison contacted her. They met up, a pair of alcoholics together, Morrison bearded and puffy from booze, forty pounds overweight. Janis was drinking White Russians, somehow believing the vodka-based cocktail's milk quotient had health-enhancing attributes. Morrison told her that he was about to go to live in Paris for a time. Rock 'n' roll was no longer for him, he insisted to her.[112]

On 1 October 1970 Janis Joplin rewrote her will, leaving half her estate to her parents, and a quarter each to her brother and sister.

The next day, Friday 2 October 1970, she received the legal documents for the prenuptial agreement she intended Seth Morgan to sign. This was planned for the next day, to be witnessed by Peggy Caserta, with whom Janis intended herself and Morgan to have a sexual threesome.

Peggy, however, who had been planning an industrial-scale marijuana shipment from San Diego to San Francisco, remained shacked up at the Chateau Marmont with another girlfriend. And Seth Morgan refused to fly down to Los Angeles unless Janis paid for his ticket – over which she took umbrage.

So on Saturday 3 October 1970 Janis Joplin's plans for a night of hedonism had fallen into disarray. She did, however, make that phone call to Bobby Womack, giving her a highly creative last day on earth.

There are other accounts of her final evening besides that of Womack. There is a claim, for example, that after finishing at Sunset Sound at around 11 p.m., she went for a couple of drinks at Barney's Beanery, the popular West Hollywood bar close to the junction of La Cienega and Santa Monica Boulevard, with organ player Ken Pearson. And that at around 1 a.m. she went into the lobby of the Landmark to purchase cigarettes – her last act before shooting up, in this version of the story of the final hours of Janis Joplin.

Is there any reason to doubt either version? Not really: it is quite possible that somehow the events in each elide into each other.

Only the desperate, tragic outcome remains.

That Sunday, 4 October 1970, road manager John Cooke was dispatched to the Landmark Hotel by Paul Rothchild after Janis had not shown up to that day's recording session. Gaining access to her bedroom, he found Janis on the floor, dead. The autopsy that was performed the next day ascribed her death to 'acute heroin-morphine intoxication due to: injection of overdose'. Joplin's ashes were scattered from a plane into the Pacific Ocean and along Stinson Beach in Marin County.

Almost inevitably, *Pearl*, the album that Janis Joplin had almost completed, became her biggest ever record.

Released in January 1970, it was the number one album in the USA for nine weeks. 'Me and Bobby McGee', written by Kris Kristofferson and taken from the LP, was also a number one single.

Finally, it seemed, Janis Joplin had received the universal acclaim and approval she had sought all her life.

JIM MORRISON

'I am the Lizard King/I can do anything'

From 'The Celebration of the Lizard King'

On Monday 7 March 1968, an incident took place at The Scene, the New York club in the Hell's Kitchen area of Manhattan. It was one in which the three participants involved – Jimi Hendrix, Janis Joplin, and Jim Morrison – seem, with the benefit of cruel hindsight, to have been brought together by fate.

Located at 301 West 46th Street, The Scene was New York City's hippest club-sized venue of the era. From 12 June to 2 July 1967 The Doors had played two sets a night there, supported each evening by the eccentric Tiny Tim. This New York residency had proved a triumph for the Los Angeles group, cementing in New York the status newly achieved by their first US number one single, 'Light My Fire'. This in turn would drive *The Doors*, their eponymously titled first album released in January that year, to the number two slot – one place beneath the Beatles' epochal *Sgt. Pepper* – on the US album charts that September, establishing their eminence as the first nationally successful propagators of what quickly had become known as acid rock.

The Doors had repeated their residency at The Scene from 1 to 5 October, a promotion for *Strange Days*, their second album, which was released that month. It reached number three in the US album charts while its predecessor was still in the Top 10. While many acts struggle with their second album, having used up most of their best material on their first release, *Strange Days* only improved on the first LP.

Jim Morrison was now embedded as a fixture at The Scene, a status he exploited when The Doors returned to New York City, to headline on 22 and 23 March with two shows a night at the newly opened Fillmore East, becoming only the second act to top the bill at the venue. Prior to these dates, The Doors played shows in Hamilton, Rochester and Boston. The concerts in March 1968 in the northeastern United States would become legendary as The Doors' greatest ever live performances. Audiences were amazed by an anti-Vietnam war film they projected to accompany the as yet unreleased song 'The Unknown Soldier', and the group played with such ferocity that they took the crowd's collective breath away. Jim Morrison, moreover, was neither too drunk nor too stoned, as he so often was, and performed at the peak of his powers in these breath-taking dates.

Based in Manhattan for this short tour of the US north-east, The Doors had arrived in the city from the West Coast early in the month, to take part in publicity and promotion.

And so it was that late on 7 March, Jim Morrison found himself at The Scene. The Young Rascals, who had already had US number one singles with 'Good Lovin'' and 'Groovin'', were playing at the club that night. Towards the end of their set they were joined on stage by Jimi Hendrix, always partial to sitting in with suitable musicians. Permanently primed for the magic potential in impromptu musical get-togethers, Hendrix plugged in the open-reel Ampex recorder that he took everywhere with him.

By the time Jimi stepped out onto the stage, Jim Morrison was demonstrably inebriated – he had already irritated Janis Joplin, also in the audience, by drunkenly knocking over her table of drinks. The Doors singer staggered his way to the front of the stage, clambering onto it. According to Danny Fields, later to manage Iggy Pop and the Ramones, Jim – who was 'very drunk' – 'wrapped his arms around Hendrix's knees and started screaming, "I wanna suck your cock." He was very loud and Hendrix was still attempting to play. But Morrison wouldn't let go. It was a tasteless exhibition of scene stealing – something Morrison was really into.'[1]

Janis Joplin had already had a brief sexual frisson with Jim in Los Angeles. But this did not curb her actions. 'Janis walked up and tried to smash a bottle over Morrison's head to get him off Hendrix,' said Fields. 'The three of them were in a tangle of broken glass, dust and guitars. The bodyguards had to send them home, each in their own limousine.'

Within under three-and-a-half years each player in this

absurd and unedifying scenario would be dead, each at the age of twenty-seven.

A poet and visionary of extraordinary ability, James Douglas Morrison, born on 8 December 1943, was one of the most intelligent of all rock stars. He was supremely talented, highly perceptive and exceptionally well educated, both formally and through his own broader studies. After first encountering the German writer's name in Kerouac's *On the Road*, 'Jimmy' Morrison – as he then was, aged sixteen – twice read Friedrich Nietzsche's *The Birth of Tragedy*, following it with the same writer's *Beyond Good and Evil*. It was from Nietzsche that Jim absorbed the notion that whatever did not kill him would only make him stronger (Nietzsche, Ray Manzarek said later, was what killed Jim Morrison). Jim Morrison is the personification of that old adage of being careful what you wish for, because you may get it.

Yet rock 'n' roll and the music industry has always been a home to dysfunctional, damaged people, many deeply so. Extremely talented rebels, often mired in – yet simultaneously driven by – their personal problems. The Doors, moreover, were the biggest American group of the second half of the 1960s: deservedly, as they certainly were one of the greatest bands there has ever been, and the definitive Los Angeles group of that era. Keyboard player Ray Manzarek, guitarist Robby Krieger and drummer John Densmore were all jazz aficionados – there always was an intellectual core to

The Doors' music. Although they recorded for only just over four years, The Doors' tight Gothic sound, married to the supreme confidence and beauty of Morrison's poetic lyrics, along with his suitably enigmatic death in a Paris bathtub in 1971, have made the four-piece one of the most legendary of all rock acts. 'The Doors were asserting themselves as the archetypal band for an American apocalypse that we didn't even know was creeping up on us,' wrote Mikal Gilmore in *Rolling Stone* in 2001. 'The real question,' he continued, 'isn't so much whether we can find the virtue in Jim Morrison's art despite the waste of his life. Rather, the question finally is: Can we separate the two? And if not, what do we make of that?'[2]

The time span of The Doors' career encompassed some of the most vivid tableaux that defined the era, the second half of the much mythologized Sixties: the youth riot on Los Angeles's Sunset Strip in 1966, two months before the release of their first album; the Summer of Love the next year in San Francisco; the emergence of Andy Warhol's New York pop art subculture; the Kent State shootings; Charles Manson and his madness; the moon landing; the murders of Martin Luther King Jr. and Robert Kennedy in 1968; the My Lai massacre and the debacle of the Vietnam War; the election of President Richard Nixon.

And the schism between Jim Morrison and his parents was equally archetypal, carrying a tremendous resonance for the group's fans, many of whom were similarly afflicted in their relationships with their families. Jim's naval officer father, for example, had allegedly disowned him for having chosen to study film at UCLA. (As the son of a Navy officer, he had been expected to attend the US Navy Academy at Annapolis, as his father had done; or perhaps to become a diplomat.) Was this why, in early publicity material, Jim Morrison claimed that his mother and father had been killed in a motoring accident? When The Doors played in Washington, DC in 1967, his mother came to the concert but the singer refused to see her, and never spoke to her again.

In the song 'The End', the final track on The Doors' first album, Jim Morrison showed his true, complex feelings about his mother and father:

> The killer awoke before dawn
> He put his boots on . . .
> And then he walked on down the hall
> And he came to a door
> And he looked inside
> Father?
> Yes, son
> I want to kill you
> Mother, I want . . .

'Morrison himself later said,' wrote Mikal Gilmore, 'that he intended the passage as a metaphor for bidding goodbye to childhood and creating your own lot in life. That's hardly an uninteresting or an improbable reading – especially given how many young people shared a similar sense in the 1960s – though the recitation also seems to depict both a lethal rage and psychic damage that possibly even Morrison himself didn't want to explore much once they had been given voice.'[3]

Unlike such San Francisco groups as Jefferson Airplane and The Grateful Dead, The Doors did not consider peace and love a philosophical priority. Instead, they threatened anarchy, apocalypse, an awfulness everywhere. And The Doors' – Morrison's, really – sense of betrayal by their parents, as evinced in 'The End', partially explains the group's immense popularity amongst US troops serving in Vietnam. One such soldier was Oliver Stone, the film director, who first heard the music of The Doors when he was serving in the First Cavalry Division. At the time he was stoned on marijuana: 'The lyrics were very clear. The music was driving and erotic and sinuous – almost Brechtian and carnivalesque at times, the organ fighting with the guitar. Their first two albums knocked my socks off – that's what the war sounded like to me.' In an irony worth noting, Jim's father, Steve Morrison, was captain – soon to be admiral – of the USS *Bonhomme Richard*, an aircraft carrier stationed in the Gulf of Tonkin in the South China Sea; from the *Bonhomme Richard*'s deck, US warplanes would daily bomb Vietnam.

'I've been reading about the problems kids have with their parents. Yeah. That's right. And I'm here to tell you – I didn't get enough love as a kid!' Jim Morrison famously hollered in 1969 during a show in Seattle.

The eldest son of an inevitably peripatetic Navy family, Jim Morrison suffered from the disruptions of the family home being ceaselessly relocated, regularly losing new groups of friends. Yet, in what could be seen as almost a Nietzschean manner, he benefited from the self-reliant, outsider status this granted him.

After Jim's birth in Melbourne, Florida, the family lived in Albuquerque, New Mexico; Los Altos, California; Alameda, California; Kingsville, Texas; and Alexandria, Virginia, a suburb of Washington, DC. In Alexandria, at George Washington High School, from which he graduated, his teachers were astonished at the breadth and depth of his reading. George Washington High School was not devoid of musical talent amongst its alumni: Mama Cass of The Mamas and the Papas, The Lovin' Spoonful's Zal Yanovsky, and Scott McKenzie, hit recorder of 'If You're Going to San Francisco (Be Sure to Wear Some Flowers in Your Hair)', had all been educated there.

Burying himself in books, and the knowledge they provided, he found a constant he could always rely on. Despite clearly being an intellectual-in-waiting, Jim Morrison was a bully towards his siblings, especially his younger brother, carrying on the behaviour that he had endured from his parents, especially his allegedly sadistic father; he had even, at the age of sixteen, taped up his brother Andy's mouth while he was sleeping.

In Clearwater, Florida, Jim Morrison went to live temporarily with his paternal grandparents while he attended St Petersburg College. In 1962 he transferred to Florida State University in Tallahassee. It was while in college in Florida that he somewhat belatedly discovered the vocal appeal of Elvis Presley, now in his post-army period; for listening to 'Return to Sender' at full volume, he was expelled from a student lodging. (The other influence on his own rich vocals to which Jim Morrison would always admit was Frank Sinatra.) In Clearwater he also met Mary Frances Werbelow, whom he would see every weekend, hitchhiking the 280 miles from Tallahassee. While at FSU he made the decision to study film at the University of California in Los Angeles, and began taking courses that would set him up for this. So, at the very beginning of 1964, he hitchhiked 2,500 miles from Florida to California and enrolled in UCLA's theater arts department.[4] Fortunately, when Jim Morrison was a young boy his father had set up a tuition fund for his eldest son, to which he had access and with which he paid for his course; fortunately, for taking this course was in direct defiance of his father's wishes. As a consequence, his father broke all contact with him.

While at FSU in Tallahassee, Jim Morrison had been arrested at the age of nineteen for being drunk and disorderly, resisting arrest and larceny. He had stolen an umbrella from a police car on the way to a football game, and received a fifty-dollar fine. It was the first indication that drink might cause Jim Morrison difficulties in life. Yet why was he so drawn to drink and, later, drugs? By the need for self-obliteration? From what was he trying to escape? Partially, one senses, Jim Morrison simply liked getting out of it: it was more fun than reality – and there is a great tradition of musicians filling the dead time spent on the road with alcohol. Yet with Jim Morrison it certainly ran deeper than that. Indubitably hedonistic, Jim Morrison's relationship with drugs and alcohol unquestionably brought about his end, directly and indirectly. It lay at the heart of his aberrant behaviour and self-created disasters.

In time, Ray Manzarek, with whom he had founded The Doors, came to see the singer as schizophrenic: there was the very nice, sensitive and creative Jim Morrison; then there was 'Jimbo', a drunken, self-indulgent hedonist, surrounded by idiotic, sycophantic lackeys. As his fondness for psychedelic drugs gave way to alcohol after the release of *Strange Days*, Jim Morrison began to justify his drinking: 'I'm not a musician, I'm a poet. And I'm Irish. The drug of Irish poetry is alcohol.'[5]

By far the most extreme example of Jim Morrison's dysfunctional behaviour was the notorious incident at a Miami show, on 1 March 1969, when he allegedly exposed himself on stage – although no one at the show, audience or band members, ever saw his penis. He may have taken it out, but (if he did) it was kept hidden behind his wafting shirt tails. All the same, it seemed no coincidence that his most extreme transgression should have occurred in his home state, where he had first lived with the parents whose behaviour appeared to haunt him.

For although ostensibly self-possessed to the point of arrogance, inside Jim Morrison was deeply vulnerable. And as is often the case, the roots of this insecurity lay within his childhood.

Prior to his Miami obscenity trial, Jim Morrison told his attorney Max Fink that he had exposed himself because 'I thought it was a good way to pay homage to my parents.' He also told Fink that as a child he frequently wet his bed, and that when he told his mother about this, she would send him back to sleep on the soaking bed linen. He was often reduced to sleeping on the floor.[6]

Even more seriously, Jim Morrison also told Fink that as a young child he had been molested by a male close to the family. Moreover, when he had attempted to inform his mother of this, she had refused to believe her son, telling him he was a liar. The trauma of recounting this to Fink reduced the 26-year-old singer to tears.[7]

The bedwetting followed a deeply disturbing incident, one widely believed to have had a profoundly formative influence on the young 'Jimmy' Morrison. When he was four years old, while driving early one day in New Mexico with his parents and grandparents, they came upon what clearly had been a recent, extremely serious motor accident: a car had ploughed head-on into a truck packed full of Native Americans. There were dead bodies strewn across the road, while those seriously injured moaned and screamed. Inevitably, the gory vision before him fascinated the young boy, as well as burning deeply into his psyche an image that resided there permanently. This was the source of the 'scattered on dawn's highway bleeding' line in 'Dawn's Highway' on the posthumous *An American Prayer*, released in 1978, seven years after Morrison had passed away. And the dead Indians mentioned in 'Peace Frog' on *Morrison Hotel* is a direct reference to this traumatic sight. When Oliver Stone came to direct *The Doors*, the biopic released in 1990, Ray Manzarek told him how Morrison would emit a screech and Manzarek would think, 'This is not the soul of a white man, there's an Indian in there.'

Taking into account the regular diet of LSD and marijuana that he began in 1964, the year he commenced film studies at UCLA, it is perhaps unsurprising that Jim Morrison continued and expanded his interest in the shamanism of Indians from the American south-west. With a friend at the university, Felix Venable, a 35-year-old Berkeley graduate and a connoisseur of the Beat lifestyle, Jim ingested LSD, then still legal. Travelling out to the Joshua Tree area by Palm Springs, they would trip, endeavouring to communicate with shamanic Indian spirits.[8] On one such occasion, Jim revealed to Venable his belief that the spirit of one of the dead Indians he had observed at the car wreck had entered his own soul. Venable subsequently connected Jim Morrison with a UCLA anthropology student who had undertaken research in Mexico with a Yaqui shaman. 'Jimmy knew someone in the department,' wrote Stephen Davis, 'and apparently made contact with Carlos Castaneda, whose dissertation would become the 1968 best-seller and counterculture bible *The Teachings of Don Juan: a Yaqui Way of Knowledge*. Poet Michael Ford was also at UCLA at the time and believes Morrison did meet with Castaneda. But no details of the meeting survive.'

Whatever transpired, as the finely pitched vocalist with The Doors, Jim Morrison took on that shamanistic role of an animal deity, in his case that of The Lizard King. He expressed this on their third album, *Waiting for the Sun*, in the song 'Not to Touch the Earth': 'I am the Lizard King / I can do anything.' The lizard's ability to shed its skin may have had some connection to the leather trousers he would constantly wear. Jim Morrison had also discovered he had an anagrammatic alter ego, Mr Mojo Risin', which he employed in his song *LA Woman*. It was a name that above all else suggested the male libido and the virility of the penis. According to author James Riordan,[9] Doors producer Paul Rothchild recalled that in the recording studio it was not unknown for an invariably drunk Jim Morrison to be found 'involuntarily talking in tongues'. 'The shaman,' said Morrison, 'was a man who would intoxicate himself. He was probably already an unusual individual. And he would put himself into a trance by dancing, whirling around, drinking, taking drugs – whatever. Then he would go on a mental travel and describe his journey to the rest of the tribe.'[10]

Jim Morrison began his studies in Los Angeles in February 1964, the month after the Beatles had so tumultuously arrived in the United States. But it was also six weeks after the death in the city of one of his inspirations, Aldous Huxley, the British author of the dystopian *Brave New World*. Huxley had died on the same day that President John F. Kennedy was murdered in Dallas, Texas. Relocating in 1948 to the then lotus land of southern California, Huxley had become a pioneering participant in consciousness-expanding experiments involving the ingestion of mescaline, peyote, and, later, LSD. In 1954 he had published an account of such experiments in his book *The Doors of Perception*.

Part of Jim Morrison's reason for beginning studies at UCLA in the then brand new discipline of film studies was to avoid compulsory service in the US military. The month that he commenced his UCLA studies, Jim had been obliged to visit his father in San Diego, where the USS *Bonhomme Richard* was docked. Although clad in appropriately preppy clothing, his hair neatly trimmed, he was immediately ordered by his father to attend the ship's barber for a further haircut.

At UCLA Jim Morrison began his course in film production. 'More than anything else,' wrote James Riordan, 'Morrison was interested in reaching the masses and film was the best medium he had found for it up to this time.'[11]

His reading expanded: as well as Nietzsche, he now loved the writing of Blake, Rimbaud, Kafka, Artaud and Baudelaire.[12] The Greek historian Plutarch became a favourite, notably his writings on Alexander the Great. (Oliver Stone, who later made a film about the great Greek leader, was similarly entranced.) He also immersed himself in studying Greek tragedy, and the manner in which its effects were achieved. Soon Jim Morrison would take on the appearance of a Greek god, one that combined oddly with his gaucho look of black leather trousers and white lace shirts. For now, however, he was pudgily overweight and not immediately impressive to look at. Wanting to move with the cool set, a sign of his ambition, he hung out with older students, especially the circle of Felix Venable, with whom he began to drink excessively and ingest LSD. Another student to whom his peers looked up was Ray Manzarek, like Venable older than many of the other students on the film course. Manzarek had already completed his economics degree at DePaul University in Chicago, where he had been born and grown up, the son of Polish parents who had themselves recently moved to the Los Angeles area, to the suburb of Manhattan Beach. Initially he had signed up at UCLA for a law degree, but quickly switched courses. Manzarek was distinctly unimpressed with Morrison's friendship with Venable, considering him 'a plain, evil mind fuck'. As a consequence of this friendship, Manzarek noted, Jim Morrison was 'starting to act a little weird. It's like those black demons were always there just waiting . . . and this guy happened to come along and swing the gate open, and they all came bowling out.'[13]

On their course was an impressive cast list of instructors: among the teachers was Jean Renoir, director of the classic

La Regle du Jeu. He was succeeded by Josef von Sternberg. And Jim Morrison certainly was a serious student of what at the time he clearly intended to be his future craft, travelling in late 1964 the 400 miles to Berkeley, outside San Francisco, to a rare screening of Jean Genet's thirty-minute film *Un Chant d'Amour*, a paean to gay love in prison. Ray Manzarek was also there. Although Manzarek and his girlfriend Dorothy were spending a few days in San Francisco, Morrison had travelled all the way simply for that short film. 'Together, as if we were fated,' wrote Manzarek. 'In the same place, at the same time, for the same art. It was simply meant to be.'[14] And it was not only esoteric foreign art films that bonded the pair: both Manzarek and Morrison were huge fans of the 1961 western *One-Eyed Jacks*, directed by Marlon Brando, rating it far higher than John Ford's revered *The Searchers*. 'We were all Dadaists in a way,' considered Manzarek. 'All a little mad, a little over the top, and all in love with life . . . Jim was a poet. I was the jazzer-musician-blues guy.'[15]

Ray Manzarek noted that Jim Morrison lived in a nice apartment on Goshen Avenue, near the Veterans Hospital complex on Wilshire and San Vicente. 'Obviously his mother and father had a couple of bucks,' thought Manzarek.[16] His book shelves bulged with the tomes of the era: French existentialists such as Sartre, Camus and Genet, as well as cultural reading list American standards like Fitzgerald, Hemingway, Faulkner and the more recent Norman Mailer. Jim Morrison was also partial to the Beat poets, and the highly stylized work of Louis-Ferdinand Céline, the French modernist novelist, whose *Journey to the End of the Night* was a clear influence on The Doors' 'End of the Night'. At his apartment, he and Manzarek would talk and drink beer and smoke pot. Jim was an excellent joint-roller, 'little works of art', according to Manzarek.[17]

Jim's girlfriend from Clearwater, Florida, Mary Werbelow – who was stunningly beautiful, according to Manzarek – had followed him out to LA looking to fulfill her ambition to become a dancer. To Jim's surprise, she had moved into her own place. Enrolling as a student at Los Angeles City College, she took a job as a go-go dancer, becoming 'Gazzari's Go-Go Girl of 1965' at the club of the same name on the Sunset Strip – The Doors would play there the next year. Mary thought this was the start of her career, unaware that it was the highest point she would reach, and that Jim Morrison was tiring of her; their relationship ended when she came to see him and found him with another girl.

Meanwhile, Ray Manzarek, an experienced, classically trained pianist who was also into the blues and modern jazz, had started to play keyboards in a surf band, Rick and the Ravens, who had a regular spot in a Santa Monica bar. Manzarek performed under the stage-name of 'Screamin' Ray Daniels, the bearded blues-shouter', and his five dollars a show earnings contributed to his tuition fees. One night, for no particular reason, he announced that audience member Jim Morrison, 'a poet from UCLA film school', would come up onstage and perform 'Louie Louie', a song that Morrison would facetiously and drunkenly call out for. 'He was good. And he loved it. He bopped around and sang himself hoarse ... That was the first time Jim Morrison ever sang onstage.'[18]

Their film course concluded in May 1965. Jim Morrison received his bachelor's degree in cinematography despite the faculty's rejection of the short film it was compulsory for all students to make. As though exemplifying Nietzsche's aphorism that that which does not kill you will only make you stronger, Jim Morrison was the only student in his year to fail this area of his course. Ray Manzarek felt the faculty's examiners simply did not get it: 'It was cinematic poetry. It was a juxtaposition of images that really didn't have any relationship to one another in a linear, narrative form. But after five minutes went by, it became a collective "whole". It became a poetic piece. I thought it was excellent.'[19]

At the end of their film course, Jim Morrison told Ray Manzarek he was intending to move to New York. Manzarek, however, told Jim his plan was to remain in LA, to make a career as a filmmaker. Gradually it dawned on Manzarek, however, that – despite his time studying – he knew no one who was actually making a living in the Hollywood movie business and had no idea how to get started. For the time being, finances were not too tight for him. Dorothy Fujikawa, his girlfriend, had basic employment, cleaning computer tape. In that post-UCLA comedown, Ray Manzarek was undergoing something of an existentialist crisis about his future. He sought to heal this by working on his tan at Venice Beach.[20]

Down on the sand one day, he suddenly saw what appeared to be a vision walking towards him: Jim Morrison, dressed only in cut-off jeans, looking like a Greek god. The chubby boy from UCLA had lost thirty pounds and now looked tremendous. He had achieved this weight loss by the simple expedient of not eating and, instead, ingesting LSD. And he had been living on the roof of an abandoned Venice office block. To Manzarek's surprise, Morrison declared he been 'writing some songs'.[21] Responding to Manzarek's cajoling, Jim Morrison sang him one of these, 'Moonlight Drive', a song of death, as expressed in its final lines: 'Baby, gonna drown tonight / Goin' down, down, down.' In other words, the first song of his that Morrison performed for Ray Manzarek anticipated his own end. And then he sang him a second song, 'My Eyes Have Seen You'. Then a third: 'Summer's Almost Gone'.

It was an inspirational burst of songwriting. Immediately, Manzarek told him they were going to form a group together, but Morrison wondered at first who would be doing the singing; clearly he lacked any belief in his own vocal abilities. Reassured by the keyboard player of his talent, Morrison was persuaded to move into the tiny Ocean Park apartment in which Manzarek and his girlfriend lived.

Both former film students were serious consumers of LSD and marijuana – major pot-heads. After Morrison had told

Manzarek what the name of their group should be – The Doors, taken from the title of Aldous Huxley's book *The Doors of Perception*, in turn taken from William Blake's poetic line 'If the doors of perception were cleansed everything would appear to man as it is . . . infinite' – they decided that the sound of their group should be psychedelic, a new concept at that time. What they needed was more musicians – as yet they lacked a guitar player and drummer. For a guitarist, Ray Manzarek wanted a player who was a rocker but with a knowledge of jazz – 'Les Paul/Chuck Berry by way of Charlie Christian.'[22]

A principal reason that Jim Morrison had wanted to study at UCLA was because it was in California, renowned since the Second World War for the most cutting edge, and sometimes downright eccentric, thinking in the United States. It was where the most extreme elements of Western culture and philosophy collided with that of the East, the next stop across the Pacific.

Maharishi Mahesh Yogi, the founder of Transcendental Meditation, arrived in Los Angeles in 1965 on his proselytizing world tour. Attracted by what he had learned about the Maharishi's simple meditation techniques, Ray Manzarek attended his series of lectures in Pacific Palisades, in west Los Angeles. There he encountered drummer John Densmore and guitarist Robby Krieger, who had already played together in a group, the Psychedelic Rangers. (Long before the Beatles' interest in the Maharishi's philosophy, therefore, The Doors' three instrumental musicians became followers of Transcendental Meditation, and continued to be so.) At first it was only John Densmore who joined up with Ray Manzarek and Jim Morrison. He suggested they rehearse together and see what happened.

In addition to being the closest geographical point in the mainland USA to Eastern philosophy, California was also the nearest American location to Vietnam, where Jim Morrison's father was stationed, soon to be an admiral in the burgeoning undeclared war. Now no longer a student, Jim Morrison was automatically eligible for the draft. (Ray Manzarek had already served his spell in the US military.) Although the assorted drugs Jim had consumed prior to his physical had little effect, when he declared (as Jimi Hendrix had done to escape the service in which he had already enlisted) that he was a homosexual, he was immediately excused from serving.[23]

Jim Morrison's future was now clear. Early rehearsals took place at Ray Manzarek's parents' Manhattan Beach home: initially they were also working with the keyboard player's brothers, Rick Manzarek (guitar) and Jim Manzarek (harmonica).

Before the four-piece had ever played a live date they recorded a demo tape, in three hours, at World Pacific Studios on Third Street in downtown Los Angeles. The demo contained several songs, notably a tune called 'Hello, I Love You', which Jim had dreamed up when a gorgeous black girl had walked past Ray Manzarek and himself on Venice Beach. Then there were 'Moonlight Drive', 'Summer's Almost Gone' and 'My Eyes Have Seen You' – the three songs Jim had sung the keyboard player when they met on Venice Beach – as well as a couple of new numbers: 'End of the Night', and 'A Little Game (Go Insane)'.

Together they shopped their demo around the record labels of Los Angeles, largely encountering utter indifference or downright disdain. They went for a meeting with Lou Adler at ABC Dunhill; as he had signed The Mamas and the Papas, they had great respect for him. But he was dismissive of their work: 'Nothing here I can use.' 'That's okay, man. We don't want to be used, anyway,' Jim Morrison immediately punched back.[24] (Ray Manzarek felt they later paid for that remark by Jim. Lou Adler became one of the promoters of 1967's legendary Monterey Pop Festival – although by then a major break-out act in the United States, The Doors were never invited to play the event.)

At Columbia Records, however, the four musicians fared far better. Newly appointed to the A&R department, with a brief to develop new acts, Billy James gave them a deal of sorts. 'They had a quality that attracted me to them immediately. I guess they appealed to the snob in me because they were UCLA graduates and I thought, "Great, here are some intellectual types getting involved with rock 'n' roll." . . . The music was so raw, so basic, so simplistic, so unlike anything I was familiar with.'[25]

As Columbia owned Vox, the instruments manufacturer, James gave his newly signed musicians carte blanche at Vox's warehouse in the San Fernando Valley. Ray Manzarek kitted himself out with a free Vox organ and amplifier.

Yet nothing more seemed to happen at Columbia for The Doors. Unbeknownst to them, Billy James had run into difficulties at the label. Newly promoted to A&R from Columbia's publicity department, he felt he lacked sufficient production experience to do credit to his new signings, and the company's more seasoned producers were all tied up with their own projects. Losing faith with the label, Ray Manzarek's brothers quit the group. This was when the guitarist Robby Krieger, whom the keyboard player had also met at the Transcendental Meditation centre, was pulled in. Trained in both classical and jazz guitar, he had experienced an epiphany when he saw Chuck Berry perform at Santa Monica Civic, immediately trading in his classical instrument for a Gibson SG, the identical guitar played by Berry. Not unconnected to his fondness for Eastern mysticism, he had also become adept on the sitar, courtesy of lessons at the Los Angeles Ravi Shankar school.

They found space for practising in Santa Monica, in a garage behind the bus depot. Soon Ray Manzarek took a small apartment in nearby Venice, where they could rehearse all day. A cloud of marijuana smoke hung over their rehearsals. Permanently high on powerful weed, The Doors found their sound quickly. 'Robby's bottleneck guitar was snake-weaving us into the fourth dimension, into a higher, expanded state of consciousness. We had gone primordial and cosmic at the same time,' wrote Manzarek.[26] Then Robby Krieger came up with the structure of a simple song that soon turned into a tune called 'Light My Fire'.

Of these times, Jim Morrison later recalled: 'In the beginning we were creating our music, ourselves, every night . . . starting with a few outlines, maybe a few words for a song. Sometimes we worked out in Venice, looking at the surf. We were together a lot and it was good times for all of us. Acid, sun, friends, the ocean, and poetry and music.'[27]

They auditioned for a bass player, but then Ray Manzarek discovered the Fender-Rhodes keyboard bass. The instrument also gave great freedom to John Densmore's drumming.

In January 1966 Jim Morrison, his UCLA friend Felix Venable, and Philip O'Leno, whom they both knew from the same college, declared their intention to drive to Mexico, only 100 miles distant, where they would commune with Native American sages and consume peyote. It is more likely that they only got as far as New Mexico, however. Somewhere along the way, while pulled up at a red stop light, Jim Morrison jumped out of their vehicle, ran over to a Mexican-American girl, kissed her on the mouth, and then leapt back into the car. Returning to Los Angeles, Jim Morrison and Felix Venable were covered in bruises; Jim told a patently untrue story of how they had beaten Phil O'Leno to death, leaving him in a riverbed. On hearing this, O'Leno's father had Jim Morrison arrested and slung into jail. He was soon bailed, and the case fell apart when O'Leno surfaced in Los Angeles. Later, it was suggested that all three had been beaten by police in New Mexico, or that O'Leno and Jim Morrison had come to blows over a girl.

In February 1966 The Doors auditioned for an utterly undistinguished club on the Sunset Strip, the London Fog. It had virtually no audience, apart from local hookers and alcoholic lowlife. But they got the gig, beginning later that month. Playing from Thursday to Sunday, The Doors performed five sets a night, for ten dollars each. (A go-go dancer, one Rhonda Lane, would dance in a cage as they played.) As had the Beatles' similar stints in Hamburg nightclubs, the rigour of these sets honed The Doors into a fine rock 'n' roll machine, especially Jim Morrison, whose initially weak vocals were becoming far stronger. He was also losing his nervousness over performing – at first he would sing with his back to the audience. 'All that singing was exercising his throat muscles and they were getting strong and thick,' wrote Ray Manzarek.[28]

About a month after The Doors had begun their London Fog residency, redheaded Pamela Courson walked into the club, having driven the thirty or so miles up from Orange County where she lived with her parents. After they had finished their set, John Densmore began to chat her up, believing he had got off with her. But then it was time for the next Doors' set. By the time they had come off stage, she had disappeared.

Some days later, at a UCLA party, Jim Morrison saw her again. She was with a man. When he finally got to speak with her, she told him she was studying art at Los Angeles Community College. Before he could ask for her number, she was distracted and disappeared.

The next weekend, however, she turned up again at the London Fog. Again, John Densmore steamed in on her. Then Jim Morrison sat down beside the pair of them in a booth at the club and leaned over and bit her on the neck. This unorthodox courting gesture caused her to become immediately smitten with him.

Early in May, however, the London Fog ran into financial difficulties and The Doors were fired. It was a time of changes for the group: realizing that nothing whatsoever seemed to be going on with their Columbia deal, they asked for the label to release them, not appreciating they were about to be dropped anyway. But a new opportunity appeared almost straight away.

Before they had finished their final week at the London Fog, Ronnie Harran, the booker for the far more prestigious Whisky A Go Go, came to the venue on Thursday 5 May 1966 and saw them play. She immediately signed The Doors as house band for the nearby Whisky, booking them to play a pair of sets a night for $135 a week each.[29]

As the Whisky house band, The Doors supported the headline act. The first week at the Whisky A Go Go, the tremendous headliner was Them, with the 'possessed Celt', as

Manzarek described Van Morrison, as front man. Invariably drunk, Van the Man, as he would become known, would pound the stage floor with his microphone stand. Jim Morrison would soon be emulating this element of his stage-craft. But, Ray Manzarek observed, that was not the only aspect of the Ulsterman that Jim Morrison, enamoured of his namesake, endeavoured to emulate: another attraction was his considerable consumption of alcohol. 'The thing that was so interesting to me was to learn how much chaos there was inside the group Them,' said Paul Rothchild, who would go on to produce The Doors. 'It's almost as if Jim studied their chaos and brought it into The Doors.'[30]

Having befriended each other, on the last night Van and Jim Morrison jammed together on stage, Jim joining in with Van on the classic 'Gloria'.[31] (Among the other acts that The Doors supported that summer were The Animals, Buffalo Springfield, The Byrds, Captain Beefheart and his Magic Band, and the Mothers of Invention.)

The exposure earned by The Doors at the hip Whisky A Go Go quickly brought them to the attention of its equally hip patrons. Arthur Lee, for example, the leader of the already revered Love, had immediately understood what The Doors were about. Love had signed to Elektra, an effort by the folk label to expand its roster into the blossoming new rock market. Now Elektra was searching for further top-quality rock acts – Buffalo Springfield had been a target, but the label lost out to Atlantic. So when Jac Holzman, Elektra's founder, came to the Whisky to watch a Love show, Lee insisted he remain and check out The Doors' next set. Exhausted after a flight from New York City, Holzman did not at first get them. Arthur Lee was so persuasive that Holzman returned to watch their next four shows, finally understanding and falling utterly for The Doors, and offering to sign them. 'Love had gotten my foot in the rock door, and now I needed a second group to give Elektra more of that kind of credibility, but The Doors weren't showing it to me,' wrote Holzman in his autobiography *Follow the Music*. 'Jim was lovely to look at, but there was no command. Perhaps I was thinking too conventionally, but their music had none of the rococo ornamentation with which a lot of rock and roll was being embellished – remember, this was still the era of the Beatles and *Revolver*, circa 1966. Yet, some inner voice whispered that there was more to them than I was seeing or hearing, so I kept returning to the club.

'Finally, the fourth evening, I heard them. Jim generated an enormous tension with his performance, like a black hole, sucking the energy of the room into himself. The bass line was Ray Manzarek playing a second keyboard, piano bass, an unusual sound, very cadenced and clean. On top of Ray, Robby Krieger laid shimmering guitar. And John Densmore was the best drummer imaginable for Jim – whatever Morrison did Densmore could follow . . . this was no ordinary rock and roll band.'[32]

Holzman was impressed by not only The Doors' inclusion

in their set of Kurt Weill's 'Alabama Song', with its elements of foxtrot and blues, but also by their arrangement of it. 'And when I heard, really heard, Manzarek's baroque organ line under 'Light My Fire', I was ready to sign them.'

Holzman offered them a one-year, one-album contract with two one-year options, with a reported initial advance of $5,000. The official signing took place in New York. Elektra flew the four musicians there, and set up The Doors' first club gigs in the city, at Ondine's, a hip venue. As though to emphasize their sophisticated roots, John Densmore and Ray Manzarek went to see Dizzy Gillespie play at the Metropole club.[33]

The group had dinner at the New Jersey home of Paul Rothchild, whom Holzman had earmarked to produce their first LP. Just out of jail on a pot charge, Rothchild was being given a break by Holzman. That evening Jim, drunk, came on very openly to Rothchild's wife, a cause of concern for the other group members – they felt Jim was like a child seeing how far he could push it with the parent figure of Paul Rothchild.[34] On the drive back to their fleabag hotel in Manhattan, Jim started to pull Rothchild's hair as he was driving. But then he transferred his attentions to Ray, doing the same thing to him.[35] Back in his hotel room Jim stripped naked and, drunkenly, stood out on the window ledge. Then he pissed on his hotel room's floor rug.[36] Shouldn't such puerile behaviour have been interpreted as a worrying sign?

At Ondine's, however, The Doors triumphed, and became

the talk of the town: Andy Warhol appeared with his entourage, a sign of a certain form of success, as did the actor Warren Beatty.

Back in Los Angeles, The Doors now had a reputation as the hottest new local group. Jim Morrison was being spoken of as a sex symbol: he took advantage of as many of the opportunities this presented to him as he possibly could. 'The word was out on the street that everyone had to see this lead singer because there had never been anything like him, with the unnatural grace of someone out of control,' wrote Pamela Des Barres, former rock and roll groupie, in her book *I'm With the Band*. 'He looked like a Greek god gone wrong, with masses of dark brown curls and a face that sweaty dreams are made of . . . It was really mind-boggling. There was no modern sexy American icon at that time and he instantly became that for me and all the girls I knew and we never missed them. I saw The Doors play a hundred times.'

All the same, Pamela Courson reigned supreme as the queen of Jim's harem. 'Pamela had reddish golden hair, porcelain skin, and lavender eyes. Their sex life was weird. Pam could take his tying her up and beating her, but what she really minded was Jim's penchant for anal intercourse,' revealed Ellis Amburn in *Pearl*, his biography of Janis Joplin.[37] Jerry Hopkins and Danny Sugerman, Morrison's first biographers, described an archetypal Morrison sexual encounter with a girl he had just met in West Hollywood's Alta Cienega

Motel, of all the sleazy lodging houses used by Morrison, the one he most favoured: 'he got her whole life story, then he butt-fucked her.'[38]

Despite the evident success of their musical project, Jim Morrison all of a sudden committed what could in retrospect be seen as an act of self-sabotage – of a kind that, as time progressed, would become increasingly common. To Ray Manzarek he declared that he had a problem with the line-up: he didn't like drummer John Densmore. Despite their clearly defined sound, Jim Morrison wanted him fired. What sparked this? Was it the jealous memory that The Doors' drummer had been the first to attempt to hit on his girlfriend? He seemed to harbour deeply rooted subconscious resentment towards John Densmore. Later, Jim came round to John and his girlfriend's apartment as he tripped on acid, virtually destroying the place and pissing in their bed.[39] Did the drummer's calm outlook on life, partially influenced by his Transcendental Meditation practice, unhinge Jim Morrison, who must have known in the core of his being that much of his own behaviour was downright dysfunctional?

Soon this whim of sacking John Densmore passed over. In August 1966, they recorded their first album in a four-track studio in six days, the songs well set into their playing psyches. This would be their biggest ever seller.

In the album's initial publicity blurbs, Jim talked about being attracted to chaos, revolt, disorder. 'I thought they'd never play our records with comments like that!' remembers John Densmore.[40] New York critic Richard Goldstein had perceptively labelled Jim's lyrics as 'Joycean Rock'. But The Grateful Dead's Jerry Garcia understood the dark side of the group. 'Everybody says the Dead are so dark,' he mused. 'Well, what about The Doors? They were the dark band of the sixties.'

By the end of the first week of September 1966, the group's debut album had been recorded. The Doors were anxious for the eponymously titled long player to be in the stores. Yet Jac Holzman advised them that, to avoid the record becoming lost in the Christmas release rush, he did not intend to put out *The Doors* until January. To mollify the anxious musicians, he assured them no other Elektra album would be released that month, thereby guaranteeing for a brief time the ceaseless attention of the record company's publicity, promotions and marketing department.

The last track on *The Doors* was the 11-minute epic 'The End', a remarkable work by any standards. Had there ever been a song of such ambition in the rock 'n' roll genre? Initially the tune was about the break-up Jim Morrison had had at UCLA with Mary Werbelow, the girl who had followed him out to Los Angeles from Florida. 'Every time I hear that song,' Jim Morrison told *Rolling Stone* writer Jerry Hopkins in 1969, 'it means something else to me. It started out as a simple goodbye song . . . Probably just to a girl, but I see how it could be a goodbye to a kind of childhood. I really don't know. I think it's sufficiently complex and universal in its imagery that it could be almost anything you want it to be.'[41]

In fact, 'The End''s Oedipal lyrics could have come straight from an extreme psychoanalytic session. Self-consciously histrionic, 'The End' evoked Greek theatre. It is impossible, really, to see the song as anything other than an exorcizing of Jim Morrison's clearly complex feelings about his parents. On first hearing, 'The End' was startling.

Inevitably, Jim Morrison had dropped acid before the recording session. But at first the song wouldn't click for the singer. Paul Rothchild and Morrison sat and talked it through all evening. The next morning the first take nailed the number. Paul Rothchild felt the recording equipment almost worked itself, in harmony with this great, extremely ambitious work. Yet it clearly had a psychological effect on the singer. That night he returned to the studio, alone, in a drink- or drug-induced frame of mind, and – after removing his boots and shirt – sprayed it with the foamy contents of a fire extinguisher.

As though signifying the breadth and depth of The Doors' music, 'The End' sat perfectly comfortably alongside blatantly commercial songs like 'Light My Fire'. ('The End' would gain legendary status when featured in Francis Ford Coppola's *Apocalypse Now*, which further embedded The Doors in popular culture.)

The Doors was released on 4 January 1967, right as that year of change kicked in. The Elektra label already had an aura of cool about it, and the centrepiece of their marketing could only confirm that: the billboards of Sunset Boulevard had long sold junk products, but now the Strip, the apogee of the band's scene, was graced with the presence of their album cover. The first time this had ever been done for a musical act, the billboard was a statement of Elektra's faith in their new signing, Holzman averred. The same day that the album came out, Elektra also released the group's first single, 'Break on Through', with its bossa nova beat, coupled with 'End of the Night' on the flip.

'Break on Through' was a failure as a single, reaching only 126 in the US national chart – although it was number eleven on the LA chart. But the next 45 fared far better. Released in April as a single, 'Light My Fire', largely written by Robby Krieger but credited to the whole group, was number one nationally for three weeks – although it took time, three months, for the single to peak, on 25 July. (In celebration, Jim Morrison bought a black leather suit to wear on stage.) Similarly, the album had steadily risen up the US album charts, until it hit the number two spot in September 1967, behind only the mighty Beatles' *Sgt. Pepper*.

In January 1967, The Doors played six nights at the Fillmore in San Francisco, important shows in the self-styled alternative culture capital of California. First they supported The Young Rascals and Sopwith Camel, for three nights. Then they opened for The Grateful Dead and Junior Wells and his All-Stars. On that occasion, however, there were signs of impending problems: for the second of those concerts, Jim Morrison was a no-show, sitting in a Sacramento cinema through three screenings of the classic film *Casablanca* and never turning up at the venue.

In March they played San Francisco's Avalon, this time topping the bill. *The Doors* was heading up the album charts and the evening was 'one stoned gig', as John Densmore described it.[42] They were supported by Country Joe and the Fish and Sparrow. This was the first time they had noticed serious audience appreciation for 'The End', as though 'they were meeting us halfway,' Densmore wrote.

Soon they also topped the bill at San Francisco's Winterland. 'When The Doors came on to do their thing,' read a review in the *New York Times* (a sign of their growing popularity), 'there was sudden silence and the crowd sat as if it were about to hear a chamber music concert.'

In Janis Joplin's apartment in San Francisco one night, Ellis Amburn wrote, Pamela Courson was present and sat and watched as Janis requested Jim's presence in her bedroom. After waiting several hours, she eventually took a cab to her hotel with Big Brother and the Holding Company guitarist Sam Andrew. Later, after that night with Jim Morrison, Janis gave the thumbs-down to the experience. 'I don't like Jim Morrison. He was okay in bed, but when he got up the next morning, he asked for a shot of sloe gin.'[43] It was the inappropriate choice of liquor that occasioned Janis's doubts about The Doors' singer.

Clearly Pamela Courson felt obliged to accept her consort's egregious rock-star behaviour. But she would get even, taking up with Tom Baker, a friend of Jim's, an actor considered a 'hunk' by girls, who would soon star in *I, a Man*, a Warhol sub-porn movie. With a pair of cohorts, he was known as one of 'the boys who fuck famous women.'[44] (After he had appeared nude in the Warhol film, Baker challenged Jim Morrison to let it all hang out at a Doors show – which eventually Jim Morrison almost did, causing himself immense problems.)

There were further examples of bad rock-star behaviour. Sitting one night that summer in a booth in New York's Max's Kansas City, Jim Morrison was too drunk to get up and urinate in the men's room. Instead, he pissed several times into an empty wine bottle. At the end of the evening, he gifted it to the waitress, telling her he hadn't time to finish the apparently half-full bottle.

On Saturday 29 April, The Doors and The Grateful Dead jointly topped the bill at a show at the Earl Warren Showgrounds in Santa Barbara, California – a pair of the leading proponents of underground rock, both with their hot debut albums recently released. The Dead's acid guru Owsley Stanley gifted Jim Morrison his specialty: purple barrel LSD.

Two weeks later, The Doors again were topping the bill at San Francisco's Avalon Ballroom. Future Doors road manager Bill Siddons saw the show: 'We ended up sitting in the audience at this show at the Avalon Ballroom, watching this maniac. What I remember is Jim on stage. I wasn't affected one way or the other by meeting him, but when I saw him on stage I was more emotionally gripped and moved and disturbed than I had ever been at any similar type of thing.

'I remember thinking, WHAT? What is he saying? What is he doing? I don't get it. And then he said something about "Awkward instant / And the first animal is jettisoned / Legs furiously pumping / Their stiff green gallop" and I went, "This guy is completely out of his mind." But I was moved by it, I could feel it. It was the first time poetry had been a movie to me, the images were so strong that they came to mind in a photo form. I could see the horses jumping off the boat. I could see them drowning.

'So what was my first impression of Jim? He scared me to death.'[45]

That same month of May, The Doors began to tentatively record their second album. The majority of the sessions would take place in August that year, however.

In New York, meanwhile, on Saturday 12 August, The Doors supported the adored Simon and Garfunkel at the Forest Hills Tennis Club before 13,000 people. It was entirely the wrong audience, as the crowd were predominantly there to watch the revered folkie duo. The Doors only played four songs, on borrowed equipment, and Ray Manzarek felt it was the worst show they had ever performed. While in the city Jim Morrison had a fling with Gloria Stavers, the editor of *16*, the teen magazine. He also brought Nico, already a member of The Velvet Underground, back to his hotel room. 'Ja, Jim ist crazy,' she later declared.[46]

In Manhattan on 11 June 1967 The Doors played a full theatre date at the Village Theater. All seemed to be going extremely well for the band, yet four days later, Jim Morrison was in a furious frame of mind. Reports were filtering in of huge crowds at the Monterey Pop Festival in California, and not only of the event's great success but of its cultural significance. Jim Morrison was incensed that they had not been invited to the festival, believing it indicated the creation of a snobbish gap between San Francisco and Los Angeles acts. Was this, as Ray Manzarek suspected, Lou Adler's revenge for the way Jim had spoken to him at their meeting at his label?

In Los Angeles in August 1967 they recommenced recording their second album. Jim Morrison had already declared in a radio interview that it would be called *Strange Days*. There was already an advance order of 500,000 for the as yet unrealized record.

In an article written while they were making the album, the celebrated writer Joan Didion observed, with considerable prescience, that Jim Morrison was suggesting 'some range of the possible just beyond a suicide pact'.[47]

There were lighter moments. Like the Manhattan photo shoot for *Vogue* in September 1967. The pictures were taken by 24-year-old Baron Alexis Alfonse von Gecman Waldeck in his Chelsea loft for that December's edition of the upmarket fashion magazine. 'In Jim Morrison I saw a peasant,' Waldeck told *Crawdaddy!* magazine. 'He could be a Russian peasant. I would love to photograph him in a wheat field in a wagon, with an open shirt. There's similarity between Nureyev and Morrison. There's that pride – you know, very much Self. They both like to see themselves. Morrison loves himself.'

The photographer's shots were complemented by words from the New York writer Albert Goldman in which he waxed lyrical about Jim Morrison as 'the one authentic sex hero of the current generation . . . the most admired figure on the American rock scene.' (In *Feast of Friends*, the documentary about The Doors directed by – among others – Jim Morrison, Goldman, a great champion of the group, is in the very first scene, in footage showing The Doors' singer speaking with him in a limousine. Goldman would go on to write hugely successful – and controversial – biographies of Lenny Bruce, Elvis Presley and John Lennon, and at the time of his death was working on a biography of Morrison.)

More than anything, it was these unexpectedly dignified *Vogue* images that led to the transmogrification of Jim Morrison, singer with The Doors, into Jim Morrison the Sex Symbol. 'If my antenna are right he could be the biggest thing to grab the mass libido in a very long time. I have never seen such an animalistic response from so many different kinds of women,' wrote *Village Voice* columnist Howard Smith.[48]

'The quality Morrison has got,' considered Gloria Staver, the editor of the million-selling *16* magazine, with whom Jim had already had a fling. 'The teenagers see their thing, the secretaries in my office have become entranced by him, the New York hippies at the Fillmore dig him. There's something for everybody. But it's still Whole. He walks through the fire and he comes out Whole.'[49]

On that same visit to New York, on 17 September 1967, The Doors appeared on the almost mythical *Ed Sullivan Show*. They were to perform 'People Are Strange' from the imminent *Strange Days* album, and 'Light My Fire', their number one hit single from the first LP. Minutes before their performance, a producer came to their dressing room: the 'Light My Fire' line 'Girl, we couldn't get much higher' would need to be changed to 'Girl, we couldn't get much better'. The Doors appeared to agree to this. Except that when Jim Morrison sang the song live on national television, he stuck to the original version of the lyrics. Afterwards the production staff informed the group that they had been ready to book them on a further six shows. Now, however, they were banned from *The Ed Sullivan Show*, seemingly forever.

Strange Days, for which the *Vogue* photo shoot and the *Ed Sullivan Show* performance had served as promotion, was in the stores in the United States on 25 September, less than nine months after the group's first LP had been released. Put out as a single, 'People Are Strange' scraped the Top 10, but failed to emulate the number one status of 'Light My Fire'. 'Love Me Two Times', the second single off *Strange Days*, only made 25 – although we will come to the curious circumstances behind this. The lack of a smash hit 45 was used as an explanation for why *Strange Days* never made it higher than the number three album slot. Memorable for its distinctive cover – featuring none of the group and shot in a New York alley – if anything, the record was even better than *The Doors*. As though it was competing with the eleven-minute version of 'The End' that concluded the first album, *Strange Days* had another eleven minute final tune. 'When the Music's Over' was an early pro-ecology epic of considerable insight:

> What have they done to the earth?
> What have they done to our fair sister?
> Ravaged and plundered and ripped her and bit her
> Stuck her with knives in the side of the dawn
> And tied her with fences and dragged her down.

But does 'When the Music's Over' possess the majesty of the impossible-to-emulate 'The End'? Perhaps not.

On Sunday 27 August 1967, The Doors had played at the Cheetah, a venue on Santa Monica Pier. Before an audience of 2,000, Jim Morrison had deliberately fallen off the stage, to be caught by the audience. Towards the end of 1967 in live shows he was moving much more spontaneously on stage as he performed his visionary, shamanic act. At the beginning of December, however, a far darker force moved into his life.

On Saturday 9 December 1967 The Doors played in New Haven, Connecticut. While making out with an 18-year-old local girl in a backstage shower stall prior to the show, Jim was interrupted by a cop who opened the door. Seeming to believe the singer was a member of the audience who had somehow snuck backstage, the officer ordered him to leave the room. As he would, Jim told the cop to fuck off. For this response, the policeman sprayed mace into the singer's eyes. In pain, Jim Morrison ran screaming to the group's dressing room. Bill Siddons then emerged to inform the cop of his error. The officer apologized, although such regret begs the question as to why he would have felt entitled to mace a member of the audience? As a metaphor for a jagged schism in an egregiously conflicted nation, in which lines were distinctly being drawn between 'straight' and 'non-straight' society, it is compelling. (Might one also not muse on Jim Morrison's awkward relationships with uniformed authority? Did such figures in any way trigger nerves that reminded him of his naval officer father?)

As though in some absurdist cartoon of precisely how not to behave at such events, local police hovered on the edge of the New Haven stage. During The Doors' last number, 'Back Door Man', Jim Morrison – who had performed the concert with stinging red eyes – told the audience the tale of what had happened backstage prior to the show. Now he taunted the police. Thrusting his mike under the nose of one of them, he commanded: 'Say your thing, man!' Almost immediately, the house lights were switched on. Police stepped forward, arresting the singer and dragging him offstage – the first time this had ever happened to an artist in the United States. The hall erupted with fury. In the ensuing riot by the audience, many fans were also arrested.

Taken to a local police station, Jim Morrison was charged with 'breach of the peace, resisting arrest and indecent or immoral exhibition'. Further arrests were made as angry protesters gathered outside the police station. At two in the morning, The Doors' singer was released from the station on a bail bond of $1,500. A trial was set for the next month.

They had started the year on the high of the release of their first album, *The Doors*. By the end of 1967, The Doors' singer seemed briefly to have become Public Enemy Number One.

After the New Haven incident, and despite the fact that all charges against the singer were very quickly dropped, the FBI opened a file on Jim Morrison. Like the actions of the mace-spraying patrolman, the fallout from this incident further highlighted the cultural schism in the United States. And that New Haven drama had another down side; although Jim Morrison should have been deemed innocent until found guilty, this was not the response of the nation's radio schedulers. 'Love Me Two Times', the second single off the *Strange Days* album, was heading up the charts, only to stumble and be held at no higher than the number 25 slot – in the wake of the onstage arrest, The Doors were temporarily banned from further AM radio play. And there was a nasty fallout within the group itself. Robby Krieger expressed to John Densmore[50] the extreme dislike that he now felt for Jim Morrison and how it seemed as though the group's other three members had now become his babysitters. As though to achieve a clearer perspective on their lives, Robby Krieger and John Densmore took a month's leave of absence from The Doors. They decided to undertake an advanced Transcendental Meditation course of some rigour in the presence of the Maharishi Mahesh Yogi. Around the same time they enrolled in Los Angeles's newly opened Ravi Shankar Kinara School of Indian Music.

Were The Doors' drummer and guitarist readying themselves for the group's next phase? For there was no time for hanging around – within the space of a year The Doors had become the biggest American group, and their workload was becoming more relentless. Yet the by now familiar brouhahas in which the group's singer seemed to become snared showed little sign of abating. In Las Vegas on 29 January 1968, in the parking lot of the Pussy Cat A Go Go, Jim Morrison feigned smoking a joint in front of a security guard. The guard called over colleagues and Morrison and Bob Grover, a *New York Times* journalist who was with him, were given a beating. Police were called and the singer was charged with 'vagrancy, public drunkenness and failure to possess sufficient identification'. In an article subsequently written by Grover, he remarked of Jim Morrison: 'His charisma was such that your ordinary upholder of the established order could be infuriated merely by the sight of Morrison strolling down the street – innocent to all outward appearances but . . . well there was that invisible something about him that silently suggested revolution, disorder, chaos.'[51]

On Monday 19 February 1968, the group went into Hollywood's TTG recording studios, at the junction of Sunset and Highland, to begin sessions for their next album. An entire side of the album was to be filled with Jim's poem 'The Celebration of the Lizard'. Yet the group's three principal musicians paid such attention to the instrumental pieces that much of the desired cohesion between them and the vocals became lost. Ultimately the notion of recording 'The Celebration of the Lizard' was abandoned.

When sessions resumed at the beginning of March, Jim Morrison showed a clear disinclination to participate in the recording process. One day he arrived in the pink Jaguar E-type of actress Sable Sperling. He was clutching a bottle of Wild Turkey and they were both on downers, the singer claiming to have swallowed some twenty Quaaludes. Jim Morrison was supposed to be there to perform the vocals on 'Love Street' and 'Summer's Almost Gone'. Unfortunately Jim could barely stand. He declared that he didn't want to sing those songs and would perform 'Five to One' instead.[52] Although everyone – especially Rothchild – expected him to keel over at any moment, he nailed the take. Ray Manzarek had noticed what seemed to be a birthmark on Sable Sperling's shapely thigh; perusing it more closely, he saw it was a long, swollen bruise. What had happened? he asked her. Oh, she replied, Jim had hit her with a plank of wood.

This was by no means the only occasion that Jim Morrison turned up drunk at TTG. He was frequently accompanied by other extremely odd people. One day he arrived with a woman who looked like the as yet unknown Charles Manson; Jim's friends pulled up her skirt and offered the assembled company the opportunity to enjoy themselves in her anus.[53] Such incidents made John Densmore declare his intention to quit the group. Paul Rothchild told him he was worried that Jim Morrison would not last long.

Midway through the sessions, Jim Morrison cut off much of his hair, badly and unattractively, as if to represent his psyche.[54] Paul Rothchild summoned a band meeting. 'Jim . . . you don't seem interested in participating much in the recording of this album. What are you doing? You don't look like a rock star anymore.' 'Stop him?' Rothchild responded later to a question from the writer Vic Garbarini.[55] 'Everybody tried to stop him. You couldn't. Strangers would stop him on the street and try to help him. We all tried to stop him. If you'd know Jim for even ten seconds, you'd know one thing: he was unstoppable. He was his own motive force, an astounding human being. There was no stopping him.'

In an interview to promote the new record, Robby Krieger remarked: 'There was a lot of Jim getting drunk and bringing drunken friends into the studio and Paul throwing them out. Scenes, heavy pill-taking and stuff. That was rock 'n' roll to its fullest.'[56]

By early March 1968, however, the studio sessions had been put to one side as The Doors headed for the East Coast and an epochal set of shows, including their performances at the Fillmore East. This was the period when, to the annoyance of Janis Joplin, Jim Morrison stumbled onto the stage at the Scene club in Manhattan as Jimi Hendrix played with The Young Rascals.

By the time they returned to the recording studio in Los Angeles, the idea of recording 'The Celebration of the Lizard' had been scrapped – although the 'Not to Touch the Earth' section was retained. The group had agreed to fund the *Feast of Friends* documentary.

This documentary was an opening salvo in a bid for independence by The Doors. In April, with an advance from Elektra, they bought out their management team, who were replaced by Bill Siddons, their nineteen-year-old tour manager. They opened an office in West Hollywood at 8512 Santa Monica Boulevard, near the junction with La Cienega. Not long after this, Jim walked into the new offices and announced to Ray Manzarek, 'I wanna quit.'[57] He told Ray he thought he was having a nervous breakdown. The keyboard player suggested this frame of mind might have something to do with being drunk all the time. And Ray persuaded him to hang on for another six months.

The recording process for what became known as *Waiting for the Sun* was arduous and painful – at times like tooth extraction, Paul Rothchild obsessing over every possible sound glitch. (John Densmore felt this may have had something to do with a jar labelled 'KD' that Rothchild kept behind his console: 'KD' stood for 'Killer Dope'.)

By the end of April, the new album was finally ready for release. Although it was named after the tune 'Waiting for the Sun', that song would not appear until 1970's *Morrison Hotel*.

In March the first 45 was issued, the controversial 'The Unknown Soldier' with its critical references to the Vietnam war. Considering the political climate in the United States, it was amazing the song received any airplay whatsoever. However, it managed to scrape into the Top 40, peaking at 39.

Early in June, the second single was released from the new album: 'Hello, I Love You', coupled with 'Love Street'.

The release of 'Hello, I Love You', one of the songs on The Doors' original demo, also met with considerable controversy, but of another kind altogether. The Doors were criticized for the release of what was condemned as an outright commercial song, possibly stolen from The Kinks' 'Tired of Waiting', and clearly aimed at the hit parade. Which, of course, it was: why on earth else would a song be chosen as a single? But it was simultaneously a perfect piece of garage band punk, driven by Manzarek's thrusting keyboards and the singer's powerful liquid baritone, and climaxing in Morrison's war whoops. And it achieved the desired effect: 'Hello, I Love You' stealthily crept up the charts until, on 3 August, it was the number one single in the United States, staying in this chart position for two weeks. (Also in the US Top 5 at that time was José Feliciano's version of 'Light My Fire'. Paradoxically, it was the success of their own version of 'Light My Fire' that had polarized their audience. Were The Doors a

Top 40 hit act or proselytizers for the revolution – whatever that revolution was?)

After the release of *Waiting for the Sun* on 12 July 1968, album sales were bolstered by the success of 'Hello, I Love You' and it went to number one in the US album charts the same week that the single hit the top slot. (The Doors had now become internationally successful – both 'Hello, I Love You' and *Waiting for the Sun* made the UK Top 20s.)

A string of major North American dates in arena-sized venues promoted the new album. On 5 July 1968, The Doors topped the bill at the Hollywood Bowl in Los Angeles, selling out all 18,000 seats. The show was recorded for the *Feast of Friends* film. The group were joined by Mick Jagger and music producer Jimmy Miller for a pre-show dinner at Mu Ling's Chinese restaurant. Whether or not he was weighted down by his extensive helping of food, Jim Morrison gave a distinctly underwhelming performance. His vocals were impeccable, but he stood static by the microphone, with none of the stage movements by now expected by The Doors' audience. 'They (The Doors) were nice chaps, but they played a bit too long,' said Mick Jagger following the show.

These dates were followed up by The Doors' first trip to Europe, for shows in England, Germany, Denmark, Sweden and Holland. The London concerts, at underground temple the Roundhouse, on Friday 6 and 7 September, were great triumphs, some of their best ever performances. There were two shows each day: on night one, they supported Jefferson

Airplane; on night two, it was the other way around. 'The audience was one of the best we've ever had,' said the singer. 'Everyone seemed to take it so easy. It's probably the most informed, receptive audience I've ever seen in my life.'

In Amsterdam Jim Morrison was indisposed. That morning while they had been in Germany he had eaten a lump of Lebanese hash given to him by Bob 'the Bear' Hite of Canned Heat. Arriving in Amsterdam, Jim had danced on stage during the Airplane set. But then the hash kicked in and he was unable to perform his role as The Doors' singer during their own set.

After the European tour, Jim Morrison and Pamela Courson rented a flat in London's Belgravia and remained there for a month. There they were visited by Michael McClure, the Beat poet and writer. He wanted Jim to play the part of Billy the Kid in a movie to be made of his play *The Beard*. While at their London lodgings, McClure came across a copy of Jim's poetry. He was impressed and suggested Jim Morrison publish a private edition, entitled *The Lords and the New Creatures*.

Jim paid a visit to Abbey Road studios, where the Beatles were recording 'Happiness is a Warm Gun' for their *The Beatles* album.

On returning to Los Angeles on 20 October 1968, it was yet again time to enter the recording studio to make another album. This set of sessions saw The Doors working at Elektra's new recording studio on La Cienega, 'the house that The Doors built', as it became known. The four musicians were not at all pleased, however, to learn they would pay almost standard rates – they were given a ten per cent discount. Jim turned his back on Jac Holzman so he wouldn't see the fury etched into his face.[58]

In early November 1968, The Doors played seven dates, mainly in the American Midwest. In Phoenix, Arizona, on 7 November, they performed to a 10,000-strong audience at Veterans Coliseum. After an onstage equipment malfunction, Jim Morrison began to berate the audience. 'We are not going to stand for four more years of this shit,' he commented on the election two days previously of a new president, the Republican Richard Nixon. He encouraged the audience to stand and come up to the stage. When some 500 kids did so, they were pushed back by police – their response was to shower police officers with garbage. Several people were arrested. The local Arizona Highway Patrol captain had come close, he said later, to arresting Jim Morrison for his use of vulgar and obscene language. Having got away with this in Phoenix, in St Louis the singer tested the local police even more during the song 'Back Door Man' – 'Fuck me, baby, fuck me, girl, suck my cock, honey, around the world,' he extemporized.

The Smothers Brothers Comedy Hour television show was known for its satirical take on current events, notably the Vietnam War. As such it was a suitable vehicle for The Doors. When the group's opportunity came, on 15 December 1968, Jim Morrison gave a *tour de force* performance on 'Touch Me' and 'Wild Child', both songs from the new album, *The Soft*

Parade. The first single off the new album, the overtly sexual 'Touch Me' raced up the US charts to number 3. Robby Krieger performed *The Smothers Brothers* TV show with a conspicuous black eye – he and Jim had traded punches with some representatives of the Old Order in a bar on Santa Monica.

The Doors' live performances in 1968 concluded with a show on home territory, at the Los Angeles Felt Forum. After the group had played 'Light My Fire', the audience began to chant 'Again, again!' Perhaps suffering from an excess of self-importance, Jim Morrison found himself irritated at such an inoffensive audience response – although gratitude perhaps would have been more appropriate. To make his point he stepped to the front of the stage and berated the crowd with all 133 lines of 'Celebration of the Lizard' before walking off for good.

Jim Morrison was doing a lot of wandering off – the increasingly eccentric singer would frequently disappear. Often he had simply checked into a cheap motel, such as the Alta Cienega, a favourite that was convenient for The Doors' office on nearby Santa Monica Boulevard – where he also had been known to regularly crash out on the couch. He was, however, adept at vanishing for longer periods.

His absences contributed to occasional controversies, as when the other three band members would be obliged to make decisions without him. For example, with Jim missing on one of his frequent walkabouts, the other three members agreed – for a considerable fee – to let 'Light My Fire' be used in a television commercial for the new Buick Opel, an economy car that Ray Manzarek felt was apt for the new time in which they were living. The advertisement would require, however, a crucial line in the song to be altered, to 'Come on, Buick, light my fire'.

Jim refused to go along with this idea, and there was a huge row, which ultimately was won by Morrison:[59] 'Light My Fire' was not used in a television commercial for the new Buick Opel.

Meanwhile, they were still recording *The Soft Parade*, playing gigs and editing *Feast of Friends* – Jim Morrison seemingly far more interested in this increasingly expensive project than in making the new album. This in itself was controversial, The Doors risking the wrath of hardcore fans by adding horns, strings and further instrumentation in elaborate arrangements.

On Friday 24 January 1969, it was time for The Doors to play a prestigious gig at Madison Square Garden in New York City. The venue held over 20,000 and was sold out for The Doors' show, for which they received $50,000. Although the Garden was beginning to host regular rock concerts, it had not adapted to the complexities of sound balance required for musical events at such a cavernous venue. Adding to the potential problems with the Garden's sound, The Doors were performing in the round. But the concert was a striking success. Lax security permitted the audience of mainly teenage girls to wander the auditorium, some even making it on stage.

Although Jim Morrison's performance was minimalist and devoid of histrionics, he seemed for the most part in perfect command of the audience. But at one point he wandered to either side of the stage, delivering a message to each in turn: 'You are life!' and 'You are death!'

While in Manhattan for the date, Jim Morrison first encountered Patricia Kennealy, the editor of *Jazz & Pop* magazine. When she went up to his suite at the Plaza Hotel to interview him, static sparks flew as they shook hands, created by the friction of her boots on the floor-covering fabric. Despite the simple scientific explanation, they both registered the symbolism. 'A portent,' said Jim. (Kennealy was a practising witch, a member of a coven, and would later 'marry' Jim Morrison in a ceremony devoid of any legal status.)

Always interested in exploring radical art forms, Jim Morrison had a high regard for the Living Theatre, the New York-based innovative drama company renowned for its productions of experimental plays. The Living Theatre was always strapped for cash and the singer donated money to help keep them going. In their 1968 production, *Paradise Now*, they showed an eagerness to abolish the gap between art and life, with the actors forcing arguments with members of the audience aiming to so alienate them that they would leave. Although the piece was often acted in the nude, when they came to Los Angeles to perform the actors had been warned by police that they would be arrested if they did so; accordingly they played it while wearing underwear.

Jim Morrison saw their every performance, including those of *Frankenstein* and *Antigone*, but it was the production of *Paradise Now*, with its confrontational tone, that most captured his imagination. Its influence would linger with him until the next Doors show the following day. 'He had a madder than usual look in his eyes, though I knew he was sober,' said Tom Baker, who had gone to the Bovard Auditorium with him. 'At one point Jim turned to me and said, "Let's start a fire in the balcony or something. Get a riot going."'[60]

On 1 March The Doors were scheduled to play in Jim Morrison's home state of Florida, at the Miami Dinner Key Auditorium in Coconut Grove. Following this date, which was to be a warm-up for the longest set of concert dates The Doors had performed, Jim, Robby Krieger and John Densmore were scheduled to briefly vacation separately in nearby Jamaica. On the morning of 1 March, Jim Morrison and Pamela Courson had such a bitter row on the way to the airport that the singer refused to let her accompany him; there was a suggestion that she had told him she was pregnant by someone else. Then he managed to miss the flight that the rest of the group had taken. Obliged to fly to New Orleans, where he would catch a connection to Miami, he drank all the way, managing to miss his Miami-bound plane in New Orleans. There he continued to drink in the bar as he waited for the next flight.

Arriving late for The Doors show, Jim Morrison was certainly the worse for wear, very drunk indeed. And the audience was rowdy, largely because it was unlawfully packed with almost twice its legal capacity of 7,000. It didn't really improve their mood when Jim Morrison began to harangue them from the stage. During 'Five to One', after challenging audience members to come up on stage and 'love my ass', he turned on them: 'You're all a bunch of fuckin' idiots. Let people tell you what you're gonna do. Let people push you around . . . How long are you gonna let it go on?' But then his mood shifted again: 'I'm talking about love your neighbour . . . till it hurts. I'm talkin' about grab your friend. I'm talkin' about love, love, love, love.'

After more rants, he made a direct reference to the Living Theatre: 'The last couple of nights I met some people who were doing somethin'. They're trying to change the world and I wanna get on the trip. I wanna change the world.'

Again and again, he challenged the audience to rush the stage. Unusually, that night Jim Morrison was wearing cotton boxer shorts beneath his leather pants. With his shirt off, the top of the boxer shorts was visible. As he stuffed it back inside his trousers, Jim inquired: 'Hey, anybody want to see my cock?'

His shirt back on, he fumbled behind its tails, as though unbuttoning his fly. Except no one could see anything at all. 'Okay, I'm gonna show it to you,' he promised. Pulling his shirt-tail swiftly to one side. 'Okay, watch now . . . here it comes!'

Still no one could see anything at all. 'Did you see it? Did you see my cock?' he inquired. 'Do you want to see it again? Watch close now.' He pulled his shirt back and forth: 'There, I did it! Did you see it? Are you happy now? Want to see it again?'

As the crowd surged forward, there was serious danger of the stage collapsing. Then Jim bellowed once again into the mike: 'Now, look close, I'm only gonna show you my cock one more time.' Once again he wafted his shirt in front of his flies. But in fact, he was revealing nothing.

'Folks, he never exposed himself. But it's become a myth, hasn't it? It's become an American rock and roll myth. And it's a lot more fun to believe the myth, isn't it? So we do,' wrote Ray Manzarek.[61]

The singer's moment of controversy over, The Doors continued their set, kicking into 'Light My Fire'. As the song progressed, Jim Morrison urged audience members to come up on stage. The stage then began to list. Security guards started to push people back into the hall off the stage. Inevitably, Jim pushed one of the security men off the stage. At which point another security guy threw Jim into the audience, where he was caught by the crowd. Working his way through them, Jim made his way to the dressing room.

The next day Jim, John and Robby took the short flight to Jamaica, while Ray Manzarek and Dorothy made their way to Guadeloupe. Jim had booked a residence in Jamaica, a former Great House, up a hill in the middle of the island, where he had intended to share the vacation with Pamela.

Now he went on his own. Alone in this former slave mansion, he became depressed. John and Robby had rented a sea-front villa in the north coast resort of Ocho Rios. One day Jim showed up there, drunk of course. He stayed for several days, annoying John Densmore, who had been seeking respite from the singer's ego, before flying back to the United States.[62] There, the Concert Hall Managers Association of the United States had issued a confidential newsletter. It warned against the 'unprofessionalism' of The Doors, singling out Jim Morrison. As a consequence, The Doors were effectively banned from live performance in the USA – all the subsequent dates on their first ever full-scale tour of the USA were cancelled. The live show cancellations occasioned by the Miami incident cost The Doors an estimated million dollars.

It was while they were in Jamaica that they learned that on 5 March Dade County Sheriff's Office had begun legal proceedings against James Douglas Morrison. He was to be charged with lewd and lascivious behaviour, a felony; indecent exposure, a misdemeanour; open profanity, a misdemeanour; and drunkenness, also a misdemeanour.

Owing to an absurdity of the American legal system, Jim was obliged to surrender to the FBI. Because he had been in Jamaica when the warrants were issued, this was deemed unlawful flight across state lines to avoid prosecution – even though he was unaware he was about to be prosecuted. He was charged with lewd and lascivious behaviour, simulating oral copulation, and indecent exposure.

'"Rallies for decency" were convened in the name of "decent, wholesome, traditional Christian values"', wrote Ray.[63] The national outrage was absurd: even though drunk, Jim Morrison had conned them all. Thirty thousand 'Teens for Decency' filled Miami's Orange Bowl two weeks after the controversial show.

Suddenly radio stations were again refusing to play The Doors. Already criticized for its orchestral arrangements, sales of the blues-based *Soft Parade* suffered: it only made number 6. The biggest single off the record was 'Touch Me', which made number 3, a substantial hit at least. None of the singles – the others were 'Wishful Sinful', 'Tell All the People' and 'Runnin' Blu' – had been written by Jim Morrison; they were all Robby Krieger compositions.

Back in Los Angeles, the group languished, reeling from the moral outrage they had provoked. Supposed to be working on the *Feast of Friends* edit, Jim instead spent much time at the Palms bar on Sunset, drinking. In an apparent attempt to hide who he was, he had grown a full beard, effectively hiding his good looks, and was putting on significant weight from his alcohol consumption.

At a meeting with the other two Doors musicians, Ray said that they had to confront Jim about his drinking. An intervention session was arranged at Robby's father's house, at 2 in the afternoon. After much collective trepidation, it was put to Jim that he was drinking too much. 'I know I drink too much. I'm trying to quit,' he replied.

On Saturday 14 June 1969 The Doors played their first live concert since the Miami debacle, at the Chicago Auditorium Theater. The next day they played in Minneapolis, and there were further shows in Vancouver, Atlanta and New Orleans. On Wednesday 25 June, they appeared on *Critique*, an hour-long PBS television show of unimpeachably serious credentials. The five numbers they played live included an epic performance of 'The Soft Parade'. In the panel discussion afterwards, writer Al Aronowitz dismissed The Doors as 'inconsequential'.

Two days later they were in Mexico City, playing four nights in the Forum, a supper club. In exchange for performing at the nightclub, they had been promised they would play a show in a Mexico City bullring. Although Jim Morrison was not a particular fan of cocaine, all the group – except John Densmore – willingly availed themselves of the large amounts of coke they were offered.[64] Then they were told the bullring show had been pulled, on 'safety' grounds.

Jim was deeply saddened by the passing of Brian Jones on 3 July 1969. 'Ode to LA while Thinking of Brian Jones, Deceased' was a 73-line poem he quickly wrote, publishing it at his own expense and giving it away to members of the audience at Doors concerts on 21 and 22 July at the Aquarius Theater on Sunset in Hollywood. The shows were recorded for the group's *Absolutely Live* album.

Unwisely, The Doors turned down a slot at that August's Woodstock festival because the singer believed the acoustics would be inadequate. But there were shows in Los Angeles, New York City, Philadelphia, Pittsburgh and Detroit. The contracts for these concerts specified that the group would lose all payment should Jim utter any obscenities whatsoever.

The summons to appear in court on the charges from the Dade County Sheriff's Department were not served on Jim Morrison until 9 November 1969. In a hearing that lasted twenty minutes, bail was set at $5,000 and a trial date was set for 28 April 1970. 'Jim seemed sobered by the ordeal,' wrote John Densmore.[65]

Two days later, on 11 November 1969, Jim Morrison was busted once again. On a flight from Los Angeles to Phoenix, Arizona, to see The Rolling Stones play, Jim and Tom Baker drunkenly mauled a flight attendant. The police had been called when they landed, and The Doors singer was charged with 'drunk and disorderly conduct' and 'interference with a flight crew'. This carried a maximum ten-year sentence. At the trial in March 1970 they were both acquitted, a case – somehow! – of 'mistaken identity'.

Whatever the future held for Jim Morrison, another album needed to be made, and so they began work at Elektra Sound Recorders on what would become known as *Morrison Hotel*. 'Roadhouse Blues' featured John Sebastian on mouth harp, who told the band his name could not go on the record because he was contracted to Kama Sutra records. Later they learned he was embarrassed to be associated with the controversial Doors.

One night Jim Morrison brought some friends down to the studio: actor Laurence Harvey and Tom Reddin, the Los Angeles chief of police,[66] whom he had met in a restaurant. Paul Rothchild swiftly hid the joint he was rolling.

While driving around downtown, Ray Manzarek happened upon the rundown Morrison Hotel. Despite protests from the owner, photographer Henry Diltz shot the group sitting in a window of the building.

Early one morning in January 1970 at The Doors' office on Santa Monica Boulevard, Jim Morrison was interviewed for an hour by Howard Smith, the columnist for the *Village Voice* who had already written so favourably of him. Jim was publicizing *Morrison Hotel*, due to be released on 7 February 1970. 'We're the band that everybody loves to hate,' the singer complained, referring to a film festival in San Francisco where a screening of *Feast of Friends* had been greeted with boos. 'They hate us because we are so good.' Jim then said of The Doors that, 'I can reasonably predict another 7 or 8 years.'

'A lot of the groups I've talked to have said they have a lot of trouble hanging on to money,' commented Howard Smith.

'That's their fault,' came Jim Morrison's facetious reply. 'They are probably spendthrifts: it's like giving whisky to an Indian . . . I've always said this,' he extemporized ironically. 'Money does beat soul every time.'

Howard Smith told Jim he felt he was being disparaging towards him. But you can feel the journalist growing nervous and edgy on tape. In fact, Jim Morrison is really being honest and open, if a little ironic – which clearly some people had trouble with.

Asked about his impending trial in Miami, Jim Morrison batted away the question: 'I might even buy a suit, a conservative dark blue suit, and a big fat tie with a great big knot. And I'll take a lot of tranquillizers. And try to have a good time. Maybe I'll write a piece in *Esquire*: my impressions of my hanging. Hey man, you're putting me on a bummer, let's talk about something light.'

Howard Smith then asked about The Doors' music having recently become more pop-orientated. 'I don't agree with that,' replied the singer. 'I think it keeps getting better and better. And gets more subtle and more sophisticated, lyrically and musically. If you keep on saying the same old thing over and over it gets boring.'

On 17 and 18 January The Doors played four concerts in New York at the 4,000-seater Felt Forum in the Madison Square Garden complex, including much material from the new album. By now Jim Morrison had shaved off his beard and lost some of his booze-induced weight. In Manhattan, he renewed his relationship with Patricia Kennealy, spending time with her at her apartment. Dates followed in San Francisco, Long Beach, Cleveland and Chicago.

Later that month, Jim Morrison reluctantly attended a party at Elektra's new West Hollywood offices. Egged on by Tom Baker, he began to wreck the place, until he was pushed out of the door onto the street.

On 7 April 1970 *The Lords and the New Creatures* was published by Simon & Schuster. These were the poems by Jim Morrison that Michael McClure had read in London. Now they had been picked up by a major publisher. McClure found Jim Morrison sitting with a pile of the just-delivered books, in tears of gratitude. 'This is the first time I haven't been fucked,' he told the writer.

Although his Miami trial had been scheduled for April, it was now postponed until August. This meant it remained hanging over his future, a permanent weight on his mind. He began to suggest that once the trial was over, he might move to another country to live.

On Saturday 29 August 1970, The Doors co-headlined the Saturday night show at the UK's Isle of Wight festival, sharing the top slot with The Who. Jim Morrison had to be in court on Monday morning in Miami. During his performance, the singer seemed desperately introverted, even refusing a blast on Roger Daltrey's then exotic peppermint schnapps. He performed like an unmoving statue. 'Jim was in fine vocal form,' wrote Ray Manzarek.[67] 'His voice was rich and powerful and throaty. He sang for all he was worth but moved nary a muscle. He remained rigid and fixed to the microphone for the entire concert. Dionysius had been shackled. They had killed his spirit. He would never be the same in concert again. They had won . . . He knew it was over.' Jimi Hendrix, who would be dead within three weeks, was also on the Isle of Wight bill.

Jim Morrison's Miami court case lasted – with occasional breaks – for almost two months. On 30 October 1970, he was found guilty of vulgar and indecent exposure and vulgar and indecent language.[68] He was found not guilty of gross and lascivious behaviour and drunkenness – absurdly, as this was all he was actually guilty of. He was sentenced to six months' hard labour in jail and given a $500 fine. He was, however, allowed out on bail to appeal.

Midway through the trial, Jimi Hendrix had died, aged twenty-seven, on 18 September 1970. This sent Jim Morrison into a fit of depression that was only exacerbated when Janis Joplin, who was the same age, also passed away, on 4 October. 'You're drinking with number three,' Jim would inform friends.

Back in Los Angeles, The Doors immediately began work on their next album, *LA Woman*. The title track contained the phrase 'Mr Mojo Risin'', an anagram of Jim Morrison. Paul Rothchild was no longer at the helm as producer: he had complained he thought some of their new material sounded like 'cocktail jazz'. But there was a larger, more complex reason for Rothchild pulling out of this job: he had been producing *Pearl*, the Janis Joplin album that would be released posthumously, and felt so stunned from her death that he wasn't up to a return to the studio.[69] Bruce Botnick, their longstanding engineer, said he would help The Doors co-produce the record, which they decided to make at their rehearsal space.

One evening Michelangelo Antonioni, the celebrated Italian film director who had made the epochal *Blow-Up*, came to see them. He was finishing *Zabriskie Point* and was searching for music for it. One of the tunes The Doors were readying for *LA Woman* was 'L'America', and it was felt this might be appropriate.[70] 'The apostrophe after L is short for Latin America,' John Densmore remembered Jim explaining the song to the film director, 'or Central America, or Mexico, for that matter. Anywhere south of the border.'

'During his monologue,' Densmore wrote in his book *Riders on the Storm*, 'I remember thinking how brilliant Jim was. God, I loved his mind. How did he continually come up with such original stuff? He still seemed creative and vibrant back then, even though he was on a downward spiral with his drinking.'[71]

Even though by then 16-track tape was available, *LA Woman* was recorded on 8-track. 'Our last record turned out like our first album: raw and simple,' decided John Densmore. 'It was as if we had come full circle. Once again we were a garage band, which is where rock 'n' roll started. We even dropped the individual writer credits, just like on our first three albums: all songs written by The Doors.'[72]

One day while they were recording, John Densmore noticed that Jim was limping as he walked into the rehearsal room after a brief adjournment to buy beers. Robby Krieger told him that while staying at the Chateau Marmont Jim had had a fall. He had tried to swing into his room off the rain gutter, slipped, and fallen on his back onto the roof of a cottage. 'God, he never used to get hurt. I thought he was indestructible,' said Densmore.[73]

The no longer indestructible Jim Morrison professed a desire to play a tour of small halls in Australia. However, The Doors would only play four more concerts again, ever: a pair in California – in Bakersfield and San Diego one weekend – and one each in Houston and New Orleans.

Although the show in Houston was apparently outstanding, when The Doors played New Orleans, on 12 December 1970, Jim Morrison's performance revealed a man shockingly at war with himself. At the end of the song 'Soul Kitchen', from their first album, Jim delivered bad jokes for some minutes: 'What did the blind man say as he passed the fish store? "Hi, girls."'

Midway through the set he slammed the microphone stand into the stage floor, over and over and over, in the manner he had learned from his namesake Van Morrison, until the wood beneath was destroyed. Sitting down on the drum riser, he then refused to perform for the remainder of the show.

'He was just plain boring. It was pathetic – an artist on the skids,' thought John Densmore.[74] 'Jim wasn't even drunk, but his energy was fading. Later Ray remarked that during the set he saw all of Jim's psychic energy go out the top of his head. I didn't quite see that, but it did seem that Jim's life-force was gone.'[75] After Jim and Bill Siddons had gone into their hotel, the other three Doors conversed outside the building. 'It's finished,' declared Ray.

The garage-band feel of *LA Woman* paid off. 'Love Her Madly' reached number 4 on the singles charts. Meanwhile, 'Riders on the Storm' enjoyed heavy FM airplay – released as a single it got to number 14. 'LA Woman' itself, which was released in late April 1971, only reached number 9 in the USA, but ultimately sold 2 million copies. (Its sales, of course, were boosted three months later, by the death of Jim Morrison, unexpected except by all those who knew him.)

Some days before the album came out, Jim Morrison had left for Paris, on 15 April. Two months earlier Pamela Courson had already arrived in the French capital. They took an apartment at 17 rue Beautreillis in the Marais section of the city, a beautiful location. He enjoyed his reflective life in the city, and seems to have written a number of poems, many of which were not discovered until over a decade and a half later. He is believed to have been working on a pair of screenplays. In April and May he and Pamela drove through parts of France, Spain and Morocco, later visiting Corsica for ten days.

But he was still drinking, thwarted by himself when he tried unsuccessfully to go cold turkey. Soon, however, he was living a similar life in Paris as the one he led in Los Angeles, he and Pamela each forming new sets of friends – in Jim Morrison's case, a bunch of drinking buddies with whom to hang out in undesirable *boîtes*. By the end of June, however, he was falling into depression.

On 2 July 1971 Jim Morrison went with Pamela Courson to a cinema to watch *Pursued*, a film starring Robert Mitchum, one of his favourite actors. Pamela Courson claimed he came back with her to their apartment from the movie and went to bed. Waking in the night from chest pains, he got up to soak in the bath tub. It was 5 a.m. when Pamela woke and found him still lying in the bath. A heart attack was what had killed Jim Morrison, it was widely circulated.

Later a story emerged that Pamela Courson had been using heroin – Paris was always a prime source for the drug. Jim Morrison, she said, had found her stash, and did some himself, which was what killed him. She told this version to Danny Sugerman, later denying to him that there was any truth in the story whatsoever. And there was another version that went the rounds: that Jim Morrison had snorted heroin in a Paris nightclub and overdosed. He had then been taken to his apartment where an attempt was made to revive him by placing the singer in a cold bath.

In conditions of great secrecy, James Douglas Morrison was buried on 8 July, 1971 at the Père Lachaise cemetery, the prestigious central Paris graveyard for artists. There was only a handful of onlookers.

ROBERT JOHNSON

Believe that my time ain't long

'Ramblin' on My Mind'

Robert Johnson (left) with Johnny Shines

Robert Johnson, the legendary bluesman who died in murky circumstances from drinking poisoned whisky on 16 August 1938, is widely considered the godfather of both rhythm and blues and rock 'n' roll.

In terms of contemporary culture, he is also the first on the list of immensely influential young men and women apparently fated to die at the age of twenty-seven following a ferocious flourish of talent. However, Robert Johnson was murdered; with the possible, but highly unlikely, exception of Rolling Stone Brian Jones, the only one on this eminent list to meet such a tragic end.

The shadowy nature of his passing, intertwined with the suggestion that he sold his soul to the Devil in exchange for his talent, has only added to his mystique as a dark figure – like a character from some Mississippi-set Jacobean tragedy reworked by Tennessee Williams. Yet nothing could be further from the truth. 'Robert was one of those fellows who was warm in every respect,' said his friend Johnny Shines,[1] 'Robert was a fellow very well-liked by women and men, even though a lot of men resented his power or his influence over women-people. They resented that very much, but, as a human being, they still liked him because they couldn't help but like him, for Robert just had that power to draw.'

So celebrated is his legend that in 1994 Robert Johnson's image appeared on the 29 cent US postage stamp, recognition of his distinguished role as a black archetype of modern American mythology. He has fuelled the dreams, fantasies, and aspirations of myriad largely white blues fans. These included a lonely young boy from Ripley in Surrey, England. 'At first the music almost repelled me,' wrote Eric Clapton, who in the mid-1960s almost singlehandedly brought Robert Johnson to the fore, in *Clapton: The Autobiography*. 'It was so intense and this man made no attempt to sugarcoat what he was trying to say, or play.'[2] In his biography *Chronicles*, moreover, Bob Dylan recalled that he broke down Robert Johnson's lyrics by handwriting them onto paper.

The seemingly eternal suffering expressed in Robert Johnson's lyrics held a library's worth of meaning for those tormented by late-teenage angst. Certainly there is an element about the white-boy worship of Robert Johnson which suggests that for some of his fans he held a position like that of an honorary noble savage.

Such a perception was reinforced initially because the bluesman's legend was established when very few facts were known about him. Now, thanks to the assiduous efforts of music historians, much of Johnson's life is reasonably well documented. The most enduring and fanciful part of the Johnson myth, based on evidence supposedly gleaned from his writing and recording of the song 'Cross Road Blues', is that one midnight at the Delta crossroads of Highway 61 and Highway 49 by Clarksdale, Mississippi, he sold his soul to the Devil in return for his extraordinary and unique guitar-playing abilities. On close examination this is a legend without any basis in fact.

Indeed, believers in the fable even got the wrong man; the blues performer who had a distinctly mutated version of this experience was not Robert Johnson, but the unrelated Tommy Johnson, his friend and fellow musician. Tommy Johnson is best known for his songs 'Maggie Campbell Blues' and 'Canned Heat Blues', and claimed to have found his sudden guitar-playing skill in such a night-time crossroads ritual, one that is integral to many African animist religions, a relic of the slavery era widely practised to this day in the United States, the Caribbean and South America.

'If you want to learn how to make songs yourself, you take your guitar and you go to where the road crosses that way, where a crossroad is,' said LeDell Johnson, Tommy Johnson's brother, to the blues scholar David Evans about Tommy's sudden guitar-playing skill and Tommy's claims of its provenance, offering a severely truncated version of what is in fact an African spiritual practice. 'Get there, be sure to get there just a little 'fore 12 that night so you know you'll be there. You have your guitar and be playing a piece there by yourself . . . A big black man will walk up there and take your guitar and he'll tune it. And then he'll play a piece and hand it back to you. That's the way I learned to play anything I want.'[3]

The 'big black man' in Tommy Johnson's account is interpreted by impressionable white Christian listeners as 'the Devil'. In other words, the 'Devil' is a big black man. And here is the unravelling of even more complex, deep-rooted prejudice; for if anything, the very notion of the black man selling his soul to the Devil at the crossroads is a white man's superstition, reliant on such northern European notions as the Faust legend.

So as well as being a fabrication, it is also indubitably racist, an easy explanation for a white audience of the extraordinary abilities of a black man. In reality, however, the truth of the life of Robert Johnson is far more prosaic. For example, his visible 'evil eye', with which he was reputed to be cursed, was most likely nothing more than a cataract.

Brought into what became the United States by African slaves, animism-based religions and thinking remained ingrained in American black society; a number of interlocking, polytheistic religions provided a core belief system that, as time progressed, frequently intersected with aspects of Christianity. And as time progressed, animistic beliefs, which became known as 'hoodoo' (perhaps because the word seemed less threatening than 'voodoo'), developed as part of the collective unconscious of the US black community.

In West Africa there are such crossroad gods as Eshu (also Esu) in Yoruban mythology, and Legba in Benin mythology – these are the figures who have been misinterpreted as the 'big black man' Devil character. The notion of Robert Johnson selling his soul to the Devil is extremely potent for young blues aficionados – like Robert Plant, who allegedly possesses a pouch of earth taken from the ground at the crossroads where Robert Johnson allegedly took part in such a ceremony. (Led Zeppelin's 1969 track 'The Lemon Song' included the line 'You can squeeze my lemon 'til the juice run down my leg', from Robert Johnson's 'Traveling Riverside Blues'.)

Even the fact that Johnson recorded 'Cross Road Blues' only demythologizes the fable. He recorded the song in San Antonio, Texas, on 27 November 1936, his first recording session. But if you listen to the lyrics, they are about trying to hitch a car ride, from the perspective of a young black man likely feeling imperilled by being alone at night in the murderously threatening atmosphere of the white-controlled, Ku Klux Klan-dominated American South. ('Hell hound on my Trail' can as readily be interpreted as the fear of a fugitive pursued by a lynch mob.)

It's all a metaphor. Eshu (and Legba) is a benign force, an encouraging entity to assist you in life's journey. So why was it replaced by 'the Devil'? Because this was the closest that followers of a polytheistic religion could come to explaining such characters as Eshu to followers of a monotheistic religion. Eshu is not an adversarial figure. Is the idea of selling your soul to learn a skill not too far from Carl Jung's notion that artistic development is always at the expense of other areas of one's character? Or could it also mean a period of vanishing into a metaphorical wilderness to find oneself?

Robert Johnson was supposed to have been a mediocre player, at first. After several years, it finally came together for him, and he gained his superior command of rhythm – and inflection – and in that combination something extraordinary began to happen.

But the very notion of Eshu is that he is the 'trickster'; so are we being tricked here? For Robert Johnson was undoubtedly aware of the world of hoodoo. In his remarkable 'Hell Hound on My Trail', he sings that 'hot foot powder' has been sprinkled all around his door, keeping him with 'a rambling mind' – as the peripatetic Johnson was so often remembered by those who knew him. 'Hot foot powder', a mixture of herbs and minerals, was available from stores that dealt in hoodoo products; it was used as a means of ridding yourself of unwelcome individuals. Most likely, Robert Johnson's mention of it is as a metaphor, but he would certainly have known his way around the products in a hoodoo store.

'These stories,' writes Catherine Yronwode, 'seem to be prescriptions for a way to contact a specific, helpful spirit – and the specificity of the crossroads spirit's power is quite apparent: he is a teacher spirit who will accelerate one's mastery of mental, manual, and performing arts. The man at the crossroads does not steal your soul or condemn you to perdition or make any unholy bargain with you. He takes your offering and then he teaches by example and transference of power.'[4]

Part of the legend of Robert Johnson is his pre-eminent position in Delta blues. The Mississippi Delta, which is not really a delta but part of an alluvial plain, should not be confused with the Mississippi River delta, which lies some three hundred miles south of this area. The region connected to Delta blues consists of the northwest section of the American state of Mississippi, as well as adjacent parts of Arkansas and Louisiana, the section lying between the Mississippi and Yazoo Rivers.

Prior to the American Civil war, fought from 1861 to 1865, it was one of the richest cotton-growing areas in the United States, the plantations dependent on the labour of black slaves. The area is still predominantly black. Following the abolition of slavery, cotton remained the principal crop; freed slaves were frequently allocated a small share (the origin of the 'forty acres and a mule' stereotype) of their former plantation and they would farm that section, very much dependent on, and vulnerable to, the largesse of the former plantation owner.

The homes of these former slaves were often places of abject poverty, exacerbated by a lack of sanitation and essential hygiene, with frequently no latrines. Moreover, the grim spectre of lynching loomed forever over the black population, especially for males, a permanent threat to any 'nigger' getting above his station. Ill-educated and outnumbered, the local poor white community felt themselves under economic threat – local blacks could be employed for even less than themselves – and their resentment would sometimes find an outlet in membership of the Ku Klux Klan.

The facts about Robert Leroy Johnson are much clearer than the myth.

He was born on 8 May 1911 in Hazlehurst, Mississippi.

His mother was Julia Ann Major Dodds. In 1889, when she was fifteen, she had married Charles Dodds, who had been born in February 1865. Both of their parents had been born into slavery.

In 1900 the federal census listed this married couple's children as twelve-year-old Louise, nine-year-old Harriet, eight-year-old Bessie, five-year-old Willie, four-year-old Lula and one-year-old Melvin Leroy. Two children had died of illness – not uncommon in those days – and two more children were born subsequently.

But Robert Johnson was not a consequence of Julia Dodds's marriage; Charles Dodds was not the father.

Charles Dodds was relatively affluent and successful. He was a manufacturer of wicker furniture and also owned farming land outside Hazlehurst, Mississippi, which was south of the state capital of Jackson, outside the Delta. Yet his position hardly saved him from conflict with local whites. Specifically, in 1909 Charles Dodds fell foul of John and Joseph Marchetti, a pair of Italian businessmen who had settled in Hazlehurst. This strife was occasioned almost entirely by Charles and Joseph both enjoying the charms of the same local woman, Serena, a mistress with whom Charles had two boys. Fleeing a white lynch mob, Charles Dodds disguised himself as a woman and managed to make it to Memphis, Tennessee, 240 miles distant. There, still feeling unsafe, he changed his name to Charles Spencer. Soon Serena and her boys joined him in Memphis, followed shortly afterwards by most of the children that Charles 'Spencer' had had with Julia Dodds.

It would have been a very different life to the one they had experienced in the Delta; the world's largest cotton and hardwood lumber market, Memphis was a rich boom town, on one hand sophisticated, on the other wild and often very dangerous. In 1921 Memphis was the murder capital of the United States, its homicide rate seven times that of the country's average; guns and knives were pulled with abandon, and poison – that staple weapon in slave rebellions against white overseers – was a regular method of dispatching rivals.

Unhappy about the living arrangements of her husband, Julia Dodds remained in Hazlehurst with two of their daughters. Yet the Marchettis soon kicked them out of their home and land.

This was clearly a bad time for Julia Dodds, only compounded by the divorce that she and her husband underwent the next year, in 1910.

Julia, who was by now thirty-six years old, then had a brief relationship with Noah Johnson, a local plantation worker who was ten years younger than her. Out of this relationship was born Robert Leroy Johnson.

The boy was born into a life of struggle. His father had quickly disappeared, and Julia needed to make money simply to survive. Working as an itinerant cotton-picker, for more than two years Julia moved from camp to camp in the Mississippi Delta region, around Tunica and Robinsonville, with her youngest daughters, Bessie and Carrie, who cared for their half-brother, the baby Robert.

Showing compassion for their plight and their poor living conditions, Charles Dodds Spencer decided around 1914 that he would bring Robert up along with his other children in Memphis, where they were joined eventually by Julia. Yet because of the birth of Robert, Charles Dodds Spencer refused to resume his relationship with her; Julia lived in the same household with her former husband and Serena, his mistress having now usurped her position in the family. However, there was apparently no tension because of this. In Memphis Robert's elder half-brother, Charles Leroy, owned a guitar, and from time to time Robert would play on it. Having started out life as Robert Johnson, the boy now found himself named Robert Spencer, bringing further confusion to an already confused life.

Memphis may have been somewhat wild, but it was also a progressive city; a powerful and vocal local movement urged the education of young black children. Robert Johnson attended elementary school there, most likely St Peter's, from 1916 to 1920.

Around 1920, however, Robert went back to live with his mother, who had returned south and settled in the town of Robinsonville, Mississippi, thirty or so miles from Memphis. When he returned to the Delta, even though he was not yet a teenager, the contrast between the sophisticated and exciting city of Memphis and the small towns of the Delta must have struck Robert Johnson forcefully.

But the sensual urbane flavour of Memphis lingered in him, its influence part of who he was. His song 'From Four Until Late' makes mention of the city, employing an identical melody to a tune by a Memphis musician, Johnny Dodd, whose 1920 hit was very similarly entitled 'Four Until Late Blues'. He would return time and time again to Memphis; Robert Johnson's later dapper appearance was always far more that of a Beale Street slicker than a Saturday night fish fry plantation worker – even when that was his actual occupation.

By this time Julia, now forty-one, had remarried, in October 1916, to twenty-two-year-old Willie 'Dusty' Willis. As a consequence Robert Johnson now became known as Little Robert Dusty, further confusing his identity.

In the early 1920s, Dusty, Julia and her son crossed the Mississippi River to the town of Commerce. The two adults were employed on the Abbay and Leatherman plantation, and a wooden shack came with their jobs. By 1924 the fourteen-year-old Robert was registered at the Indian Creek school.[5]

On arriving at the school, he had demonstrated that he was already a very proficient musician. His contemporary, Willie Coffee, recalled that they would regularly play hooky from school, hiding under a local church. There Robert would 'blow his harp and pick his old Jew's harp for us and sing.' When discovered by their teacher, as they inevitably were, the truant schoolboys would each receive five lashes. Contrary to the claim that Robert Johnson had no education whatsoever, Johnny Shines maintained he had beautiful handwriting, a product of his creative long fingers.

During this time Robert Johnson is recalled making a 'diddley bow', a wire stretched with nails, on the side of their plantation shack that abutted onto the levee. It would be played by hitting it with a stick as a glass bottle was slid along to change notes, and Robert would be heard playing on it late into the night.[6]

After playing around with the Jew's harp, Robert moved on to the harmonica, practising it for the next few years until he bought an old guitar, so battered that it only had four strings – he saved up his pennies for the remaining two strings. Out on the edge of the road that ran alongside the levee holding back the waters of the Mississippi, as other kids played with marbles, he would struggle to play this instrument. One of his favourite songs, which he would strive to replicate, was 'How Long, How Long Blues', by Leroy Carr.[7] Taught by Harry 'Hard Rock' Glenn, he also learned one of his first guitar songs, 'I'm Gonna Sit Down and Tell My Mama'.[8] In addition he picked up a certain ability with piano and pump organ.[9]

By now the clearly intelligent, quietly self-assertive boy was aware of his ancestry, and of his true name, which he began to use. He would slip away at night, travelling to nearby towns like Lake Cormorant, Pritchard and Banks, playing guitar in juke joints – frequently black-owned stores that converted at night into small semi-nightclubs. He would also travel up to Memphis, to spend time with Charles Spencer and his family.[10]

Wherever he went, however he travelled, Robert Johnson was known for somehow always looking well turned out, well pressed. As the guitarist Johnny Shines, with whom he would trek and play as a duo in the last years of his life, explained to Alan Greenberg, 'We'd be on the road for days and days, no money and sometimes not much food, let alone a decent place to spend the night . . . And as I'd catch my breath and see myself looking like a dog, there'd be Robert, all clean as can be, looking like he's just stepping out of church.'[11]

For his parents there were worries he might have been going off the rails. By contemporary standards his mother Julia, by then in her late forties, was considered aged – in 1920 life expectancy for non-white Americans, who were ninety per cent black, was only just over forty-five years. Yet together with her new husband Dusty Willis, Julia had endeavoured to imbue her son with solid, God-fearing values, setting him on a straight course, they hoped, for adulthood. Robert did not always get on with his step-father, however; Dusty Willis held no truck with the boy's penchant for picking at his guitar, when instead he should have been out breaking his back picking cotton in the fields.

His fastidiousness about his on-the-road appearance was not necessarily reflected in other aspects of his demeanour; fond of a drop of moonshine, Robert was known to grow amorous under the influence of alcohol. Johnny Shines later recalled their needing to hotfoot it out of towns after Robert found himself becoming over-affectionate towards another man's girlfriend or wife.[12] How must his parents have felt when in 1926, when he was only fifteen, Robert Johnson began a relationship with a divorced mother? The woman, Estella Coleman, was ten years older than Robert; was this perhaps a subconscious adherence to the pattern of behaviour displayed by his own younger father with his mother? And by her relationship with Dusty Willis, less than half her age? 'Robert followed my mother home,' Estella's son said later about an affair that would continue, one way and another, for the next ten years.[13]

Estella Coleman's son's name was Robert Lockwood, Jr. He was only four years younger than his mother's lover. When he was eight, Robert Lockwood had started to play organ in his father's church. When Robert Johnson arrived with his guitar, however, he switched to that instrument. Whenever he put down his guitar and went out, Robert Lockwood would pick it up and try to copy what he had seen him doing. On discovering this, Robert Johnson resolved to tutor the younger boy, the only person whom the usually secretive Robert is believed to have so instructed. Robert Johnson even made Robert Lockwood a guitar. 'The first thing he taught me,' said Robert Lockwood, 'was "Sweet Home Chicago" . . . He was like pennies from heaven for me, because he taught me how to make my living. My mother loved him and he taught me to play, so I have to say I loved him too.'[14] Later Robert Johnson would also teach him the rudiments of stage-craft. (The ultimate consequence of this exposure to his mother's lover was that by 1948, after many years of assiduous application to his craft, during which time he himself had already become a celebrated blues musician, Robert Lockwood had been transformed into what Robert Palmer described in his 1981 book *Deep Blues* as 'the Delta's first modern lead guitarist'.[15] As though repaying his debt of instruction from Robert Johnson, Robert Lockwood later taught guitar to the man who became B.B. King.)

Most other bluesmen worked in guitar duos, but 'Robert came along and he was backing himself up without anybody helping him, and sounding good,' Lockwood recounted in *Deep Blues*.[16] Lockwood's assessment of Johnson's playing differed from the common local view, which was utterly dismissive of his skills. Pounding the floor with his feet to push along the rhythm, Robert Johnson made his guitar sound as though it was being played by two men, somehow managing to simultaneously play rhythm and lead parts. His high, keening vocals, sometimes riding up to a reedy falsetto, were far from the deep baritones employed by many bluesmen. Still in his mid-teens, Robert was in the process of developing his style and abilities to a point where he would revolutionize the form.

He was surrounded by prospective mentors. Settled in the area, for example, was local bluesman Willie Brown, from whom Robert Johnson already had endeavoured to glean as many musical insights as he could. Robert emulated Willie Brown, learning some of his tunes, notably 'The Jinx Blues'; and Willie Brown is referenced in Robert Johnson's song 'Cross Road Blues', when Robert calls for help from his 'friend Willie Brown'.

Willie Brown was an acquaintance of Charley Patton, born in either 1887 or 1891, one of the earliest and greatest – and best-educated – of the Delta blues artists. Already celebrated, Patton was distinguished by his gravelly, raucous voice and showmanship; he was an early exponent of that chitlin circuit specialty of playing his guitar behind his head and between his knees. Between 1929 and 1930, Charley Patton recorded forty-three tunes, more than any other blues artist up to that point; altogether he would record over sixty songs. He wrote stories about his life and the lives of those around him, about women running off, about problems with the law, about life on plantations and work and chain gangs, and about a seemingly casual racism; his song 'High Water Everywhere' was about how the flooding of the Mississippi in 1927 changed the geography of the entire Delta. 'Would go to the hilly country but they got me barred', he sang of how the local police made sure only white folks made it to the high ground. (In Patton's 'Dry Well Blues', it was the turn of drought to bring devastation.)

Charley Patton was, in fact, the first blues superstar. 'Patton was the first one that matters,' wrote Charles Shaar Murray. 'The basic Delta blues style – from which the post-war Chicago style was primarily derived – was, by all contemporary accounts, essentially Patton's style: Son House, Bukka White, Mississippi Fred McDowell and – by extension – Robert Johnson, Muddy Waters et al were following in his footsteps . . . His [Patton's] signature tunes, "Pony Blues" and "Banty Rooster Blues", are basic building blocks of Delta blues . . . If any one artist could be truthfully described as the true father of Delta Blues, he's yer man.'[17] Frequently in the area, playing the juke joints, Patton would often be in a duo with Willie Brown; when they performed Robert Johnson would literally sit at their feet.

Life was providing Robert Johnson with the kind of songwriting material eagerly sought by bluesmen. A handsome boy, girls flocked to him, notwithstanding that half the time he was living with Estella Coleman. Then in 1929, at the age of nineteen, Robert Johnson married Virginia Travis.

Perhaps he was seeking a more stable life than he had so far experienced, believing he could create a family of his own. Virginia herself was only fourteen when they wed. Robert and Virginia moved in with his half-sister Bessie and her husband on the Klein plantation east of Robinsonville. He tried hard to be a loving, devoted husband, reprimanding his brother-in-law for his bumpy automobile driving when it was discovered that Virginia had fallen pregnant. Although the newly-married Robert endeavoured to make a go of share-cropping, however, he couldn't put down his guitar, and was often away from home, playing for money. But that was Robert Johnson; on one hand searching for a warm, loving environment, but on the other holding any such world at arms' length, off leading his own slippery existence, the one in which he had learned to survive.

And so it was that when Virginia went into labour with their first child, Robert was on the road. When he arrived home to Virginia's parents' home, where she had been taken when she had gone into labour, he found that both his by then sixteen-year-old bride and baby had died during child-birth, on 10 April 1930. The full wrath of the Travis family came down on him; his devotion to the dark practice of musicianship was believed by them to have contributed to Virginia's death.

'According to some researchers,' wrote Elijah Wald,[18] 'this was a major trauma for him and set him to his life of rambling, but as far as I know this is pure speculation.' Indeed,

Robert already seemed to be living the peripatetic life of the musician.

The tragedy of Virginia's death was alleviated to an extent when, around this time, Robert Johnson met Son House, nine years older than himself, who – following on from Charley Patton – would serve as a further musical inspiration.

'Robert Johnson was the man who brought the Mississippi Delta blues to its absolute peak of refinement, sophistication and self-conscious artistry.' wrote Charles Shaar Murray. 'Muddy Waters was the man who transformed the Delta troubadour's art into an urban ensemble music. And Eddie James "Son" House Jr was the man who inspired and tutored both of them.'[19]

Son House, a Baptist preacher since the age of fifteen, was a bluesman of considerable mystique. Although he did not begin to learn the guitar until he was in his twenties, his blues career, which he alternated with preaching, had been interrupted by a two-year spell in the Parchman Farm prison camp for shooting a man dead.

In 1930 Son House had moved to Robinsonville, Mississippi, where Robert Johnson was living. This move was largely motivated by his friendship with local bluesman Willie Brown, and with Brown's friend Charley Patton. Almost as soon as he arrived in Robinsonville, Son House began playing in a duo with Willie Brown. Charley Patton had taken Son House and Willie Brown to Grafton, Wisconsin, to a Paramount recording session. Now House and Brown were playing at local dances. Of a film made of Son House when he was in his sixties, Elijah Wald wrote that on this evidence his 'best performances remain the strongest – indeed perhaps the only – argument for the blues musician as a sort of secular voodoo master'[20].

Son House recalled how he would play at Funk's Corner Store in Robinsonville on Saturday nights. It was an open-air venue, the audience seated on wooden benches pulled up in front of the store. 'Robert, he would be standing around, and he would listen too, and he got the idea that he'd like to play. So he started from that and everywhere that he'd get to hear us playing for a Saturday night ball, he would come and be there.'[21]

Although the younger man was inspired by Son House's presence, this was hardly reciprocated. 'Such another racket you ever heard!' was how he described Robert Johnson's first attempts at performing in public. 'It made people mad, you know. They'd come out and say, "Why don't y'all go in there and get that guitar from that boy! He's running people crazy with it."'[22]

Moreover, according to Son House, Robert Johnson's parents were aghast that he was frequenting such lowlife joints as Funk's Corner Store: 'Guys would fight all the time, kill up each other, shoot each other . . . So they got afraid and they didn't want him to be out to those kind of places. But he got involved with it so well, and he didn't like to work anyway, because his father and mother they were farmers.'[23] Accordingly, Robert

Johnson would resort to that staple strategy of errant progeny, climbing out of the window when his family was asleep.

'He used to play harmonica when he was 'round about fifteen, sixteen years old. He could blow harmonica pretty good . . . But he got the idea that he wanted to play guitar. He used to sit down between me and Willie.'[24] When Son House and Willie Brown would take a break, stepping outside into the cooler air, Robert would pick up their instruments 'and go to bamming with it, you know? Just keeping noise, and the people didn't like that.'

Although berated for his seeming lack of talent by Son House, Robert Johnson was undeterred. Every time he and Willie would take a break, the boy would be picking up their instruments again: '"BLOO-WAH, BOOM-WAH" – a dog wouldn't want to hear it!'[25]

Scolded by his peer musicians and his step-father, Robert Johnson eventually lit out of the area: 'Went somewhere over in Arkansas,' Son House inaccurately recalled.[26]

Perhaps the death of his wife Virginia triggered thoughts of his own origins. In 1930, soon after she had passed away, Robert Johnson went in search of his real father, journeying the 200 or so miles back to Hazlehurst, where he had been born. While hunting for Noah Johnson he came across Ike Zinnerman, who would become his mentor.

Isaiah 'Ike' Zinnerman had been born four years before Robert Johnson in Grady, Alabama. His family were farmers, and at first he had followed that line of work. From an early age, however, music dominated his life. He began to play juke joints in the area, until he headed south, ending up at the village of Beauregard, Mississippi, in an area known as The Quarters, next to the local cemetery. There Ike worked on road construction, a beneficiary of early efforts to end the crippling financial depression by building highways through the region. To an extent, this endeavour was a success, increasing the flow of cash to the local stores.

While visiting his brother Herman, who lived a few miles away in tiny Martinsville, Ike Zinnerman first encountered Robert Johnson in a juke joint store known as One Stop, on the corner of Martinsville Road and Highway 51. Robert himself had come over from Hazlehurst, six or seven miles away.

Needing a bed for the night, Robert went back to Ike's two-bedroom house in The Quarters, where Ike lived with his wife Ruth. Both Ike and then Ruth had taken an instant shine to the highly likable teenager. For a time he virtually moved into their home, and was assiduously coached by Ike Zinnerman in guitar-playing technique, Ike teaching him everything that he knew. Ike also gave him further instruction in harmonica-playing, at which Robert already was relatively proficient.

When Ruth was sleeping, Ike and Robert would walk over to the cemetery and play there, deep into the night, in order not to disturb the Zinnerman family. Here, it can be claimed, lie the origins of the allegations that Robert Johnson sold his soul to the Devil.

What is true about Robert Johnson is that he seemed to have what would come to be termed a 'photographic memory'. He would only need to hear a tune once on the radio or on one of the new jukeboxes to be able to play it perfectly, note-for-note – not even immediately after having heard it, but a day or so later. He was, quite clearly, a very gifted man.

Among the songs he and Ike Zinnerman would play were 'Walking Blues' and 'Ramblin' on My Mind', which Ike allegedly had written but which were later credited to Robert. Together they were said to have written 'I Believe I'll Dust My Broom' and 'Come on in My Kitchen', later credited to Robert Johnson alone. There are even suggestions from Ike Zinnerman's children that their father actually wrote those two himself. Learning from Ike, Robert Johnson began keeping a notebook, in which he etched the lyrics to his songs. The influences on his new songs were clear: Kokomo Arnold, Peetie Wheatstraw, Lonnie Johnson, Skip James and Scrapper Blackwell.

In May 1931, at the local courthouse, he married Calletta 'Callie' Craft, who was ten years older than him, with three young children from her two previous marriages. Callie doted on her young husband, sufficiently for her not to object to the nights he spent away with Ike Zinnerman.[27] (Was Callie unaware of the child he had fathered in the neighbourhood with one Vergie Mae Smith?)

Along with Ike Zinnerman, Robert was soon playing juke joints and work camps from Saturday evening until Sunday night. 'As time went by, and he became more confident of his abilities, he played more by himself,' wrote Stephen LaVere.[28] Callie would frequently accompany him to these shows, but he told no one that the doting woman with him was his wife. Perhaps he was concerned that information would cramp his style with other women. Occasionally Tommy Johnson, who was a neighbour, would play, and during other acts' performances, Robert Johnson would display his flair as a tap dancer, for which he was noted.[29]

Still learning about himself and his art, Robert Johnson often played around Hazlehurst under an assumed name; to many he was known simply as 'RL',[30] which he said stood for Robert Lonnie, a reference to the great Okeh recording artist Lonnie Johnson, a particular hero of his who had begun recording in 1925.[31] Lonnie Johnson's early records were the first guitar recordings displaying a single-note soloing style with string bending and vibrato – the origin of blues and rock solo guitar. Some of Robert Johnson's recordings would genuflect stylistically to Lonnie Johnson.

Perpetually suffering from itchy feet, he then took Callie and her kids from south Mississippi to Clarksdale. But Callie was not as hale and hearty as she appeared. Uprooted from her home and friends and family, she went into decline, physically and mentally. Robert deserted her, and she called home to Hazlehurst for her family to retrieve her. Callie died some years later, and though Robert did return to Copiah County, neither she nor her family ever saw him again.

Son House estimated the length of Robert's disappearance at six months, after which he returned with a new guitar. Others recalled it differently; that he remained in Mississippi, but went further south, staying away for up to two years, they claimed. Whatever; away from those who knew him, Robert Johnson had more opportunity to be himself.

Upon his reappearance, however, Son House was astonished – Robert Johnson had come back with an extra, seventh string on his guitar. He also had become a fantastic player, juxtaposing shuffling rhythms and slide guitar leads. 'And when that boy started playing, and when he got through, all our mouths were standing open. All! He was gone!'[32] It was now that local people would say that to acquire such skills, which they adjudged supernatural, he had sold his soul to the Devil. And Robert Johnson, who clearly had a sense of showbusiness mythology, was happy to encourage this; if they wanted that explanation they could have it.

For another seven days or so, Robert Johnson was in Robinsonville, but he was anxious to go on the road. Son House took it upon himself to explain to him the perils of life as a travelling musician, notably alcohol and girls. Robert Johnson, however, paid no heed: 'He was awful moufy – a terrible big chatterbox – proud as a peafowl.'[33] For a time Johnson's 'hangout', according to House, was in Bogalusa, Louisiana, home to the Great Southern Lumber Company, and almost 300 miles south.

Now it was around 1931. Robert Johnson was twenty years

old. He still looked very young, yet considered himself to be a man. Those he met found him extremely likable. Even though he was round-shouldered and small, he was a good-looking fellow. Always well dressed, the rigours of spending much of his life on the road never seemed to affect Robert's spruce appearance. 'He seems to have impressed everyone with his self-possession and confidence, his air of knowing what he was about, both on guitar and on the road,' wrote Elijah Wald.[34] When he started to play, you would notice his fingers. 'His sharp, slender fingers fluttered like a trapped bird,' said the bluesman Johnny Shines.[35]

In fact, Robert Johnson seemed a man of considerable paradox; for example, he consumed large amounts of alcohol, yet never appeared drunk. 'He was very bashful, but very imposing,' said Shines.[36] Although warm and amicable, he could also be moody and withdrawn. All who knew him considered him a loner, someone always on the move. Robert Johnson became noted for his ability to disappear suddenly, even walking offstage in the middle of a song, not to be seen again for a couple of weeks, recalled Johnny Shines.[37]

He probably had good reason to slink away; Robert Johnson clearly had several simultaneous relationships with women. But he also loved moving from town to town, some new adventure always on the edge of the horizon.

The permissive town of Helena, Arkansas, just across the Mississippi, was a favourite destination for Robert Johnson, as it was for most musicians, and he regularly played its Kitty

Kat Club. Robert Lockwood's mother Estella lived in Helena, and Robert Johnson made camp in her home. From there he would play all over the Delta and in the years leading up to his death he would take his music to many parts of the United States, in taverns, in speakeasies, in mining and levee camps – even as far as New York and Canada.

Johnny Shines, whose mother was another girlfriend of Robert Johnson, was a man who shared a similar wandering minstrel heart. Johnny Shines had been born in 1915 in Memphis, where he started playing slide guitar at an early age, performing for money on the streets; Charley Patton had been an inspiration. When he moved to Hughes, Arkansas, in 1932, Johnny Shines started farming instead. After a chance meeting with Robert Johnson, he returned to music, working with Robert.

Most nights Robert Johnson was playing shows in the environs of West Helena, Arkansas. When Shines was taken to see him by a friend, he thought 'Robert played a good guitar . . . about the greatest guitar player I'd heard.'[38]

The pair went on the road together, even though Johnson's style was to keep everyone at arm's length. From 1935 to 1937, Robert Johnson and Johnny Shines toured all over the eastern United States. Blues duos were commonplace, but Robert and Johnny rarely played together. They were travelling companions; on arriving in a town, they'd set up in opposite ends of a park, or on separate street corners, establishing a mood by their very presence. By the evening they might be playing one after the other in some local juke joint. Often 'jukes' would be set up in people's homes, the furniture shifted to one side. Artists like Robert Johnson and Johnny Shines earned as much as six dollars a night; lesser acts would only get a dollar and maybe a meal. As the year wound down, there was money to be earned; in the fall it was the harvest for cotton and corn farmers. From September until January was the time to pull in money.

Jumping trains, they travelled to New York, where they played in speakeasies. They also journeyed to Chicago, Texas, Kentucky, Indiana, Canada. 'I tagged along with him 'cause I knew he was heavy and I wanted to learn,' said Shines.[39]

As soon as people saw them in the street carrying their instruments, and then heard them play a snatch of a tune, they would be offered gigs. There were many fights, one or other of the pair waking up with a black eye or a loose tooth. ''Cause he'd jump on a gang of guys just as quick as he would one, and if you went to defend him, why, naturally you'd get it!'[40]

And what did Robert Johnson play? The purest blues? No, not at all; he played what people wanted to hear: polkas, Bing Crosby hits, country and western and hillbilly songs, show tunes, pop hit ballads.

Yet above all Robert Johnson wanted to have his own work recorded; an ambitious man, he knew this was the only way for his songs to be heard on a large scale. And there was only one man in the Delta who he knew could help him in this –

H.C. (Henry Columbus) Speir, who owned a music store in the black district of Jackson, Mississippi, a white man with an awareness of the black community's distinctly separate tastes, to which he specifically catered. Speir essentially was a talent scout, and provided artists for – amongst others – Columbia, Victor, Okeh, Decca, Paramount, and Vocalion. Already he had been involved in the recording of Charley Patton, Son House, the Mississippi Sheiks, Skip James and Tommy Johnson, as well as other noteworthy bluesmen. (Ultimately H.C. Speir would come to be seen as one of the most influential figures in modern American music.)

In 1936 Robert Johnson came into Speir's store, seeking him out in the hope that he could start transferring the songs he had written to discs. In his shop Speir had a machine for vanity recording, for which he would charge five dollars a song. It was onto this device that prospective artists also would record demonstration discs. The songs would be recorded onto hardened beeswax on a metal plate for the master recording and sent to whichever company Speir was then working for. If they liked them, they would arrange for a session in a recording studio in one of the larger nearby cities such as Memphis. At the time that Robert Johnson approached him Speir was working for ARC, the American Recording Company. ARC's preferred southern recording location was Texas. Robert was given an address in San Antonio, Texas, and sent a train ticket. The bluesman was extremely excited that Speir was taken with what he had recorded for him, and that he was sending him to the Texas city to record. 'I'm going to Texas to make records,' he proudly told his sister Carrie.[41]

The broad catalogue of material that the bluesman had become accustomed to performing live stood him in good stead. 'Johnson was the first bluesman who systematically learned from records (as opposed to reworking his local traditions),' wrote Charles Shaar Murray, 'and he seemingly conceived his songs as records in the first place. Rather than simply string out a series of common-stock verses over standard riffs and changes, he composed tight, set-piece songs custom-designed for the three-or-so-minute limits of a 78 rpm single.'[42]

The first Robert Johnson recording session was held on Monday, 23 November 1936, in room 414 of the Gunter Hotel at 205 East Houston Street in San Antonio. The sessions were set to conclude on Friday, 27 November. Don Law was the A&R man in charge, with Ernie Oertle the engineer.

At Law's suggestion, Robert also provided guitar backing for two groups of Mexican musicians, led by Andres Berlanga and Francisco Montalvo, and by Hermanos Barzaza. Suffering from nerves, he played with his back to the other musicians. Absurdly, this has been interpreted as further proof of his alleged diabolic leanings; rather, it seems simple proof of his nervousness on what was the biggest day of his life so far. And there is another, equally plausible explanation for Robert Johnson's insistence on recording while facing a corner of the room, with his back to everyone else present – that he had figured out that the natural reverberation of his voice and guitar bouncing off the two walls would make them sound larger on the mike.

On that first day Robert recorded eight songs. These included 'Sweet Home Chicago', 'I Believe I'll Dust My Broom', and 'Terraplane Blues'.

The next day, however, Tuesday, Don Law had to bail Robert out of the Bexar County jail. He was in on a vagrancy charge, a common problem for black Americans wandering the streets of southern cities during the daytime – why weren't they off picking cotton someplace? Later Robert called Don Law from his hotel room, saying he was lonesome. And that as a consequence of this lonesomeness he had someone with him, a woman, who required fifty cents, while Robert didn't even have a nickel to his name.[43]

On the Thursday, Robert Johnson recorded '32-20 Blues'. The next day, Friday, 27 November 1936, he put another seven tunes on wax. These included 'Cross Road Blues', the song that became inseparable from the curious mythology established around the soon-to-be-legendary bluesman.

Returning home, Robert Johnson was flush, with hundreds of dollars in his pocket – more cash than he had ever had in his life.

'Terraplane Blues' was released as a 78 rpm single, becoming a regional hit and selling over 5,000 copies. Now Robert Johnson could be heard on the new invention, the jukebox.

He was a star and celebrity. The song seemed to be an ode to a desirable car, the Terraplane, but is actually a metaphor for sex. Manufactured by Detroit's Hudson Motor Car Company, the Terraplane was inexpensive but powerful, with sensual deco lines; John Dillinger and Baby Face Nelson's getaway vehicle of choice, its very name carried a certain outlaw cachet.

Pleased with the success of 'Terraplane Blues', ARC booked a second set of sessions with Robert Johnson on 20 and 21 June 1937, on the third floor of a warehouse in the Vitagraph building in the business district of Dallas, Texas. The sessions were scheduled for a Saturday and Sunday – specifically, so that traffic noise in the bustling Texan town would be at a minimum.

It was a typically hot Texas June day. Pails of ice were brought into the studio. Robert Johnson recorded in between the Crystal City Ramblers and Zeke Williams and his Rambling Cowboys, appropriate company for a man for whom rambling was – as he had sung in the San Antonio sessions – always on his mind.

Arguably, the second of these two Robert Johnson recording sessions was even more successful than the first. Out of it, for example, came 'Hellhound on My Trail' – 'universally recognized as the apogee of the blues'.[44] It was released as a 78 rpm single on the Vocalion label in September 1937, after Robert Johnson's death.[45]

In Dallas on 20 June, he recorded ten songs: 'Hell Hound

on My Trail', 'Little Queen of Spades', 'Malted Milk', 'Drunken Hearted Man', 'Me and the Devil Blues', 'Stop Breakin' Down Blues', 'Travelling Riverside Blues', 'Honeymoon Blues', 'Love In Vain Blues' and 'Milkcow's Calf Blues', in that order. As at the San Antonio sessions, second takes were made of most of the numbers.

Robert Johnson's recording success probably hastened his end. Always adored by women, this was only enhanced by the success of 'Terraplane Blues'. His complex web of girlfriends, their husbands and boyfriends, these older women, mother figures off whom he would live – or, at least, survive – seemed to be circling him, like vultures. Ironically, he faced deadly danger after an entanglement with a younger woman.

The demise of Robert Johnson has spawned a pair of theories other than that he was poisoned to death: that the true cause was death from syphilis, which was possibly hereditary; that he died of Marfan syndrome, a connective tissue disorder. Unfortunately for these imaginative speculations, there were credible witnesses to the events leading up to the end of Robert Johnson on 16 August 1938. Specifically, Robert's fellow bluesmen David 'Honeyboy' Edwards, with whom he was booked to play at a dance on Friday 12 August 1938, near Greenwood, Mississippi, and Sonny Boy Williamson, who was also on the bill.

In July 1938, Robert Johnson had started an affair with the young wife of Ralph Davis, a 39-year-old sawmill worker and juke joint proprietor. Robert would rendezvous with the woman every Monday at the home of her sister, in Baptist Town in Greenwood, and they would spend the day together.

During this period Robert Johnson stayed with friends who lived on the nearby Star of the West Plantation, playing dances around the neighbourhood.

For the night of 13 August, Robert was offered a dance at Ralph Davis's country juke joint at the intersection of Route 49 and Route 82; he was, in other words, going down to the crossroads.[46]

Around eleven in the evening, after he had been playing in Davis's juke joint for two hours, Robert Johnson paused for a break. He was handed a jar of corn whisky – bootleg whisky, as this was a dry state – by Craphouse Bea, the very woman with whom he had been having the affair, the wife of Ralph Davis. Unbeknownst to Bea, her husband had dissolved mothballs in the liquor; he was fully aware of the sexual relationship between his wife and the bluesman, and now he was taking his revenge. But did Ralph Davis intend to kill Robert Johnson? Possibly not – mothballs in alcohol was a common method of administering poison, though it was not usually fatal. Sometimes it was used to remove drunkenly troublesome individuals from bars – they would vomit and almost pass out, but generally recover after a few days. 'This man had a good looking woman, and he didn't want to lose her. And Robert was about to take her away,' said Honeyboy Edwards.[47]

Robert Johnson returned to the stage, where he resumed

playing. At around two in the morning, however, he became violently ill. A man called Tush Hog, who had become friends with him, took him back to his home on the plantation. Although the estate had a doctor on call, the cause of Robert's illness could not be identified, and the attendance of the medical practitioner was not requested by the plantation owner.

With his immune system weakened by the effects of the poisoned whisky, Robert Johnson caught pneumonia.

Robert Johnson's mother told the blues archivist Alan Lomax that she was present at her son's death. 'When I went in where he at, he layin' up in bed with his guitar crost his breast. Soon's he saw me, he say, "Mama, you all I been waitin for." "Here," he say, and give me his guitar. "Take and hang this thing on the wall, cause I done pass all that by. That what got me messed up, Mama. It's the devil's instrument, just like you said. And I don't want it no more." And he died while I was hangin his guitar on the wall.'[48]

All things considered, some might expect Robert Johnson's mother to provide such a lyrical description of her son's end.

However, it was pneumonia that the pioneering bluesman succumbed to on Monday 16 August 1938. An affair between Robert Johnson's older mother and a younger man had brought him into life. Now his own cuckolding of an older man had brought about his end.

It was just the kind of subject matter that inspired people to write blues songs.

NOTES

AMY WINEHOUSE

1. *Guardian* blog, 24 July 2011
2. *Amy Winehouse: The Biography*, Chas Newkey-Burden (John Blake, 2008)
3. *Observer*, 22 April 2007
4. *Daily Mail*, 18 November 2007
5. *Arena*, BBC TV, 23 July 2011
6. *Daily Mail*, 18 August 2007
7. *Daily Mail*, 18 November 2007
8. *Sun*, 2011
9. www.theartsdesk.com, 26 October 2014
10. *Guardian*, 5 December 2003
11. *Word* magazine, March 2004
12. *Camden Review*, 28 July 2011
13. Bryony Gordon, *Telegraph* blog, 16 February 2007
14. www.markborkowski.com, 4 June 2007
15. *Daily Mail*, 31 July 2011
16. World Entertainment News Network interview with Amy Winehouse, 29 June 2007
17. ITN interview with Amy Winehouse, January 2004
18. Amy Winehouse obituary, *Daily Telegraph*, 23 July 2011
19. *Time Out*, 29 January 2007
20. *Daily Mail*, 30 November 2008

KURT COBAIN

1. Jon Savage interview tapes, courtesy Jon Savage
2. Ibid.
3. Azerrad, page 17
4. Azerrad, page 21
5. Ibid.
6. Jon Savage interview tapes, courtesy Jon Savage
7. Azerrad, page 23
8. Cross, page 51
9. Azerrad, page 26
10. True, page 20
11. Azerrad, page 31
12. Jon Savage interview tapes, courtesy Jon Savage
13. Ibid.
25. True, page 20
26. True, page 77
27. Cross, page 285
28. Jon Savage interview tapes, courtesy Jon Savage
29. True, page 100
30. True, page 123
31. Cross, page 142
32. Cross, page 157
33. Azerrad, page 170
34. Azerrad, page 179
35. Azerrad, page 193
36. Cross, page 202
37. Cobain, *Journals*, page 207
38. Jon Savage interview tapes, courtesy Jon Savage
14. Ibid.
15. True, page 29
16. Azerrad, page 41
17. Jon Savage interview tapes, courtesy Jon Savage

18. True, page 31
19. Jon Savage interview tapes, courtesy Jon Savage
20. True, page 71
21. True, page 71
22. True, page 103
23. Azerrad, page 59
24. True, page 72
39. www.featureshoot.com/2009/01/michael-lavine-new-york/
40. Cross, page 225
41. Cross, page 229
42. Cross, page 249
43. Cross, page 268
44. Cross, page 276
45. Ibid.
46. Cross, page 303
47. *Last Days of Kurt Cobain* documentary
48. True, page 552
49. True, page 557
50. Cross, page 329

BRIAN JONES

1. Jackson, pages 135–6
2. Ibid.
3. Paul Gorman, *The Look: Adventures in Rock and Pop Fashion* (Adelita, 2006), page 35
4. Jackson, page 63
5. Ibid.
6. Jackson, page 6
7. Jackson, page 5
8. Jackson, page 8
9. Jackson, page 11

10. Jackson, page 17
11. Jackson, page 21
12. Jackson, page 26
13. Jackson, page 33
14. Jackson, pages 52–3
15. Ibid.
16. Jackson, page 53
17. Booth, page 38
18. Wyman, page 105
19. Ibid.
20. Wyman, page 116
21. Wyman, page 105
22. Jackson, page 163
23. Jackson, page 165
24. Jackson, page 167
25. *BEAT Magazine*
26. Gorman, page 109
27. Booth, page 104

JIMI HENDRIX

1. Full name: James Allen Hendrix, he was known as 'Al'
2. Cross, page 55
3. Cross, page 79
4. Courtesy Alan Douglas/Hendrix Estate
5. *Rolling Stone*, 16 May 2012
6. Cross, page 46
7. Cross, page 47
8. Cross, page 51
9. Courtesy Alan Douglas/Hendrix Estate
10. Ibid.
11. Ibid.

12. Cross, page 60
13. Ibid.
14. Ibid.
15. Courtesy Alan Douglas/Hendrix Estate
16. Ibid.
17. Ibid.
18. Ibid.
19. Ibid.
20. Ibid.
21. Ibid.
22. Ibid.
23. Ibid.
24. Cross, page 106
25. Courtesy Alan Douglas/Hendrix Estate
26. Cross, page 205
27. August 1965 letter home
28. Cross, page 127
29. Cross, page 139
30. Cross, page 147
31. http://www.djnoble.demon.co.uk/ints/ANDYSUM.ME0.html
32. Ed Vulliamy, *Observer*, 8 August 2010
33. Cross, page 179
34. Notably, this house had previously been occupied by the composer Handel
35. http://www.mitchmitchell.de/mitchsounds71.htm
36. Ibid.
37. Ed Vulliamy, *Observer*, 8 August 2010
38. Ibid.
39. Courtesy Alan Douglas/Hendrix Estate
40. Cross, page 215
41. Courtesy Alan Douglas/Hendrix Estate
42. Ibid.
43. Ibid.

44. Murray, page 201
45. Jimi Hendrix, *Life* magazine, 3 October 1969
46. Shapiro and Glebbeek, page 342
47. Courtesy Alan Douglas/Hendrix Estate
48. Ibid.
49. Courtesy Alan Douglas/Hendrix Estate
50. Ibid.
51. Ibid.
52. Ibid.
53. Ed Vulliamy, *Observer*, 8 August 2010
54. Courtesy Alan Douglas/Hendrix Estate
55. Ibid.
56. Ibid.

JANIS JOPLIN

1. Womack, page 156
2. BBC Radio 4, *Front Row*, September 2012
3. Womack, page 158
4. Ibid.
5. Ibid.
6. Womack, page 161
7. Womack, page 162
8. Joplin, page 21
9. Joplin, page 23
10. Joplin, page 201
11. Joplin, page 71
12. Amburn, page 8
13. Joplin, page 44
14. Amburn, page 15
15. Amburn, page 16
16. Amburn, page 14

17. Joplin, page 60
18. Joplin, page 56
19. Joplin, page 69
20. Joplin, page 77
21. Joplin, page 79
22. Joplin, pages 80–1
23. Joplin, page 82
24. Amburn, page 33
25. Joplin, page 84
26. Joplin, page 86
27. Joplin, page 87
28. Joplin, page 94
29. Joplin, page 97
30. Joplin, page 107
31. Joplin, page 108
32. Joplin, page 113
33. Joplin, page 120
34. Joplin, page 121
35. Joplin, page 124
36. Willett, page 52
37. Joplin, page 139
38. bbc.com/history.html
39. Joplin, page 160
40. Joplin, page 179
41. Graham, page 165
42. Joplin, page 190
43. Joplin, page 171
44. Joplin, page 220
45. Joplin, page 188
46. Joplin, page 234
47. Joplin, page 192
48. Willett, page 81
49. Ibid.

50. Joplin, page 261
51. Joplin, page 263
52. Joplin, page 264
53. Joplin, page 267
54. Joplin, page 271
55. Joplin, pages 234–5
56. Joplin, page 235
57. http://www.rollingstone.com/music/pictures/r-crumb-the-complete-record-cover-collection-20111221/cheap-thrills-big-brother-the-holding-company-0362927#ixzz2I88xxu00
58. Rasa Gustaitis, *Los Angeles Times*, 24 November 1968
59. Joplin, page 236
60. *Janis Joplin & Big Brother – 900 Nights*, Sky Arts, 16 January 2012
61. Joplin, page 237
62. Joplin, page 240
63. Joplin, page 241
64. Clos and Mory, page 96
65. Stewart, page 96
66. Joplin, page 253
67. Amburn, pages 194–5
68. Amburn, page 196
69. Amburn, page 197
70. Joplin, page 253
71. Joplin, page 248
72. Hubert Saar, *Newsweek*, 24 February 1969, page 84
73. Ibid.
74. Ralph Gleason, *San Francisco Chronicle*, 24 March 1969
75. Amburn, page 219
76. Amburn, page 216
77. Amburn, page 220
78. Amburn, page 221
79. Joplin, page 308
80. Townshend, page 179

NOTES

81. http://www.robertchristgau.com/get_artist.php?name=Janis+Joplin
82. Amburn, pages 228–30
83. Joplin, page 263
84. Friedman, page 177
85. Joplin, page 264
86. Amburn, page 244
87. Amburn, page 245
88. Joplin, page 278
89. Joplin, page 279
90. Joplin, page 280
91. Joplin, page 282
92. Joplin, page 282
93. Amburn, page 258
94. Joplin, page 277
95. Amburn, page 263
96. Amburn, page 267
97. Amburn, page 272
98. Joplin, page 290
99. Joplin, page 291
100. Joplin, page 292
101. Joplin, page 295
102. Joplin, page 294
103. Joplin, page 298
104. Ibid.
105. Joplin, page 299
106. Ibid.
107. Joplin, page 300
108. Joplin, page 302
109. Joplin, page 303
110. Joplin, page 305
111. Joplin, page 307
112. Amburn, page 293

JIM MORRISON

1. Riordan, page 231
2. *Rolling Stone*, 30 August 2001
3. Gilmore, page 253
4. Riordan, page 51
5. Riordan, page 236
6. Davis, page 9
7. Davis, page 9
8. Davis, page 52
9. Riordan, page 197
10. Riordan, page 191
11. Riordan, page 53
12. Riordan, page 191
13. Riordan, page 62
14. Manzarek, pages 73–4
15. Manzarek, page 75
16. Manzarek, page 77
17. Manzarek, page 80
18. Manzarek, page 87
19. Manzarek, page 55
20. Manzarek, pages 90–1
21. Manzarek, page 94
22. Manzarek, page 131
23. Riordan, page 69
24. Manzarek, page 153
25. Riordan, page 84
26. Manzarek, page 143
27. Riordan, pages 88–9
28. Manzarek, page 183
29. Riordan, page 85
30. http://www.doorshistory.com/doors1966.html
31. Manzarek, page 190

32. Holzman, pages 162–3
33. Densmore, page 81
34. Holzman, page 81
35. Densmore, page 81
36. Densmore, page 82
37. Amburn, page 135
38. Hopkins and Sugarman, page 166
39. Densmore, page 134
40. Densmore, page 95
41. Hopkins, page 496
42. Densmore, page 108
43. Amburn, page 137
44. Ibid.
45. http://www.doorshistory.com/doors1967.html
46. Densmore, page 119
47. Didion, page 131
48. Howard Smith, *Village Voice*, December 1967
49. Michael Horowitz, 'The Morrison Mirage', *Crawdaddy!*, April 1969
50. Densmore, page 148
51. http://www.doorshistory.com/doors1968.html
52. Manzarek, page 284
53. Densmore, page 163
54. Densmore, page 162
55. Riordan, page 234
56. Densmore, page 163
57. Manzarek, page 287
58. Manzarek, page 302
59. Manzarek, page 308
60. Riordan, page 291
61. Manzarek, page 315
62. Densmore, page 218
63. Manzarek, page 319
64. Densmore, page 226

65. Densmore, page 230
66. Manzarek, page 354
67. Manzarek, page 340
68. Densmore, page 247
69. Densmore, pages 251–2
70. Densmore, page 254
71. Ibid.
72. Densmore, page 256
73. Densmore, page 258
74. Densmore, page 261
75. Ibid.

ROBERT JOHNSON

1. Wald, page 117
2. Clapton, page 40
3. Evans, page 22
4. www.luckymojo.com/crossroads.html
5. Wald, page 107
6. www.robertjohnsonbluesfoundation.org/node/244
7. Stephen LaVere, liner notes to Robert Johnson, *The Complete Recordings*
8. www.robertjohnsonbluesfoundation.org/node/244
9. Ibid.
10. Ibid.
11. Palmer, page 121
12. Ibid.
13. YouTube interview with Robert Lockwood Jr.
14. Ibid.
15. Palmer, page 205
16. Palmer, page 179
17. Murray, pages 32–3

18. Wald, page 108
19. Murray, page 36
20. Wald, page 108
21. Wald, page 107
22. Cobb, page 289
23. Wald, page 109
24. Ibid.
25. Wald, page 108
26. Ibid.
27. LaVere, liner notes
28. Ibid.
29. Ibid.; http://www.tdblues.com/2011/10/ike-zimmerman-more-details-around-the-legend/
30. LaVere, liner notes
31. He was not the only musician to change his name on account of Lonnie Johnson; after he had toured the UK in 1952, Tony Donegan, also on that tour, changed his name to Lonnie Donegan
32. Wald, page 109
33. Wald, page 111
34. Wald, page 112
35. Ibid.
36. Ibid.
37. Wald, page 113
38. Wald, page 111
39. Wald, page 114
40. Wald, page 115
41. Guralnick, page 34
42. Murray, page 50
43. Guralnick, page 36
44. Guralnick, page 44
45. 'Hellhound on My Trail' was actually an adaptation of Skip James's 1931 song 'Devil Got My Woman'
46. Many accounts claim this final performance was at a place

called Three Forks; however, Jason Rewald's account stems from scrupulous research, and he is adamant that this is where this performance took place <www.tdblues.com/2009/07/facts-around-johnsons-poisoning-killers-revealed/>

47. http://www.motherjones.com/riff/2010/06/music-monday-blues-robert-johnson-honeyboy-edwards
48. Ibid.

BIBLIOGRAPHY

KURT COBAIN

Azerrad, Michael, *Come As You Are: the Story of Nirvana* (New York: Doubleday) 1993

Cobain, Kurt, *Journals* (London: Penguin) 2003

Cross, Charles R., *Heavier than Heaven: a Biography of Kurt Cobain* (New York: Hyperion) 2001

The Last 48 Hours of Kurt Cobain, dir. John Dower, World of Wonder, 2007 (television documentary)

True, Everett, *Nirvana: The True Story* (London: Omnibus) 2006

BRIAN JONES

BEAT Magazine, 15 July 1967

Booth, Stanley, *Keith: Standing in the Shadows* (New York: St. Martin's Press) 1995

Gorman, Paul, *The Look: Adventures in Rock & Pop Fashion* (London: Penguin) 2006

Jackson, Laura, *Brian Jones: The Untold Life and Mysterious Death of a Rock Legend* (London: Piatkus) 2009

Wyman, Bill, *Stone Alone: The Story of a Rock 'n' Roll Band* (New York: Da Capo Press) 1997

JIMI HENDRIX

Cross, Charles, *Room Full of Mirrors: a Biography of Jimi Hendrix* (New York: Hyperion) 2006

Henderson, David, *'Scuse Me While I Kiss the Sky: the Life of Jimi Hendrix* (London: Omnibus Press) 2003

Mitchell, Mitch, 'Sounds Talk-In' (accessed December 2012): http://www.mitchmitchell.de/mitchsounds71.htm

Murray, Charles Shaar, *Crosstown Traffic: Jimi Hendrix and Post-war Pop* (London: Faber & Faber) 1989

Pepin, Elizabeth, and Watts, Lewis, *Harlem of the West: the San Francisco Fillmore Jazz Era* (San Francisco: Chronicle Books) 2005

Richman, Robin, 'An Infinity of Jimis', interview with Jimi Hendrix, *Life*, 3 October 1969

Shapiro, Harry, and Glebbeek, Caesar, *Jimi Hendrix: Electric Gypsy* (London: William Heinemann) 1990

Summers, Andy, 'Andy Summers on Jimi Hendrix' (accessed December 2012): http://www.djnoble.demon.co.uk/ints/ANDYSUM.ME0.html

Vulliamy, Ed, 'Jimi Hendrix: You never told me he was that good', *Observer*, 8 August 2010

JANIS JOPLIN

Amburn, Ellis, *Pearl: The Obsessions and Passions of Janis Joplin: a Biography* (New York: Warner Books, Inc.) 1992

BBC Radio 4, *Front Row*, September 2012

Big Brother and the Holding Company website (accessed January 2013): http://bbc.com/history.html

Christgau, Robert, *Robert Christgau: Dean of American Rock Critics* (accessed January 2013): http://www.robertchristgau.com/get_artist.php?name=Janis+Joplin

BIBLIOGRAPHY

Clos, Patrice, and Mory, Olivier, 'Chelsea Hotel # 2 (1972–93)', Leonard Cohen Prologues website (accessed January 2013): http://leonardcohen-prologues.com/chelsea_hotel.htm

Friedman, Myra, *Buried Alive: The Biography of Janis Joplin* (New York: Random House Inc.) 1992

Gleason, Ralph, *San Francisco Chronicle*, 24 March 1969

Graham, Bill, and Greenfield, Robert, *Bill Graham Presents: My Life Inside Rock and Out* (Cambridge, MA: Da Capo Press Inc.) 2004

Gustaitis, Rasa, 'Janis Joplin', *Los Angeles Times*, 24 November 1968

Joplin, Laura, *Love, Janis* (New York: HarperCollins) 2005

Saar, Hubert, interview with Janis Joplin, *Newsweek*, 24 February 1969

Stewart, Rod, *Rod: The Autobiography* (London: Century) 2012

Sullivan, James, 'R. Crumb: The Complete Record Cover Collection', *Rolling Stone*, 21 December 2011 (accessed January 2013): http://www.rollingstone.com/music/pictures/r-crumb-the-complete-record-cover-collection-20111221/cheap-thrills-big-brother-the-holding-company-0362927#ixzz2I88xxu00

Townshend, Pete, *Pete Townshend: Who I Am* (London: HarperCollins) 2012

Willett, Edward, *Janis Joplin: Take Another Little Piece of My Heart* (New Jersey: Enslow Publishers) 2008

Womack, Bobby, *Bobby Womack: My Autobiography – Midnight Mover* (London: John Blake Publishing Ltd.) 2006

JIM MORRISON

Amburn, Ellis, *Pearl: The Obsessions and Passions of Janis Joplin: a Biography* (New York: Warner Books, Inc.) 1992

Davis, Stephen, *Jim Morrison: Life, Death, Legend* (New York: Gotham Books) 2004

Densmore, John, *Riders on the Storm: My Life with Jim Morrison and the Doors* (New York: Delacorte Press) 1990
Didion, Joan, *The White Album: Essays* (New York: Farrar, Straus and Giroux) 1990
The Doors Interactive Chronological History website (accessed June 2013): http://www.doorshistory.com/doors1966.html; http://www.doorshistory.com/doors1967.html; http://www.doorshistory.com/doors1968.html
Gilmore, Mikhal, *Stories Done: Writings on the 1960s and its Discontents* (New York: Free Press) 2008
Holzman, Jac, and Daws, Gavan, *Follow the Music: The Life and High Times of Elektra Records in the Great Years of American Pop Culture* (Santa Monica, CA: FirstMedia Books) 2000
Hopkins, Jerry, 'Jim Morrison' in Wenner, Jan, and Levy, Joe (eds), *The Rolling Stone Interviews* (New York: Back Bay Books) 2007
Hopkins, Jerry, and Sugerman, Danny, *No One Gets Out of Here Alive* (New York: Warner Books) 1995
Horowitz, Michael, 'The Morrison Mirage' in *Crawdaddy!*, April 1969, issue no. 21
Manzarek, Ray, *Light My Fire: My Life with The Doors* (New York: G.P. Putnam's Sons) 1998
Riordan, James, and Prochinky, Jerry, *Break on Through: the Life and Death of Jim Morrison* (New York: William Morrow & Co) 1991
Smith, Howard, *Village Voice*, 14 December 1967, vol. XIII, no. 9

ROBERT JOHNSON

Clapton, Eric, *Clapton: the Autobiography* (London: Century) 2007
Cobb, James C., *The Most Southern Place on Earth: the Mississippi Delta and the Roots of Regional Identity* (Oxford: Oxford University Press) 1992

BIBLIOGRAPHY

Dylan, Bob, *Chronicles Volume One* (New York: Simon & Schuster) 2004

Evans, David, *Tommy Johnson* (London: Studio Vista) 1971

Guralnick, Peter, *Searching for Robert Johnson* (New York: Dutton) 1982

Jones, Kloc, 'Fact-checking the Life and Death of Bluesman Robert Johnson', *Mother Jones*, 21 June 2010 (accessed November 2013): http://www.motherjones.com/riff/2010/06/music-monday-blues-robert-johnson-honeyboy-edwards

LaVere, Stephen C., liner notes to Robert Johnson, *The Complete Recordings* (Columbia Records) 1990

Murray, Charles Shaar, *Blues on CD: the Essential Guide* (London: Kyle Cathie) 1993

Palmer, Robert, *Deep Blues: a Musical and Cultural History* (New York: Penguin) 1982

Rewald, Jason, 'Ike Zimmerman – More Details Around the Legend', (accessed November 2013): http://www.tdblues.com/2011/10/ike-zimmerman-more-details-around-the-legend/

Rewald, Jason, 'Facts around Johnson's Poisoning – Killers Revealed' (accessed November 2013): http://www.tdblues.com/2009/07/facts-around-johnsons-poisoning-killers-revealed/

Robert Johnson Blues Foundation website (accessed November, 2013): http:www.robertjohnsonbluesfoundation.org/node/244

Wald, Elijah, *Escaping the Delta: Robert Johnson and the Invention of the Blues* (New York: Harper Paperbacks) 2005

Yronwode, Catherine, 'The Crossroads in Hoodoo Magic and the Ritual of Selling Yourself to the Devil' (accessed November 2013): www.luckymojo.com/crossroads.html

YouTube interview with Robert Lockwood, Jr. (accessed November 2013): http://www.youtube.com/watch?v=Z0JMmr00G3Q